Library of
Davidson College

LAW & FORCE IN AMERICAN FOREIGN POLICY

EDWIN C. HOYT

UNIVERSITY
PRESS OF
AMERICA

LANHAM • NEW YORK • LONDON

327.73
H868l

Copyright © 1985 by

University Press of America,™ Inc.

4720 Boston Way
Lanham, MD 20706

3 Henrietta Street
London WC2E 8LU England

All rights reserved

Printed in the United States of America

Library of Congress Cataloging in Publication Data

Hoyt, Edwin C. (Edwin Chase), 1916-
   Law and force in American foreign policy.

   Bibliography: p.
   Includes index.
   1. United States—Foreign relations—1945-
2. Intervention (International law) 3. International
law—United States. I. Title.
JX1417.H69   1985   327.73   84-21969
ISBN 0-8191-4430-4 (alk. paper)
ISBN 0-8191-4431-2 (pbk. : alk. paper)

All University Press of America books are produced on acid-free
paper which exceeds the minimum standards set by the National
Historical Publications and Records Commission.

86-8843

TO PHILIP C. JESSUP

who inspired and encouraged my work on this topic

CONTENTS

INTRODUCTION 1

PART I. THE PRINCIPLES OF WORLD ORDER

I. WORLD ORGANIZATION AS AN AMERICAN
   POLICY OBJECTIVE 7
   1. From Isolationism to the United Nations 7
   2. The Shift of Official Interest to "Containment" of the
      Soviet Union 11

II. PRINCIPLES OF WORLD ORDER TODAY 17
   1. Legal Limits on the Use of Force 17
   2. No Interference in the Internal Affairs of Other States 19
   3. The Current State of the Law of Neutrality 21

PART II. THE APPLICATION OF THE PRINCIPLES

III. DECISIONS THAT RISK NUCLEAR WAR 29
   1. The New Dimension of Risk 29
   2. Games of "Chicken" Over Berlin and Cuba 31

IV. "LIMITED WAR" IN KOREA 42
   1. American Policy Concerning Korea Before June 1950 42
   2. The Decision to Use Force to Repel the North Korean
      Attack 45
   3. The Conflict Escalates 48
   4. Formosa (Taiwan) 57
   5. Non-Recognition as a Diplomatic Weapon 71

V. THE POLICIES OF EISENHOWER AND DULLES 82
   1. The Attempt to Save Indochina from
      "International Communism" 82
   2. Non-Recognition as an Excuse for Intervention in the
      Chinese Civil War 98
   3. Secret Illegal Operations 102
   4. Suez: the United States Supports the Rules of the Charter 107

VI. VIETNAM: THE AMERICAN MILITARY
    INTERVENTION 112

CONTENTS

VII.	COMBATTING REVOLUTIONS IN LATIN AMERICA	119
	1. The United States and the Cuban Revolution	119
	2. Preventing "another Cuba"	127
	3. Counter-Revolutionary Intervention, as Practiced by the Soviet Union and the United States	145
VIII.	DECISIONS CONCERNING AFRICA	149
	1. The UN Intervention in the Congo	149
	2. The Issue of Peacekeeping Costs	161
	3. Africa after the UN Operation	167
IX.	IRAN AND AFGHANISTAN	178
	1. Iran as a Pawn in the Two World Wars	178
	2. The Struggle Between Britain and Iran, 1949-1953	183
	3. The American Intervention	185
	4. The Iranian Revolution	189
	5. Soviet Intervention in Afghanistan	197
X.	QUESTIONS OF NEUTRALITY	202
	1. Relations with India and Pakistan	202
	2. Argentina's Seizure of the Falklands (Malvinas)	210
XI.	SUMMING UP	216
	NOTES	235
	INDEX	265

When CIA chief Allen Dulles proposed to the President of the United States that our government finance and sponsor an invasion of Cuba by one thousand Cuban expatriates in clear violation of previous treaty commitments, there was no need . . . for a series of endless White House meetings to examine the proposal . . . The answer . . . should have been promptly and finally negative.

Chester Bowles

I would find a proper legal cover and I would go in. There are several legal justifications that could be used, like protecting American citizens living in Cuba and defending our base at Guantanamo.

Richard Nixon

INTRODUCTION

Growing national debates about our weapons policy and the risks of nuclear war, and about the wisdom of American military involvement in Central America, invite re-examination of the premises on which our foreign policy has been based. Few people are satisfied that our policies have been successful. Over the last thirty years they have seemed to lack any consistent guiding principle. The nearest approach to one, perhaps, has been opposition to communism. But even there consistency fails, for communist Yugoslavia received American aid as soon as it asserted its independence from Russian control, and communist China came to be appreciated as almost an ally. Balance of power might be supported as the key principle, but we created the United Nations out of appreciation of the inadequacy of balance of power as a way to prevent war. American policy has swung back and forth, between confrontation and detente, between the search for a preponderance of power and the search for an assured balance through arms control, between defending the UN rules against the use of force and undermining them, between forcible intervention in Latin America and denouncing Soviet intervention in Eastern Europe, between attacking communist China and helping communist China, between support for human rights and support for right-wing dictatorships which deny human rights.

The UN Charter states a set of principles about how international relations should be conducted, foremost among which is the illegality of the use of force except in individual or collective self-defense. It was probably inevitable, given the independent power of national governments, that nations generally would continue to put their own national interests ahead of abstract allegiance to the UN principles, and many nations, including all of the permanent members of the Security Council have violated those principles when they considered that their national interests required it. This book focuses on the American record in applying those principles. The United States has been less guilty of violating the UN principles than many nations, and it may seem unfair to single out this country by concentrating upon its violations. It would be advantageous for the world if all nations made a greater effort to abide by the UN principles. However, this is a book

2 INTRODUCTION

about American foreign policy. It does not purport to be a treatise on the application of the UN principles by nations generally. It does show that there has been a progressive departure of American policy from its original commitment to the UN principles, and the reasons for that development. It deals with the use and misuse of international law, and with its relevance to our contemporary situation. It re-examines the question whether it is in the American national interest to limit our use of force in international relations in accordance with the UN principles.

The focus is on the history of American decisions, since World War II, about whether and when to use force as a tool of policy. Part I traces the evolution of American thinking on issues of world order between 1900 and 1949, followed by consideration of the extent of contemporary international consensus on principles to govern the use of force. This Part gives the reader information about international law which will assist him or her in evaluating official policy. Part II examines specific situations and decisions, ranging from the Korean War to the current crisis in Central America.* This study of cases illustrates the ways in which international law can affect political decisions, and the ways in which it can be manipulated or avoided.[1]

It should be noted that legal considerations compete and interact with other factors influencing the policy process. The power of a Congress independent of the executive branch is a feature of foreign-policy-making peculiar to our system. Presidents must secure Congressional support for their major foreign policy decisions. Members of Congress are attentive to the concerns of special interest groups which are powerful in their constituencies. A President, too, must be attentive to group interests that are part of the coalition to

---

* Except for the Suez Crisis, American decisions relating to the conflict between Israel and the Arab states are not considered in this book. That conflict reflects the inherent difficulty of establishing a Jewish state in the center of an Arab region. Compassion for the suffering of the Jewish people in the holocaust and the need to provide a homeland for its survivors generated international support for and recognition of the Israeli state. But until the Egyptian-Israeli peace treaty of 1979, none of the Arab states had accepted Israel's right to exist. The struggle between Israel and the Palestinian Arabs continues to have an internal as well as an international dimension. Moreover, American decisions regarding Israel are influenced to a high degree by the intense interest of much of the American Jewish community in issues affecting Israel. For all of these reasons, the subject of American decisions concerning Israel merits a separate study.

which he owes his office. In certain specific cases decisions may be affected by the pressure of corporate interests, though direct influence of that kind is not often evident in crisis decisions on the use of force. Our economic system's influence on our foreign policy is more apparent in the general free-enterprise ideology which affects the world view of decision-makers both in Congress and in the executive branch, as well as that of most Americans. Those other influences on foreign policy are not examined here in any detail. This book focuses only on the policy relevance of international law.

PART I

THE PRINCIPLES OF WORLD ORDER

CHAPTER I

WORLD ORGANIZATION AS AN
AMERICAN POLICY OBJECTIVE

1. FROM ISOLATIONISM TO THE UNITED NATIONS

The conventional impression that U.S. foreign policy was isolationist down to the first World War is an oversimplification. It was isolationist only in its rejection of further involvement in the politics and the wars of Europe. The course of neutrality which was charted by Washington and Jefferson when war broke out again between France and England became settled American policy. When it came to economics, however, Americans were by no means isolationist. They were, as John Adams remarked, lovers of commerce and "as aquatic as the tortoises and sea fowl."

It is clear that American statesmen of the 19th century did not think they had any responsibility to maintain international order. Like the leaders of other small countries, they accepted the international system as they found it and focused their attention on protecting their nation's interests within that system. If they thought about appropriate forms of international organization, it was in terms of international law, which accorded the highest value to national independence and left it to the individual nations to decide whether to relate to each other according to the international law of peace, or to resort to belligerent action governed by the international law of war. As attention to legal norms was the way for a nation to avoid unnecessary disputes, the study of legal precedents was the State Department's habitual first step in considering how to react to any new situation.

On the American continent, however, the United States followed from the start a vigorous expansionist policy, seizing Indian lands and aggressively pressing border claims against Spain and Mexico. In issuing his "doctrine" in 1823, President Monroe reiterated the United States' intention to take no part in European conflicts and voiced opposition to any new European intervention in the Western Hemisphere. But nothing was said about American policy towards the other American nations. The deliberations preceding the President's Message to Congress indicate that Monroe and most of his advisers, including former Presidents Jefferson and Madison, would have been willing to join in a general pledge of non-intervention in the former Spanish colonies, which the British government proposed, but that Secretary of State John Quincy Adams was unwilling to make that commitment. Adams had stated his opinion, and intimated to the British minister in Washington, that "the continent of North America" should ultimately be considered as the "proper dominion" of the United States.

So long as the United States remained a small power the threat of American expansion was only felt by its immediate neighbors. But by 1890 the United States had surpassed England, France and Germany in population and in gross national product and was potentially one of the great powers. The question whether it should now play a more active role in world politics was a subject of increasing debate. With imperialism then in fashion, many Americans were tempted to "take up the white man's burden," as Kipling urged them, and to share in the responsibilities of governing the black and brown and yellow races. The debate in the Senate over the treaty which ceded the Philippines to the United States focused on the issue whether rule over peoples not intended to become American citizens was consistent with the principles of the American Revolution and the Declaration of Independence. The expansionists won that debate and the United States embarked on its first experiment in imperialism, which lasted until the reaction which followed the first World War.[1]

By intervening decisively in that conflict, the United States invited new responsibilities. For the next thirty years discussions of American foreign policy would focus on issues of world order.

It was Woodrow Wilson who defined the issues. Wilson first began to think about questions of world order in the context of U.S. relations with Latin America. He was an anti-imperialist who disapproved of the high-handed way Theodore Roosevelt had acquired the Canal Zone, and he was opposed to any use of American power to gain special privileges for American business. But his sense of outrage at the coup d'etat perpetrated by General Victoriano Huerta in Mexico, and the ensuing murder of Mexico's elected president and vice-president, led Wilson into an attempt to compel Huerta's resignation. He decided to use the full influence of the United States within the hemisphere to promote "orderly processes of just government based upon law, not upon arbitrary force." That, he declared on March 11, 1913, was the only basis on which there could be inter-American cooperation and friendship. Wilson's refusal to recognize the Huerta government, and his calls for its overthrow, brought defiance by Huerta and increasing conflict which led to the American military action at Vera Cruz in 1914. Not only in Mexico, but also in Haiti and the Dominican Republic, Wilson's attempt to compel the observance of constitutional legitimacy led to United States military intervention. He ultimately came to recognize that unilateral intervention, far from promoting his objective of friendly partnership with Latin America, inevitably produced national resentment in the target countries and involved the United States in too much conflict with its neighbors. He turned to an effort to accomplish his aim through a multilateral alternative—a "Pan-American Treaty of Mutual Guarantee." He explained in a speech on January 9, 1916 that the mutual guarantee was intended as a replacement for the Monroe Doctrine. That expression of policy, he said, had been seriously defective in its failure to say anything about North-South relations within the hemisphere. The result had been "an implied and partial protectorate" by the United States and fear and suspicion in Latin America. The collective guarantee would remedy the deficiency.

The key article of Wilson's projected treaty would state:

> That the high contracting parties hereby join one another in a common and mutual guarantee of territorial integrity and of political independence under republican forms of government.

There followed other articles which provided for arbitration of disputes and one whereby the parties would undertake to prevent the departure from their jurisdictions of any expedition hostile to the established government of any of the parties, or the export of arms destined for the use of any persons in revolt against an established government.[2]

Wilson particularly sought support for his treaty project from Argentina, Brazil, and Chile, which had acted as mediators in the impasse between the United States and Mexico. Negotiations continued until the United States entered the war against Germany. But the phrase about "republican forms of government" aroused Latin American apprehension that the treaty might be used as an excuse for intervention.[3] The other governments politely expressed approval "in principle," but they were in no hurry to sign. With the United States a belligerent in Europe, Wilson's Latin American project was superseded by planning for the League of Nations, a treaty of mutual guarantee in universalized form.

The central idea of the League of Nations Covenant was "collective security." Renouncing more limited alliances, all of the nations would collectively guarantee against external aggression the territorial integrity and political independence of each of them. For Wilson, the anti-imperialist, such an enterprise would be worthy of American participation. Through the League, the United States could put its power to work in the service of its ideals—to permanently secure world peace, national independence, and the rule of law. It would emerge from isolation, not to engage in imperialist ventures or balance of power politics, but to create a better system.

Wilson's attempt to lead the United States into the League of Nations was assailed by American traditionalists, who argued for a foreign policy limited to the protection of American interests. The only realistic ways to limit the destructiveness of war, in their view, were neutrality and non-intervention. "Collective security" would just make local conflicts into universal ones.[4] Wilson failed to secure Senate approval of U.S. entry into the League, but despite the isolationist mood of Congress in the inter-war era, the ideal had evoked an enthusiastic response in the minds of many influential Americans. The Kellogg-Briand pact of Aug. 27, 1928 was almost unanimously approved by the Senate. It did not commit the United States to any kind of enforcement action, but it expressed international agreement on the principle that war was no longer acceptable as a way to solve international controversies or as an instrument of national policy. In the nineteen-thirties the debate between Wilsonians and isolationists increased in intensity over the issue of whether the United States should actively collaborate with the League to curb the aggressions of Japan, Italy, and Germany. When the United States entered the Second World War it seemed that the Wilsonians had finally won the debate, for the re-creation of a world security organization, called for by Roosevelt and Churchill, was overwhelmingly endorsed by the U.S. Senate and House of Representatives in 1943, and when the UN Charter was submitted to the Senate in 1945 it was approved by a vote of 89 to 2.

2. THE SHIFT OF OFFICIAL INTEREST TO "CONTAINMENT" OF THE SOVIET UNION

It later became evident that the initial enthusiasm for the UN concealed substantial differences among segments of American opinion. The only thing that had been really settled was that the United States would henceforth play an active part in world politics. As the leader of the coalition which had defeated Germany and Japan, in military occupation of most of Germany and Austria with its British and French allies who were heavily dependent on American support, and in sole occupation of Japan, the United States had little choice about whether to play a world role. But beneath the surface there remained differences between those whose primary interest was in expanding American influence in China and Latin America, and those who stressed close association with the Western European democracies, and between those who thought American leadership should be exercised through world organization, accepting the restraints on national freedom of action which that implied, and those intellectual descendants of the American imperialists who welcomed assumption of "world responsibility," but were impatient with multilateral restraints. Their impatience was magnified by the fact that the UN approach required negotiation and collaboration with communists.

The costs of our new responsibilities as a world superpower were slow to appear. Indeed, part of the initial attraction of the United Nations for the American public was that it seemed to offer a way to avoid the hard responsibilities and costs of world leadership. It was tempting to think that, having created the world organization, we could let "it" handle the problems of maintaining world order. This was, of course, an illusion. The United Nations was not intended to be a world government and it possessed no independent power. It was merely a channel through which member nations could act, and might be able to persuade other nations to act with them. The organization might follow American leadership, given American willingness to back collective decisions with American military and economic resources, but those who thought the UN would relieve the United States of burdens were doomed to disappointment.

Cooperation between the Soviet Union and the Western allies did not survive much beyond the German surrender. The power vacuum which that left in Germany inexorably induced conflict, while the fear and suspicion with which Americans viewed all communists quickly reasserted itself, and it was reciprocated by Stalin's assumption of the inevitability of conflict between the opposing camps of socialism and capitalism.

Stalin was determined that Russia should have a free hand in the Eastern European countries which the Russian armies had occupied. He was receptive to the kind of compromise that he and Churchill agreed upon in their "percentages agreement" of 1944—Russia to be dominant in Romania and Bulgaria, balanced by British dominance in Greece, while neither should have predominant influence in Yugoslavia and Hungary (their agreement said influence in those countries should be shared on a 50-50 basis).[5] Such a deal, seemingly oblivious of the interests of the peoples concerned, was unacceptable to the United States, which wanted agreement on general principles applicable to all the small countries of Eastern Europe. General language of the kind the United States preferred was inserted in the declarations on liberated Europe and on Poland which were agreed upon at Yalta. The declaration on Poland called for consultation by the Soviet foreign minister and the American and British ambassadors with the Russian-sponsored Polish provisional government in order to reorganize that government on a broader democratic basis, and eventually to hold free elections. With respect to the other liberated peoples, the allied declaration called for the formation of interim governments "broadly representative of all democratic elements," and pledged to holding early free elections. Stalin, who lived up to his commitment to Churchill not to interfere in Greece, evidently regarded those declarations as merely propagandistic concessions, but, when the Russians intensified their grip on Poland, Romania, and Bulgaria, Truman indicated that he regarded the Yalta declarations as important commitments to be insisted upon according to the Western meaning of democracy. As the Russians remained intransigent on Polish and German issues, disagreements between the two sides became more and more acrimonious, and were reflected in the United Nations, where Russia exercised its veto power to block decisions favored by the Western majority. These developments caused many initial supporters of the United Nations to lose faith in the UN principles. They concluded that the hope of collective security on a world scale was illusory and forsook that ideal, replacing it with faith in a coalition of like-minded, anti-communist nations, which would be led by the United States.

President Truman's principal advisers on foreign policy were quite skeptical of the value of the United Nations. As Senator Fulbright observed:

> ... one suspects now that, like the League of Nations before it, the United Nations was orphaned at birth.... So far as I know, none [of President Truman's advisors] was a strong supporter of the plan for a world organization, as Cordell Hull had been. The Under-Secretary of State, Dean Acheson, was assigned to lobby for Senate approval of the United Nations Charter, and he later recalled that "I did my duty faithfully and successfully, but always believed that the Charter was impractical."[6]

After his retirement Acheson expressed his convictions in the following terms:

> ... It would be a great and dangerous mistake to mold political or military policy or action out of a fancied necessity of 'reconciling' it with the United Nations Charter.
>
> It is true that Article II calls upon all members to settle their disputes by peaceful means and to refrain from force against the territorial integrity or political independence of any state. Whatever these words may mean, we cannot accept from them any limiting obligation not reciprocally accepted by our opponents. The rules must be the same for all. The words in question did not inhibit the part played by the Soviet Union in Korea and Hungary. We cannot permit them to foreclose us from action which we might consider wise and requisite in countering the use of force against us. Whether the force is used on a considerable scale by a great power through a satellite, or whether it is used on a smaller scale by a small power to interfere with vital interests previously recognized and established, the Charter as interpreted by others leaves us free to meet this force as we think best. The Charter may be a factor in determining what we think best; but it can have no more determinative authority with us that it does with others. To regard ourselves as inhibited by its words because we argue unsuccessfully that others should be so governed, or in order to set an example for those who have not the least intention of following it, seems to me a very bad bargain indeed.
>
> The United Nations and its Charter are neither an aid nor an impediment in determining military policy. A sounder guide lies in political and military considerations.[7]

Another adviser who thought the UN to be a delusion and who favored a return to freedom of national action unhindered by UN rules, was George Kennan, whose proposed policy of "containment" of the Soviet Union was enthusiastically embraced by Truman's advisers and applied by them on a wider scale and in a more military way than Kennan intended.

The North Atlantic Treaty of April 4, 1949 was the principal instrument of the new policy. It proclaimed the parties' devotion to the purposes and principles of the UN Charter and stated that the treaty was defensive in nature and thus an exercise of the right of individual or collective self-defense recognized by Article 51 of the Charter, and it also provided that measures to defend against an attack that were taken under the treaty would be reported to the Security Council and would be terminated when the Security Council had acted to restore peace. Nevertheless, the North Atlantic Treaty marked a definite shift of American attention away from the United Nations.

The insertion in the North Atlantic Treaty of that language recognizing the preeminence of UN obligations may owe something to public criticisms of President Truman's 1947 request for a $400 million program of military and economic aid to Greece and Turkey, as well as to convictions held by other parties to the treaty. In his speech to Congress, of March 1947, calling for the aid to Greece and Turkey, Truman had asked for a demonstration of American determination "to support free peoples who are resisting attempted subjugation by armed minorities or by outside pressures." Greece, which had border disputes with Albania, Yugoslavia, and Bulgaria, was involved in a civil war between its rightist government and a communist-dominated rebel group known as the E.A.M. The rebel army used bases and supplies provided by the three communist countries to the north. The administration had decided to take up the role of protector of local governments in the Eastern Mediterranean that Britain had previously performed, but which the British had told Washington they were financially unable to continue.

A considerable share of the aid to Greece which Truman requested Congress to approve was to take the form of weapons and military advisers to help the Greek government defeat the rebellion against it. Criticism of the program, in the press and in Congress, focused on the fact that Truman was proposing unilateral American action, outside the United Nations. The UN Security Council had had the Greek question on its agenda for several months. In December 1946, the Council had established a commission of investigation, with all members of the Security Council represented on it, which was continuing its work in Greece at the time of Truman's message. The report of the commission, issued on June 25, 1947 and concurred in by all of its members except those from Poland and the USSR, found that Yugoslavia, and to a smaller extent Albania and Bulgaria, had in fact supported the Greek rebels. A draft resolution which would have created a commission to aid the four countries in settling border problems, and called on them to refrain from supporting armed bands formed in any of the four and crossing into the territory of another, was defeated by a Soviet veto. The question was then removed from the Security Council agenda and transferred to that of the General Assembly, which, after debate, adopted a resolution of Oct. 21, 1947, which called upon Greece's three northern neighbors to do nothing which could furnish aid to Greece's guerrilla rebels and established a special committee on the Balkans to observe compliance and be available to assist the four governments in settling the problems of borders and refugees. Seats on the committee were held open for the USSR and Poland. They, however, refused to participate. President Truman had made his proposals for American aid to Greece without waiting for the report of the UN investigating commission. His speech did refer obliquely to the action of the Security Council.[8] Under-Secretary of State Acheson, who had taken a principal role in advising the President, said later that "since time was so short [the President] had not been advised to go through the futility of appeal to an organization in which the Soviet Union would veto action and where in any event any help must come from the United States."[9] Senator Vandenberg, the Republican who was chairman of the Senate Foreign Relations Committee, supported the aid plan in substance, but tried to bring it "as far as possible within the United Nations."[10] His amendment to the aid bills, which was adopted, noted that the UN Security Council had recognized the seriousness of the conditions on Greece's northern border and might subsequently assume responsibility for that part of the problem, and directed the President to withdraw aid if the General Assembly, or a majority of the Security Council, should find the continuance of American aid unnecessary or undesirable.

The controversial feature of the administration's plan was not the economic aid, but the military intervention in the Greek civil war. Beside the provision of weapons, aircraft, and supplies, 250 American officers, headed by General Van Fleet, advised the Greek army, sometimes in the front lines. British advisers continued to train the Greek forces. E.A.M. decided to discontinue the armed struggle in October, 1949. The major factor in the collapse of the rebellion was the conflict between Stalin and Tito, and the expulsion of Yugoslavia from the Cominform, which took place in June 1948. This left Tito in a vulnerable position, and he turned to the United States for economic support. He ended his support of the Greek guerrillas, and closed the frontier in July 1949. The remnants of the rebel army fled into Albania and Bulgaria.[11] But this change in the external political situation in the Balkans was generally lost sight of. Greece was remembered as a successful precedent of American intervention on the side of a government fighting a communist rebellion. It had the effect of encouraging American decision-makers to repeat the effort elsewhere.

CHAPTER II

PRINCIPLES OF WORLD ORDER TODAY

1. LEGAL LIMITS ON THE USE OF FORCE

Can it be said that there remains today any international consensus concerning the principles of world order? Despite the considerable number of instances where nations, including our own, have by-passed the United Nations and acted in spite of its rules, there is much evidence that the nations do still agree that the use of force in international relations is illegitimate. We start with the UN Charter, to which all UN members profess adherence. In Article 2, paragraph 3 the Charter restated the commitment contained in the Kellogg-Briand Pact, that only peaceful means should be employed for the settlement of international disputes. Article 2, paragraph 4 stated the obligation of member nations "to refrain in their international relations from the threat or use of force against the territorial integrity or political independence of any state." To enforce that rule the Security Council was empowered to authorize collective military action, if that should be necessary, to maintain or restore international peace and security. In Article 51 it was recognized that, pending such action, states retained "the inherent right of individual or collective self-defense" if there should occur an armed attack against a member state. The Charter also affirmed the sovereignty of each of its member states and their right to be free from outside interference, even by the UN, in matters within their domestic jurisdiction (Art. 2, para. 7).

These basic principles are repeatedly reaffirmed in other declarations and agreements linking all kinds of states. One example was the "Declaration on Principles of International Law Concerning Friendly Relations and Co-operation among States" which the General Assembly adopted unanimously on Oct. 24, 1970.[1] The threat or use of force, that declaration said, was a crime for which there was responsibility under international law.[2] (The declaration went on to deal with the problem of non-intervention which will be discussed in a moment.)

On December 14, 1974 the General Assembly adopted a detailed Definition of Aggression, after many years of trying.[3] It listed various forms of forcible action which would constitute aggression, while specifying that it was not intended to prejudice the right of peoples under colonial or racist regimes, or other forms of alien domination, to struggle for self-determination.

The North Atlantic Treaty restated the parties' adherence to the UN principles, declared its strictly defensive purpose, and invoked Article 51 (the right of collective self-defense pending action by the Security Council) as its justification. It specified that measures taken pursuant to the collective guarantee should be reported to the Security Council and would be discontinued when the Security Council took effective action to restore peace. The Warsaw Pact of May 1955 was similarly defensive in its terms, and indeed copied the language of the North Atlantic Treaty in its article providing for joint action in case of an armed attack on one or more parties. The Pact of the League of Arab States (1945) forbade recourse to force for the settlement of disputes among the member states and declared that they would each respect each other's form of government and abstain from any action seeking to change it. The Charter of the Organization of American States (1948) reaffirmed the principles of the UN Charter and stressed the illegitimacy of any interference or intervention, forcible or otherwise, by any state in the internal (or external) affairs of any other state.[4] The Organization of African Unity, founded in 1963, also reaffirmed its members' commitment to the UN principles, including non-interference in the internal affairs of states and condemnation of subversive activities on the part of neighboring or other states. Statements of respect for these principles are to be found also in the Sino-Soviet alliance of 1950, the India-China agreement of 1954,[5] the Shanghai Communiqué issued in February 1972 by President Nixon and Premier Chou En-lai, and in countless other bilateral treaties and declarations as well. There is thus every indication that there is a genuine international consensus on the duty to refrain from force and to respect national independence. Application of the consensus in practice, as distinguished from acceptance in principle, is nevertheless difficult because of the self-judging feature of international law.

Since the end of World War II there have been comparatively few instances of the old type of military conflict that was purely international in nature. Abstention from such conflict by the great powers has been reinforced by their fear of nuclear war. There have been a few conflicts over unsettled borders, such as the ones between

India and China, between China and the Soviet Union, and most recently the long war between Iraq and Iran.[6] In several instances the USSR (in Hungary, Czechoslovakia, and Afghanistan) and the United States (in the Dominican Republic), invaded the territory of neighboring states to overthrow governments they did not like. Despite routine efforts to compose *post facto* justifying legal arguments, these appear to have been conscious decisions to act regardless of legality in areas which the superpower rivals considered in a particular way their special spheres of influence. They indicated no general intention to renounce the basic rule. And while the superpowers indulged in "covert" interventions, those were always conceded to be illegal.

Where clear violations of the accepted principles occurred, they were regularly denounced by the international community. One flagrant violation was Vietnam's 1978 military conquest of Kampuchea (Cambodia) in order to install a more compliant government there. Though Vietnam was protected by Russia's veto from condemnation by the Security Council, its disingenuous claim that the overthrow was the product of a popular uprising was emphatically rejected by the other Security Council members, as was China's claim that its subsequent punitive military action against Vietnam was an act of collective self-defense which was justified by Article 51.[7] The Soviet intervention in Afghanistan at the end of 1979 was again condemned by virtually the entire international community. Argentina's claimed right to take the Falkland Islands by force was rejected by the Security Council, which demanded withdrawal of the invasion force.

2. NO INTERFERENCE IN THE INTERNAL AFFAIRS OF OTHER STATES

The most difficult problem relating to the application of the no-force principle concerns internal or civil conflicts.[8] The inability to prevent or regulate civil conflict was from the beginning a serious but inescapable gap in the Charter. Many nations are badly governed and civil unrest is common. Rebel groups naturally seek arms and assistance abroad. International peace is thus endangered, for outside states are tempted to intervene and are influenced by the opinion that in order to avoid loss in competition with their rivals they must be no less aggressive than the latter. Yet, short of world government, there is no complete answer to the civil war problem. The right of peoples to alter or abolish governments which they consider oppressive, which was affirmed in our own Declaration of Independence, is among the most basic rights of man. The UN Charter, therefore, proscribed only the use of force in the members' *international* relations.[9] With respect to civil conflict it could only say that nations must respect each other's political independence.

Over the years since the Charter was written there have been attempts to spell out in more detail the meaning of the non-intervention principle. In 1965, in a unanimous resolution, the General Assembly declared: "No State shall ... interfere in civil strife in another State," or assist or finance "subversive terrorist or armed activities directed towards the overthrow of the regime of another State."[10] It added, however, an affirmation of the right of self-determination of peoples which stated the obligation of all states to contribute to the complete elimination of racial discrimination and colonialism and declared, "The use of force to deprive peoples of their national identity constitutes a violation of their inalienable rights and of the principle of non-intervention." Similarly, the 1970 Declaration on Principles of International Law Concerning Friendly Relations and Co-operation among States,[11] while it stated in explicit terms the illegality of any state's intervention in the domestic affairs of other states, whether by aiding trans-border incursions of armed men or by assistance to activities directed to overthrow the regime of another state or to interfere in civil strife or to interfere with the freedom of any state to choose its political, economic, or social system, stated also that every state had a duty to aid in the realization of the principle of self-determination of peoples by ending the subjection of peoples to alien subjugation. In this respect these declarations reiterated the principles of the 1960 Declaration on the Granting of Independence to Colonial Countries and Peoples,[12] and were a concession to the overwhelming voting power in the General Assembly of the newly independent states. The 1970 declaration affirmed that the territory of a colony or a non-self-governing territory had a status separate from the territory of the state administering it, but conceded that the self-determination principle should not be construed to encourage dismemberment of any state possessed of a government which represented the whole people belonging to the territory without distinction as to race, creed or color. The Definition of Aggression adopted by consensus on Dec. 14, 1974, as we have noted, also contained the proviso that nothing in it was intended to affect "the right" of peoples under colonial and racist regimes or other forms of alien domination "to struggle [for self-determination] *and to seek and receive support.*" (Italics added.) The members of the Organization of African Unity, in particular, have insisted on a right to give military help to Africans still under colonial rule, equating the struggle of a people against colonial domination with the right of self-defense.[13]

The largely unopposed declarations that we have cited show that in two cases—where a rebellion is a struggle for independence against colonial rule, or where it is the revolt of a people which is denied participation in government by an ethnic minority which maintains its dominance by racial laws (as in South Africa and formerly in Rhodesia)—the new consensus regards the government as illegitimate and condones foreign aid to rebels.

Governments have from time to time claimed a right of military intervention to rescue their citizens if their lives are threatened in a foreign country or if they are being held hostage by terrorists. While there is considerable support for that justification in the case of a hit-and-run rescue, it is not considered an acceptable excuse for the overthrow of a government or military occupation of a country.

3. THE CURRENT STATE OF THE LAW OF NEUTRALITY

Expressions of the new consensus have generally avoided specific reference to neutrality. That concept, important in the international law which prevailed before the United Nations came into being, was discredited by the doctrine of collective security, which assumed that the international organization would take action in any international conflict. Under the old rules, belligerents had been required to notify third states of the existence of a state of war. Those other states must then choose either the status of a co-belligerent or the status of a neutral. They would normally choose the latter. Since 1945 third states do not always have that choice in the case of an international conflict, since the Charter provides (Art. 2, para. 5):

> All members shall give the United Nations every assistance in any action it takes in accordance with the present Charter, and shall refrain from giving assistance to any state against which the United Nations is taking preventive or enforcement action.

In those circumstances neutrality would not be a permissible option. But it soon became clear that the UN would not be able to act to deal with every breach of the peace. In cases where the United Nations was unable to take a position, owing to disagreement among the great powers, each state would be left to decide for itself whether there had been an act of international aggression which justified it in intervening on the side of the victim, as an act of collective self-defense. And in the case of *civil* conflict, neutrality seemed to be a positive obligation in view of the consensus as stated in the General Assembly's Declaration on the Inadmissibility of Intervention: "No State shall... interfere in civil strife in another State."[14]

In the application of the traditional rules of neutrality to civil wars, three stages of conflict were envisaged. Civil unrest was normally considered a matter within the sole domestic jurisdiction of the established government of a country. If unrest reached a stage of serious rebellion, outside states might recognize a state of insurgency, which meant that the insurgents were regarded as legal contestants rather than mere law-breakers, but did not prevent the recognizing state from sending arms to the established government. A third stage was reached if the rebels occupied substantial territory, with an identifiable governmental authority waging armed conflict according to the laws of war. Outside states wishing to remain at peace should then recognize the rebels as belligerents and choose the status of neutrality, avoiding governmental assistance to either side.

We must note, however, that the concepts of neutrality and the legal obligations of neutrals have received very little attention since the Second World War. Even before that, technological change affecting war-making capacity, and the growth of government control over private economic activity had made parts of the old law of neutrality unsuited to contemporary conditions. Under the traditional rules a belligerent government might seize contraband of war in transit to its enemy on neutral ships, but other goods which were the property of neutrals were immune from seizure despite enemy destination. Contraband was narrowly defined as including weapons and munitions. But under modern conditions of warfare, many other articles were equally vital to a nation's capacity to wage war, and the distinction between government and private activity became impossible to maintain. In the two world wars belligerents expanded the definition of contraband to allow seizure of goods of every description in transit to their enemy. Under the old rules, apart from the liability to seizure, it had been considered a violation of neutral duty for a neutral government to furnish weapons or munitions of war to either one of the belligerents. That obligation is no longer respected today. Under modern conditions of warfare munitions are expended at such a rapid rate, that, taking the case of the 1973 war in the Middle East, Israel would not have been able to fight for more than a very few days without resupply by the United States, or Egypt without resupply by the USSR. The armies of both sides were completely dependent, for spare parts as well as ammunition, upon the nations from which they had bought equipment in peacetime. Not willing to condemn their friends to defeat, the United States and the USSR, even while seeking a cease-fire, continued sending arms to the belligerents. But while they were unwilling to be bound by the old rules of neutrality in that respect, they avoided participation in military hostilities.

A survey of contemporary practice has shown that the customary law of neutrality is still being invoked, both by third states claiming neutral rights and by belligerents claiming rights of blockade and seizure of contraband destined for their enemies.[15] In the wars between Israel and the Arab states, some third states formally declared their neutrality. Others, including the United States, preferred to call themselves "non-belligerent." Thus, when Secretary of State Rusk was asked at a press conference during the 1967 Middle East war what position was being taken by the United States, and was pressed to admit that the United States was a neutral, he responded evasively:

> We are in a situation where several governments have declared war. We are not a belligerent.... We are making a maximum effort in the Security Council to bring about a cease-fire.... Any use of this word "neutral"... is not an expression of indifference.[16]

The fact that changes in the conditions of warfare require changes in the old rules of neutrality is not sufficient to explain the almost total neglect of that aspect of international law in the United States since 1945. It has seemed to reflect, not the difficulty of adapting the law to new conditions so much as the rejection of neutrality as a *policy* for the United States. Whether neutrality indeed served American interests had been the subject of the long interwar debate between isolationists and internationalists. Neutrality had been presented as the alternative to American assumption of world leadership. Proponents of collective security stressed the opposition of the world community to any aggressor. It was thought that the obligation to support the world organization in action it would take to restore international peace would foreclose the option of neutrality. The eventuality of civil conflict received little attention.

Neutrality had also been discredited by its association with appeasement of Hitler and Mussolini during the Spanish Civil War of 1936-1939, when neutrality of the Western democracies was accompanied by aggressive intervention of Italy and Germany on the insurgent side. Not only German weapons, but also units of the Italian army and German and Italian air forces aided Franco. The Spanish navy had gone over to his side and war supplies were sent to Franco through Portugal. The Republican government in Madrid obtained some weapons and aircraft from the Soviet government and was aided by individual volunteers from the democratic countries. But it was given no help by the governments of Britain, France, and the United States. The U.S. Congress insisted upon a complete embargo against private shipment of arms to either side. Fear of communism prevented the British government from reacting strongly against the blatant intervention of Germany and Italy. Britain and France were concerned above all else to prevent the Spanish war from growing into a European international conflict. They obtained the signature of the other powers on an ostensible non-intervention agreement, but only the democracies observed it. Going beyond the requirements of neutrality, their complete embargo deprived the Spanish government of a source of supply to balance the aid given to Franco. The fact that the democracies tolerated without counter-action the armed intervention of Italy and Germany against the Spanish government, and papered over their acceptance of that aggression by the sham non-intervention accord, led many to consider non-intervention an ineffective policy, or to equate it with appeasement.

Finally, when American faith in peace-keeping by the United Nations faded, it was replaced by the belief that world politics was essentially a power struggle between "world communism" and "the free world." Those possessed by that image rejected neutrality since they believed that the Soviet Union would seize every opportunity to take sides in any local or civil conflict and that any increase in influence of local communists would be an increase in the power of the Soviet Union. In consequence, it was thought that the United States must assert its influence and should not shrink from intervention in civil conflicts.

But if that image of monolithic world communism did not accord with reality, if revolutionaries in other countries would continue to put their nations' interests ahead of those of the Soviet Union, and if nationalism could be relied upon to splinter the communist world and preserve the independence of nations, the wisdom of intervention in purely local or civil conflicts became questionable. While outside members of the United Nations must work, along with the UN, to mediate and to press the world interest in ending conflicts, both for humanitarian reasons and to prevent them from involving other nations, neutrality might be the best foundation for peace-making efforts.

In modern practice, however, foreign governments have frequently given military assistance to an established government to help it suppress an internal rebellion. They claim that military intervention is not illegal if it is in response to a request from the government in question, and they counter accusations of unneutral use of force by refusing to recognize an insurgent group as a belligerent authority even though their rebellion may assume large proportions, and by claiming that aid given to such a faction by other states makes their own assistance to the established government an instance of collective self-defense. Premature recognition of insurgents as the government of the state in question (recognition before the military issue is finally decided) has also sometimes been resorted to in an effort to justify aid to the insurgents. Premature recognition, however, is generally conceded to be a hostile and aggressive act.

The consensus resulting from two world wars, that the use of force in international relations was now illegal, subjected the whole international legal system to enormous pressure, for the possibility of legal resort to war had formerly operated as a kind of safety valve for that part of international law which regulated the peaceful relations of nations. Instead of declaring war, there was now strong temptation to find a way around the rules, and evasive justifications were encouraged by the fact that nations can generally avoid having any international tribunal rule on questions of their international legal obligations. The option given to them to accept compulsory jurisdiction of the International Court of Justice, on a reciprocal basis, has not been extensively exercised (except with major, often crippling, reservations). The United States and the other permanent members of the UN Security Council can also use the veto, if necessary, to avoid any Security Council ruling on their actions. They are thus able indefinitely to claim legality for their international actions, no matter how much they may be criticised abroad. It is this self-judging feature that makes international law different from municipal law, which always provides for authoritative settlement of disputes about subjects' legal obligations.

If nations can continue to insist on their own interpretations of their legal obligations, is there any reality to international law in this area of regulation of the use of force? What effect have legal principles had, and what effect should they have, on the calculations of the decision-makers? The examination of American decisions which is contained in Part II will provide evidence on the nature of the relationship between this part of international law and U.S. policy.

PART II

THE APPLICATION OF THE PRINCIPLES

CHAPTER III

DECISIONS THAT RISK NUCLEAR WAR

1. THE NEW DIMENSION OF RISK

An indispensable prerequisite of decision-making with respect to the use of force under today's conditions is an appreciation of the new magnitude of risks resulting from the fact that the major powers are armed with nuclear weapons.

We know that nuclear war between the Soviet Union and the United States, no matter who started it and whether or not the Soviet Union was more heavily damaged than the United States, would mean immediate or lingering death of many millions of Americans — the exact number is impossible to predict with any assurance of accuracy. It would also result in enormous destruction of our natural resources and economic capacity and permanent damage to the environment in which we live. There is a distinct possibility that it might cause the extinction of life on earth.[1]

Until quite recently most officials concerned with American security felt reasonable confidence that "Mutual Assured Destruction" made nuclear attack by either superpower quite unlikely. That confidence was well expressed in a 1969 article by McGeorge Bundy, who had been National Security Adviser to two Presidents. He wrote:

> In light of the certain prospect of retaliation there has been literally no chance at all that any sane political authority, in either the United States or the Soviet Union, would consciously choose to start a nuclear war. . . . For sane men on both sides the balance of terror is overwhelmingly persuasive. . . . there is no prospect at all that the Soviet Government could attack the United States without incurring an overwhelming risk of destruction vastly greater than anyone but a madman would choose to accept. Conversely, even the most cold-blooded of American planners has always understood, at least since 1954, that the concept of a strategic first strike by the United States is wholly unacceptable because of the prospect of Soviet retaliation.[2]

Bundy was confident that the Soviet Union was effectively deterred from risking war in Europe, as well as from attacking the United States:

Maybe [with regard to Europe] the American nuclear commitment is not as firm as it seems—but what sane Soviet leader wants to put the whole Soviet society in the scales to find out?[3]

That confidence in the unlikelihood of nuclear war has now been severely shaken by alarm at increasing Soviet armaments and apprehension of possible Soviet intrusion into the oil-producing Persian Gulf area. Since the collapse of the regime in Iran which was firmly allied with the United States, and the Soviet intervention in Afghanistan (both of which will be considered in some detail in later chapters), there has been a realization that the United States could not compete with the Soviet Union in any major war in the area of the Persian Gulf unless it were willing to use nuclear weapons. It became official policy to threaten to do so. But was such a threat believable? Strategists and officials talked of possible use of Soviet nuclear power to "blackmail" the United States. What they meant was a Soviet ability to deter the United States from escalating a non-nuclear conflict to the nuclear level. To make the American threat of possible resort to nuclear weapons more believable, in the face of the enhanced Soviet missile forces, both the Carter and the Reagan administrations developed plans for fighting a protracted nuclear war if one should begin. With the addition, on both sides, of new generations of missiles of such accuracy as to suggest that either side might hope to gain a decisive advantage by striking first, confrontations between the superpowers were becoming ever more dangerous.

Game theorists gave the name of "Chicken" to the coercive bargaining that takes place in confrontations between the superpowers. It is a game played with awareness that both sides have a strong interest in avoiding mutual destruction in nuclear war. But each sees important interests at stake, each would like the other to make the necessary concessions to avoid conflict, and each believes that any evidence of weakness will be exploited. This produces a competition in risk-taking. Each tries to demonstrate to the other that it is fully committed and cannot back down. The danger of loss of control is always present.[4] Moreover, the risks in such crises are cumulative, and in repeated plays of the coercive bargaining game the pressure to go to the brink is increased by the knowledge that the party which refuses to take risks today is likely to be taken advantage of in the next round of conflict.

2. GAMES OF "CHICKEN" OVER BERLIN AND CUBA

The first trial of strength over Berlin, in 1948-49, when the Soviet government tried to force the Western powers to alter their separate arrangements for West Germany by blocking their land access to Berlin, came during the period before the Russians had nuclear weapons. The Western allies were convinced that they had solid legal rights to remain in Berlin, derived, as they told Moscow, "from the defeat and unconditional surrender of Germany," supplemented by Four-Power agreements — rights which were fully co-equal with Soviet rights in Berlin.[5] They refused to concede that the Soviet Union had any right to impose new regulations upon air transport into Berlin.

At the end of June President Truman made a firm decision that the United States would remain in Berlin despite the blockade. His determination was demonstrated by sending 60 B-29 bombers to bases in England. The Berlin airlift was begun on an emergency basis, and an Allied counter-blockade also began to put pressure on the Russians. General Clay, the American military governor, proposed in July that an armed convoy should be sent through the Soviet Zone to insist on the right of land access to Berlin, but Truman's other advisers thought that kind of action was too risky.[6]

The United States set out to persuade the British and French that the case should be taken to the UN Security Council. It was then the opinion of the State Department that Article 37 of the UN Charter made reference to the Security Council a legal obligation in the case of a dispute likely to endanger international peace if the parties should fail to settle it by negotiations or other peaceful means.[7] The Allies made the request for consideration by the Security Council on September 29. The Soviet Union objected on the basis of Article 107 of the Charter, which provided that the Charter did not apply to action of any of the Charter signatories relating to states which were their enemies during World War II. The Allies responded that that article was not intended to prevent disputes among the victorious powers from coming before the Council. Although the Soviet Union announced that it would not participate in the discussion, the Council did take the matter up. The USSR vetoed a draft resolution put forward by all of the non-permament Security Council members, but agreed to the creation of a committee of financial experts nominated by the non-permanent members of the Council to study the Berlin currency problem. It was the introduction of the new West German currency in Berlin which the Russians had given as the reason for their restrictions.

The success of the airlift confronted the Russians with a new choice, and though they threatened to hold air maneuvers in the corridors to Berlin, they ultimately chose to accept the failure of their attempt to change the German *status quo* rather than further escalate the crisis, and through direct Soviet-American negotiations begun behind the scenes at the UN they eventually agreed to terminate the blockade, obtaining in exchange only Western agreement to participate in a new meeting of the foreign ministers which would discuss the German problem as a whole.[8]

By 1958, West Germany was independent, economically prosperous, and a member of the North Atlantic alliance, while communist East Germany was being weakened by a steady drain of resources and workers to the West. Emboldened by Russia's new nuclear capability, Khrushchev now precipitated another confrontation over Berlin.[9] In November 1958 the Soviet Government announced that it would insist upon revision of the existing regime. It argued that the military occupation had never been intended to be permanent, and that the agreement made at Potsdam in 1945 to treat Germany as an economic unit had been violated by the Western Powers so that instead of a single Germany two states came into being, with different political and economic systems and participating in opposing military alliances. In addition, the Western-occupied sectors of Berlin had become a center of tension and subversion in the middle of the German Democratic Republic (the East German state). The Soviet note of November 27, 1958 said that this situation could no longer be tolerated. The best way to resolve the problem, it said, "would be for the western part of Berlin ... to be reunited with the eastern part and for Berlin to become a unified city within the state in whose territory it is situated." It said that if the Western powers were opposed to such a solution, an acceptable alternative would be for West Berlin to be given the status of a free city, independent of both German states. Its existence and neutral status, and unhindered communications with both East and

West Germany, would be guaranteed by the four powers and by the German Democratic Republic. The Soviet note called for negotiation of this kind of arrangement within six months. If the Western powers should fail to use that time to reach such an agreement, the Soviet Government said it would itself negotiate such a settlement with the German Democratic Republic. The latter would then assume full sovereignty over its territory, and the Western powers would have to deal with that government on questions of access to Berlin. It warned that the Soviet Union was committed by the Warsaw Pact to go to the aid of the German Democratic Republic in the event of any violation of its frontiers. "Only madmen," it said, "can go to the length of unleashing another world war over the preservation of privileges of occupiers in West Berlin."[10]

The governments of the United States, Britain, and France saw the threat of war as coming entirely from the Soviet side. As before, an element in their perception of the situation was the conviction that they had a clear legal right to hold their positions in Berlin. As the United States Government repeatedly stated,[11] its rights in Berlin were independent of the Potsdam Agreement of July 1945, on which the Soviet legal case was based. The allied rights resulted from the military victory over Nazi Germany to which they had all contributed jointly. Occupation zones had been agreed upon by the Allies before the German surrender. Berlin was never part of the Soviet Zone, but was to be a separate special area under joint occupation of the allied powers, the forces of each of them occupying a designated sector of the city. When Germany surrendered, the American armies were in actual occupation of a considerable part of what had been designated as the Soviet zone, but in accordance with the agreements on occupation zones, U.S. forces withdrew from the Soviet Zone of Germany at the same time as they entered Berlin, on July 1, 1945. Agreements on access routes were made also at that time. Disclaiming responsibility for the breakdown of the Potsdam arrangements for joint policy-making for Germany as a whole, the Western powers said the Soviet Union had no right to abrogate unilaterally the agreements on rights of access to Berlin which were part of their occupation rights. They said they were willing to seek a negotiated settlement of the problem of divided Germany, but they insisted that they could not be forced to give up existing rights without their consent.

The confrontation which was thus initiated was not a simple replay of the confrontation of 1948-49, because physical conditions had changed. Berlin, industrialized, now required many times the supplies that were sufficient to sustain it in 1948-49. The airlift, which had worked so well then, would be much more vulnerable now in case of a renewed blockade. It was thought that the Russians now had the capacity to jam the air traffic communications system, if they chose, and thus block an airlift without forcibly attacking any aircraft. This would leave as the only remaining alternative means of resisting a blockade an attempt to force through a convoy by land (General Clay's proposal of 1948). Furthermore, the military balance had changed, for the United States' nuclear monopoly had ended and the Russians were now claiming possession of intercontinental ballistic missiles. American intermediate-range missiles had been sent to Britain, but they were still not operational in the spring of 1959.[12] The U.S. capacity for retaliation, represented by its Strategic Air Command, was still formidable, but with the more even balance of nuclear capability it was questionable whether the Soviet leaders would believe American threats of nuclear war over Berlin.

While Eisenhower consulted with Secretary Dulles in the period from Krushchev's November demands until the following April, when Dulles' deteriorating health forced his resignation (he died May 14, 1959), neither Dulles nor Eisenhower made any mention of possible use of nuclear weapons, as they had done in earlier Far Eastern crises.* Eisenhower was both skeptical about the likelihood of Khrushchev's taking any serious risk of nuclear war and conscious of the very exposed position of the Western Allies in Berlin. His distaste for the situation was later expressed in his memoirs:

> Inevitably, despite intimate acquaintance with it, the question kept coming back to me: "How, or rather why did the Free World get into this mess? How did we ever accept a situation in which our only feasible response to an attack on a thirteen-thousand-man garrison surrounded by numerous Communist divisions would likely mean the initiation of World War III?"[13]

Khrushchev's "ultimatum" had caused public alarm. It was suddenly realized that America's nuclear strike capability was a questionable deterrent. "For the first time," wrote Henry Kissinger, "there exists

---

* The Far Eastern crises are discussed in chapter 5.

grave doubt about our willingness to run risks on behalf of our allies
... Newspapers, officials and opposition leaders in both Germany and France constantly raise the question: What objective in Europe would seem to the United States worth the destruction of Washington and New York . . .?"[14]

Eisenhower's handling of the problem was cautious and low-keyed. On November 14, 1958, four days after Khrushchev first stated his demand to end the occupation of Berlin, when three U.S. army trucks were detained for more than eight hours by the Russians, Norstad, the U.S. general commanding NATO forces, proposed to send through "a test convoy" and to back it with "mimimum force necessary" if it were detained. That proposal was sidetracked to allow time for consultation with Britain and France. The President preferred "some sort of low-key announcement that the United States would stand on its commitments," a task which was performed by press secretary Jim Haggerty.[15] The Joint Chiefs of Staff then recommended forcible action to insist on the right of passage "with a fairly substantial force—one division—on the day the first truck convoy should be stopped."[16] But Eisenhower and Dulles both opposed escalation at that point. On January 29, 1959 the President and his advisers agreed on plans to keep all options open, while starting with measures considerably short of the use of force:

> The plan, as I approved it . . . , included these steps: (a) A refusal to acquiesce in any substitution of East Germans for Soviet officials in checking the Western occupying powers movement to and from Berlin. (While it would be permissible to show an East German official a pass for identification purposes, such official would not be permitted to stamp a pass); (b) A decision to begin quiet military preparations in West Germany and Berlin prior to May 27, sufficient to be detected by Soviet intelligence but not sufficient to create public alarm; (c) Should there be any substitution of East German officials for Soviets, a small convoy with armed protection would attempt to go through, and if this convoy were stopped, the effect (sic) would be discontinued and the probe would fire only if fired upon; (d) Transit would then be suspended and pressure would be brought to bear on the Soviets by publicizing the blockade and taking the matter to the United Nations Security Council and, if necessary, to the General Assembly. In these circumstances our further military preparations would be intensified by observable means such as the evacuation of dependents from West Berlin and possibly from all Germany; (e) In the event that this moral and other pressure was not sufficient, use of additional force would be subject to governmental

decision; (f) We would at once attempt to bring about a foreign ministers' meeting with the Soviet Union to be held about the middle of April.[17]

At a news conference on March 11, 1959 Eisenhower rejected the opinion of critics such as Dean Acheson that the crisis required any substantial reinforcement of American troops and tactical air strength in Europe. "What good," he said, "would it do to send a few more thousands or even a few divisions of troops to Europe? You couldn't possibly, between now and summer, any time, put the kind of divisions from all the countries of the world to meet that kind of a threat." Asked whether he would resort to nuclear war, if necessary, to defend West Berlin, he responded:

> The United States, and its allies, have announced their firm intention of preserving their rights and responsibilities with respect to Berlin. If... any push in the direction of real hostilities is going to occur, it's going to occur from the side of the Soviets.
>
> Now, if that would become reality, and I don't believe anyone would be senseless enough to push that to the point of reality, then there would be the time to decide exactly what the Allies would, in turn, expect to do.[18]

Eisenhower was conscious of the need to avoid putting Khrushchev in a corner by the use of threatening rhetoric. He would make no decision whether to resort to force until he had to. While declaring that the West would not accept any deadline for agreement, or any unilateral termination of Western rights, he did agree, after consultation with the British and French, to a lengthy foreign ministers' meeting held at Geneva from May to August 1959, at which the Western powers made a four-part compromise proposal:

1. They declared their intention "to limit the combined total of their forces in Berlin to the present figure (approximately 11,000) and to continue to arm these forces only with conventional weapons as at present."

2. They called for agreement by the four occupying powers "that there shall continue to be free and unrestricted access to West Berlin by land, by water and by air for all persons, goods and communications, including those of the French, United Kingdom and United States forces stationed in West Berlin. The procedures applicable shall be those in effect in April 1959." Given Soviet agreement on this point, and "without prejudice to existing basic responsibilities," the Western Powers would accept that these procedures might be carried out "by

German personnel," but all disputes with respect to access were to be settled between the four powers, which would establish a quadripartite commission in Berlin to examine any difficulties.

3. Measures should be taken to avoid propaganda and intelligence activities in any part of Berlin which might either disturb public order "or amount to interference in the internal affairs of others." This was meant to include the East German state which the West had not recognized.

4. It should be agreed that these arrangements would continue in force until the re-unification of Germany.

The Western powers also said they were willing to consider a significant UN role in Berlin, which should start with the monitoring of propaganda activities which might affect the rights of others.[19]

The Eisenhower administration seemed to have de-fused the issue by continuing negotiations, but Khrushchev had perhaps been encouraged to expect ultimate Western concessions. He no longer insisted on any time limit for negotiations, and these were still pending when the big four summit meeting scheduled for May of 1960 was broken off by Khrushchev in indignation over the U-2 incident.[20] He would wait to discuss the Berlin situation, he said, with the next American President after January 1961.[21]

President Kennedy thus had ample warning, before he took office, that the Berlin issue would have to be dealt with in his administration. At the beginning of January 1961, Khrushchev again spoke of a necessity to end the occupation regime and of his determination to sign a peace treaty which would turn over control to the German Democratic Republic. At their get-acquainted summit meeting in Vienna in June, Khrushchev reiterated that the Soviet Union would conclude the treaty by the end of 1961, and after that any violation of East German borders would be met by force. Kennedy replied firmly that the United States would stand on its established rights in Berlin.

An intensive review of policy options had already been begun. Kennedy had requested a special study of the problem by Dean Acheson. According to Schlesinger, Kennedy "thought of little else that summer."[22]

Acheson saw no possibility of compromise. If Khrushchev went ahead with his East German treaty, Acheson advised acceptance of administration of access procedures by East Germans, but he recommended that at the first actual interruption of access to Berlin the Western allies should show willingness to face war by sending an armed force down the *Autobahn*. To convince Khrushchev that to challenge the West in this way really would risk nuclear war, Western conventional and nuclear forces in West Germany should be significantly reinforced. Kennedy called on the Secretary of Defense to develop a plan for a non-nuclear military response large enough to give time for negotiation, but he was in basic accord with Acheson's viewpoint. On July 25, 1961, in a televised report to the nation, he publicly committed himself to a very firm stand. He spoke of Khrushchev's intention "to bring to an end, through a stroke of the pen, first, our legal rights to be in West Berlin and, secondly, our ability to make good on our commitment to the two million free people of that city. That we cannot permit." Reviewing the historical background, he continued:

> West Berlin . . . has now become . . . the great testing place of Western courage and will . . . It would be a mistake for others to look upon Berlin, because of its location, as a tempting target. The United States is there, the United Kingdom and France are there, the pledge of NATO is there, and the people of Berlin are there. It is as secure as the rest of us, for we cannot separate its safety from our own. . . . We do not want to fight, but we have fought before. . . . We cannot and will not permit the Communists to drive us out of Berlin.

To be ready to resist with force, he announced that he was requesting from Congress considerable increases in military appropriations and in active duty armed forces, a doubling and tripling of draft calls, and a ground alert for 50 per cent of the nation's B-52 and B-47 bombers.

In the face of this determined stand, the Soviet Union turned to a local solution for the drain of East German resources through Berlin. Without further challenge to the Western sectors of the city, it closed the sector borders between East and West Berlin on Aug. 13, and soon afterwards began the construction of the Berlin Wall. This did contravene the post-war undertakings to treat Berlin as a united city, but no more so than the earlier separate plans for the Eastern and Western Zones of Germany had contravened the original undertakings to treat all Germany as an economic unit. It was far less of a challenge to established Western rights than Khrushchev's earlier proposals, and while the United States and its allies protested the division of the city, no one proposed that the West should initiate the use of force to oppose it. Both sides were content to let the crisis fade away. When Kennedy announced his missile quarantine of Cuba, in October 1962, there were no Soviet reprisals against Berlin.[23]

In 1971 the Berlin issue was happily resolved, thanks largely to a sustained effort by Chancellor Willy Brandt, for which he received the Nobel peace prize. The key was his government's willingness to accept the existing frontiers in Eastern Europe, and to recognize the legitimacy of the German Democratic Republic as a sovereign state. In August of 1970 he concluded a treaty between the Federal Republic and the Soviet Union which declared both parties' respect for the existing frontiers and the territorial integrity of all states in Europe, and the parties' intent to be guided in their mutual relations by the aims and principles of the UN Charter, including peaceful settlement of disputes and avoidance of the threat or use of force. In November of the same year came the Treaty on Normalization of Mutual Relations between the Federal Republic of Germany and the Polish People's Republic. The two parties agreed that the existing border along the Oder and Lusatian Neisse Rivers constituted Poland's western state frontier, and they pledged that they would advance no territorial claims against one another and would abide by the UN principles concerning peaceful settlement of disputes. Ratification of the two treaties was held up by the Federal Republic pending conclusion of a definitive agreement on Berlin. There followed negotiations among the four occupying powers which culminated in a Quadripartite Agreement on Berlin, signed on Sept. 3, 1971, but to be brought into effect only after further detailed arrangements were negotiated between "the competent German authorities." The Quadripartite Agreement gave assurances that access to West Berlin would not be interfered with, that force or threats of force would not be used in the area, and that "the situation which has developed in the area . . . shall not be changed unilaterally." The Soviet Union further declared,

> that transit traffic by road, rail and waterways through the territory of the German Democratic Republic of civilian persons and goods between the Western Sectors of Berlin and the Federal Republic of Germany will be unimpeded; that such traffic will be facilitated so as to take place in the most simple and expeditious manner; and that it will receive preferential treatment.

On their part, the Western governments declared that the Western Sectors of Berlin were not part of the Federal Republic or to be governed by it, and they authorized the establishment of a Soviet consulate in West Berlin. The preamble specified that all of this was "without prejudice to [the parties'] legal positions."[24] The ensuing negotiations between the FRG and the GDR proved difficult, but two agreements were concluded, on December 17 and 20, 1971, one on arrangements to facilitate transit traffic and the other, more difficult to negotiate, giving West Berliners the opportunity to visit relatives in East Germany.[25] A protocol bringing the whole package of agreements into effect was signed on June 3, 1972, and the following year the two German states were simultaneously admitted to the United Nations.

In the matter of Berlin the United States and its allies had considered the maintenance of the *status quo* worth the risk of war. The fact that their position had a firm legal foundation was a consideration that made it more likely they would insist on their rights, and made their willingness to risk war more credible to the Russians. One would have to say that this confrontation was won by the West.

The United States precipitated a new round of "chicken" in October 1962 over Soviet nuclear missiles in Cuba. A great deal has been written about that crisis, including a specific study of its legal dimension.[26] Demanding removal of the missiles and backing his demand with a clear threat to use force, if necessary, if work on the missile bases was not stopped, President Kennedy succeeded in giving this demand a better color of legality when the Organization of American States acted on his request to make the demand for removal of the missiles a collective measure of the hemispheric organization.* However, the actions which the Soviet Union had taken, with the consent of the Cuban Government, had not seemed in advance to contravene any American legal right. The stand taken by the United States was not given credibility, as it had been with respect to Berlin, as a stand in defense of legal rights which a great power could not be expected to give up under threat. Positions in this respect were almost reversed. To make his threat to use force credible in this instance, President Kennedy had to rely on considerations that were political, strategic, and psychological, rather than legal. They were nevertheless persuasive:

1. Starting with his address to the nation on October 22nd, at which he revealed the presence of the Soviet missiles, he took a very determined stand — one from which it would be almost impossible for

---

* The legal element in Kennedy's quarantine decision is discussed in chapter 7.

him to retreat without incalculable damage to his personal political influence as President of the United States.

2. He stressed the fact that the Soviet Union was for the first time intruding militarily in "an area well known to a have a special and historical relationship to the United States."It was not hard to compare American concern for this area with Soviet concern about security in Eastern Europe. This was an area of confrontation in which the United States had a psychological advantage. All the world knew that the people of the United States were far more concerned about control of the Caribbean than were the people of the Soviet Union.

3. It had become clear that the United States knew that it had at this time a commanding superiority over the Soviet Union in nuclear retaliatory power, and much greater conventional superiority in the area in dispute.

The President and his advisers were nevertheless uncomfortably conscious that they had come altogether too close to the brink of nuclear war, and that with an attack on the Soviet missile bases which was the next logical American move, a process of escalation might set in that would be hard to stop.[27] Kennedy was therefore anxious not to push Khrushchev too far. In return for Soviet removal of the missiles, he pledged that the United States would not invade Cuba, and he also conveyed to Ambassador Dobrynin, through Robert Kennedy, informal notice that he had decided to remove American missiles from bases close to the Soviet Union in Turkey and Italy.[28]

Another confrontation of this type occurred in October 1973 when the USSR seemed preparing to send Soviet troops to Egypt unless Israel stopped its advance across the Suez Canal, and the United States responded by alerting U.S. forces, to emphasize their determination to prevent Soviet intervention. The balance of interests and commitments of the two superpowers was more nearly equal than it was in the Cuban situation. The sense of acute crisis brought a quick end to the fighting between Israel and Egypt, aided by U.S. insistence that Israel stop its offensive and acceptance by all parties of Security Council resolutions calling for a cease-fire and the creation of a neutral UN peace-keeping force to supervise its observance.[29] Something similar is reported to have occurred in June 1982, when pressure from the Reagan administration, after warning from the Soviet Union, forced Israel to accept a cease-fire ending its offensive against the Syrian army in Lebanon.[30]

CHAPTER IV

"LIMITED WAR" IN KOREA

1. AMERICAN POLICY CONCERNING KOREA BEFORE JUNE 1950

To the end of the war with Japan, Korea figured in American planning as little more than an afterthought. The Korean peninsula was not in itself of any importance to the United States. It was easy to support the general principle that the country, which Japan had annexed in 1910, should have its independence restored. President Roosevelt assumed that a period of "tutelage" under an Allied trusteeship would be necessary. Consequently, at Cairo and Potsdam, the Allies agreed that Korea should become free and independent "in due course." But if Korea was unimportant to the United States, it was of great interest to China, Japan, and Russia. Their three-cornered struggle over Korea had caused two wars in 1894-5 and 1904-5.

Until Japan surrendered it seemed likely that all of Korea would be occupied by Russian forces, which entered the war, as had been agreed at Yalta, three months after the German surrender. They immediately launched an offensive into Korea. At the last moment, when it became evident that the Japanese would surrender much sooner than anyone had anticipated, officials in Washington proposed that Korea be divided at the 38th parallel between Russian and American occupation zones. The object of this move was to keep as much of Korea as possible from falling under Russian occupation. The proposal was made on August 13 and was accepted by Stalin. Before the first American troops reached Korea on September 8, Soviet forces had in fact reached Seoul. When the Americans arrived, the Soviet forces withdrew north of the 38th parallel.

Soviet-American rivalry greatly magnified internal dissension in Korea. Korean Communist exiles returned to their country with the Russians. In the South the American occupation authorities were neither prepared nor qualified to deal with Korean politics. There was one point on which all Koreans were in agreement. They expected and desired immediate independence and they bitterly opposed the idea of trusteeship. Just before Tokyo's surrender, the Japanese tried to transfer power to a Korean government. They first approached a leader of the right wing of the Korean nationalists, who refused to deal with them. Then they turned to a leader of the nationalists' left wing, Lyuh Woon-hyung. Lyuh organized a "Committee for Preparation of Korean Independence." Under its auspices a "National Assembly" of some 1000 delegates, from the North as well as the South, met in Seoul two days before the Americans arrived and declared itself to be the government of "The People's Republic of Korea." Chairmanship of the Republic was offered to Syngman Rhee, a figure of great prestige among Koreans. He had founded a "Provisional Government of Korea" in exile in China and was regarded as "the embodiment of the Korean independence movement." Lyuh was to be vice-chairman. The People's Republic had also created provincial committees for local government and in the North the Russians supported these instead of setting up a military government. But the American commander had no authority to deal with any Korean government, as none had been anticipated. His State Department adviser considered Lyuh to be a Communist. Insisting that only the military government would govern, the Americans rejected the People's Republic, encouraged the proliferation of political parties, and favored a right-wing coalition as insurance against Communist control. Syngman Rhee, who returned from exile on October 16, refused the chairmanship that the People's Republic had offered him and became the leader of the rightists.[1]

General Hodge, the American commander in Korea, became deeply disturbed about future prospects. Three months after the occupation began, he sent a report to Washington which said that dual occupation had made "any talk of real freedom and independence . . . purely academic." The Koreans, he said, "want their independence more than any one thing and want it now." They would actively resist the imposition of a trusteeship. His report concluded:

> Under present conditions with no corrective action forthcoming I would go so far as to recommend we give serious consideration to an agreement with Russia that both the U.S. and Russia withdraw forces from Korea simultaneously and leave Korea to its own devices and an inevitable upheaval for its self purification.[2]

The government in Washington did not take up General Hodge's radical suggestion. At a meeting of the Allied foreign ministers in Moscow in December 1945 it proposed the creation of "a unified administration under the two military commands acting jointly" to deal with problems of the economy, communications, and displaced persons, and four-power discussions to work out a trusteeship agreement. In place of this suggestion, Secretary of State Byrnes accepted a Soviet counter-proposal to create a joint commission of United States and Sovet representatives to consult with "Korean democratic parties and social organizations," to prepare the way for an all-Korean provisional government.

The next two years were taken up by fruitless Soviet-American negotiations to give effect to this Moscow agreement. It would be hard to say which of the two great power rivals was more responsible for blocking the attainment of a unified independent Korea. The Russians seemed determined to accept no formula for unification which would not insure a Korean government that they could control. On the side of the Americans, the refusal to accept the "People's Republic" and the rejection of General Hodge's proposal three months later showed an equal unwillingness to take risks that might eventuate in Communist control. So long as the Soviet-American deadlock persisted, there was no prospect of ending the partition of the country.

In September 1947 the United States abandoned the effort to negotiate directly with the Russians and decided to refer the Korean problem to the UN General Assembly. Over Soviet opposition, it persuaded the Assembly to establish a UN temporary commission on Korea, which was directed to consult the Korean people, north as well as south of the 38th parallel, and to prepare for election of a Korean National Assembly in March of 1948. By the terms of the resolution which created it, the UN commission was authorized to consult the Interim Committee of the General Assembly (a committee of the whole intended to function between the regular sessions of the General Assembly) as to the application of its mandate. The members of the Soviet bloc had opposed the establishment of the temporary commission and also that of the Interim Committee and refused to participate in either body. Predictably, the temporary commission was denied permission to enter North Korea. It then asked the Interim Committee for advice on the question whether it should proceed with the elections to a national assembly in the U.S. zone alone. Following American leadership, the Interim Committee advised the temporary commission to go ahead. Some members of the temporary commission, and some delegations in the Interim Committee, questioned the wisdom of proceeding under these conditions, fearing that it would make the unification of Korea more difficult, but by vote of a majority the commission decided to hold the election. It took place under UN supervision on May 10, 1948, and the General Assembly (again over opposition of the Soviet bloc) endorsed the result. It declared, in a resolution of Dec. 12, 1948,

> that there has been established a lawful government (the Government of the Republic of Korea) having effective control and jurisdiction over that part of Korea where the Temporary Commission was able to observe and consult and in which the great majority of the people of all Korea reside; that this government is based on elections which were a valid expression of the free will of the electorate of that part of Korea and which were observed by the Temporary Commission; and that this is the only such Government in Korea . . .

It recommended that the occupying powers should withdraw their forces, and it established a new UN commission to function in Korea, to observe conditions there and to continue the effort to bring about Korean unification in accordance with the prior resolutions.[3] In North Korea, the establishment of "The Democratic People's Republic of Korea" was announced on September 9, 1948. Soviet troops were withdrawn at the end of 1948, and American troops in June 1949. Rival North and South Korean armies faced each other instead.

This American attempt to use the United Nations to solve the Korean problem without Soviet agreement had not brought unification any closer. It did involve the UN in the Korean problem and it did confer legitimacy upon the new Korean government south of the 38th parallel. The UN commission which remained in Korea was able to provide authoritative reports on the nature and scale of the attack when the North Koreans invaded South Korea on June 25, 1950.

2. THE DECISION TO USE FORCE TO REPEL THE NORTH KOREAN ATTACK

When South Korea was invaded, to call for an immediate meeting of the UN Security Council and to associate the United Nations with whatever American action should be taken was a semi-automatic response. This was so because the UN was already involved in the Korean problem and also because the North Korean attack was perceived as a flagrant violation of the UN principle forbidding resort to force[4] and a critical challenge to the world organization.

To support the United Nations was one of the reasons for President Truman's decision to commit American forces to South Korea's defense.[5] The challenge to the UN was comparable to the one Italy had presented to the League of Nations with its 1935 invasion of Ethiopia. If the UN did not rise to the challenge, worldwide confidence in it would collapse and it would go the way of the League. The President and his advisers were determined to show that the history of the 1930s would not be repeated.

There were also other, non-UN reasons for a vigorous American response. These were the intent to "contain" communism, the need to maintain the "free world" coalition by demonstrating willingness to stand by small countries dependent on American support, and the particular U.S. responsibility for South Korea because it had become independent under American tutelage and sponsorship.

For all these reasons, Truman boldly decided that the United States must fight in Korea, and tactical considerations also indicated associating the military effort with the UN. Strong support of the UN membership for vigorous American leadership seemed assured. To mobilize the maximum international support was clearly desirable. The President and his advisers were therefore of one mind in treating the defense of South Korea as a United Nations action.

While the United States was now indisputably engaged, as Senator Robert A. Taft said in the Senate, in "a *de facto* war with the Northern Korean Communists," President Truman did not ask Congress to declare the existence of a state of war or to approve the use of American armed forces in Korea. Taft and other Republican leaders announced that they would support such a resolution, but the President concurred with the advice of Secretary Acheson that he had power enough to act in his capacity as commander in chief without asking for Congressional approval.[6] A Department of State memorandum argued that the President's constitutional obligation to "take care that the laws be faithfully executed" was sufficient authority for him to take forcible action to carry out U.S. obligations under the UN Charter, a treaty to which the United States was a party.[7] Failure to ask Congress to approve the U.S. military action may have been a mistake. It was an important step in the assumption of power by the executive to involve the United States in undeclared war.

The Korean War called attention, for the first time, to the possibility of "limited war." Previous consideration of possible conflict between the United States and armies of the Communist bloc had assumed that this would be a third world war, in which the decisive battle would be between the United States and the Soviet Union, and diversion of land forces to Asia would be strategically unwise. Truman and his advisers were willing to face the risk of a third world war, but they doubted that the Russians meant to precipitate one, and they immediately saw that they should try to keep the conflict localized. To supplement the UN's summons to "the authorities in North Korea" to cease hostilities and withdraw, the United States approached the Soviet government directly. "In view universally known fact close relations between USSR and North Korean regime," it told the USSR, "US Govt. asks assurance USSR disavows responsibility for this attack and that it will use its influence with North Korean authorities to withdraw their invading forces immediately." The Soviet reply encouraged the hope that wider war was not imminent. It asserted that the conflict had been provoked by the South Koreans and said that the Soviet government was adhering to "the principle of the impermissibility of interference by foreign powers in the internal affairs of Korea."[8]

The Soviet government failed to send its representative to the initial meetings of the Security Council, continuing until August its previous policy of refusing to participate in Council meetings so long as the new communist government of China was denied its right, as they saw it, to fill China's seat. Because of that Soviet absence, Security Council resolutions recommending that the other members of the UN send military assistance to help South Korea repel the attack, and requesting the United States to designate the commander of the UN forces, were adopted without encountering the Soviet veto, and when the Soviet representative returned in August, lacking any support, he had no way to reverse the course of action. The UN authorization did bring significant moral and material support for the American military effort, and it stimulated a brief revival of State Department enthusiasm for the United Nations as a security organization. In November 1950 the "Uniting for Peace" resolution, sponsored by the United States, passed the General Assembly. It provided a way to call the General Assembly into immediate emergency session in case of a future aggression and to enable it to authorize collective military action by the use of its recommendatory powers if a majority of the Security Council should be blocked from acting solely by exercise of the veto by one of the permanent members.

American and UN action to defend South Korean was, in its initial phase, a striking success. After a rearguard action by the first American units, the UN and South Korean forces held a perimeter around Korea's southernmost port of Pusan while a counterattack was prepared. On September 15th MacArthur's landing at Inchon dramatically turned the tide and routed the North Koreans. By the end of September they had been driven out of South Korea. It had been demonstrated that the UN Charter would be enforced, that the history of the 1930s would not be repeated, and that the United States would protect its smaller allies. As a result, support for the United Nations in American opinion polls registered its historic high. In the world, the prestige of the United Nations and of the United States were also at all-time highs. The tragedy of the Korean War is that the decision-makers of the Truman administration did not stop with this success but allowed the conflict to escalate into a war between U.S. and Chinese forces. The lessons of the Korean War relate to the difficult task of preventing limited conflict from escalating.

3. THE CONFLICT ESCALATES

The escalation of the Korean conflict resulted from mistakes of both China and the United States. On the one side was a failure of the Chinese Communists to convey, in timely and credible form, their intention to protect North Korea from incursion by United States or UN forces. On the American side, the crucial mistake was the decision, after the invaders had been defeated and expelled from South Korea, to continue the UN offensive in an effort to bring North Korea under UN control.

The Security Council, in a resolution which had been drafted by the United States, provided for the establishment of a unified command "under the United States," and asked the United States to designate the commander of the UN forces. It authorized use of the United Nations flag and requested the United States "to provide the Security Council with reports as appropriate on the course of action taken." The effect of this resolution was to leave the Security Council itself as the only UN agency charged with political direction of the operation. When the representative of the Soviet Union returned to the Council in the month of August the Council was effectively hamstrung in this respect, and when the forces fighting under the UN flag went on the offensive, the United States was therefore in sole control of the limits to be placed on military operations.[9] There was some consultation with the British and French governments. Other allies received only briefings on the military situation.

The UN military action had been authorized by two Security Council resolutions, of June 25 and June 27, 1950. The first called upon the authorities in North Korea to cease hostilities and to withdraw their forces to the 38th parallel. The second noted that the North Koreans had not complied and recommended that the members of the United Nations "furnish such assistance to the Republic of Korea as may be necessary to repel the armed attack and to restore international peace and security in the area." At the start American policy makers thought of no objective beyond compelling North Korean withdrawal. Secretary Acheson declared on June 29th that the action was "solely for the purpose of restoring the Republic of Korea to its status prior to the invasion." And President Truman said later that he had given directions on June 29th "that operations above the 38th parallel should be designed only to destroy military supplies, for I wanted it clearly understood that our operations in Korea were designed to restore peace there and to restore the border."[10]

The first person to question the initial assumption was John Allison, director of the Office of Northeast Asian Affairs in the State Department, who wrote on July 1 to Dean Rusk, assistant secretary for Far Eastern Affairs:

> I understand that there has been some suggestion that in the speech which is being prepared for President Truman to make on the Korean situation there should be included a statement to the effect that United States forces and presumably South Korean forces will only attempt to drive the North Koreans back to the 38th parallel and will not go any farther. I most strongly urge that no such statement be included in the speech.... I believe there is ample justification in the last part of the second Resolution of the Security Council for any action which may be deemed appropriate at the time which will contribute to the permanent restoration of peace and stability in that area. I am convinced that there will be no permanent peace and stability in Korea as long as the artificial division at the 38th parallel continues....[11]

Rusk noted his agreement in the margin. Allison was also suported by State Department consultant John Foster Dulles, who wrote on July 14:

> The United Nations has, from the beginning, insisted that justice and equity require a united Korea. The 38th Parallel, if perpetuated as a political line, and as providing an asylum to the aggressor, is bound to

perpetuate friction ... If we have the opportunity to obliterate the line as a political division, certainly we should do so in the interest of "peace and security in the area." (UN Resolution)[12]

He argued that the question whether to cross the parallel should be left to be decided eventually on the basis of expediency.

The question of the 38th parallel then became the subject of prolonged and intensive discussion within the government. On July 13th Acheson issued instructions that no more public statements should be made about it. The matter was referred to the Policy Planning Staff which, in a memorandum of July 22, drew a distinction between two parts of the Korean problem: the effort to bring about the unity and independence of Korea, which had been a long-standing UN concern, and the current enforcement action. The purpose of the latter was only to bring the cessation of the hostilities and the withdrawal of the North Korean forces to the 38th parallel. The memorandum noted that the Korean peninsula was strategically important to Russia. One of its conclusions was that "if UN forces were to continue military ground action north of the 38th parallel ... the danger of conflict with Chinese communist or Soviet forces would be greatly increased." It also concluded that "UN military action north of the 38th parallel, except to the extent essential for tactical requirements as fighting approaches that line, would require a new Security Council resolution." It ended with the recommendation:

> It should be kept constantly before world opinion that U.S. forces in Korea are acting as a part of UN forces in response to Security Council resolutions; that they are acting in support of the moral principle of repelling aggression; that their immediate purpose is to bring about the cessation of hostilities and the withdrawal of the North Korean forces to the 38th parallel; and that other measures in regard to Korea which might be necessary or desirable, once the aggression has been brought to an end, would be a subject for UN consideration.[13]

A memorandum from the Department of Defense expressed an opposing viewpoint. It noted that the Security Council "did not specifically limit ground operations of the unified command to the area south of the 38th parallel." Therefore any of three courses of action "could be interpreted as in consonance with the Security Council resolutions:"

1. A minimum offensive effort to force the North Koreans north of the 38th parallel.

2. The occupation of Pyongyang (the North Korean capital) and the narrow part of the peninsula, leaving an unoccupied zone between there and the Chinese and Soviet frontiers.

3. A maximum effort to occupy and pacify all of Korea.[14]

By the end of August, after many meetings and drafts designed to prepare an agreed policy recommendation for the National Security Council, all participants had conceded that the June 27th resolution could be given either a narrow or a broad interpretation, and the focus of attention had become the degree of risk of Soviet or Chinese intervention. On August 25th the State Department group decided not to object to operations north of the 38th parallel, if it was understood that they should keep well clear of the Russian frontier. A paper prepared for use in tripartite talks with the British and French during a foreign ministers' meeting to be held early in September expressed the American position at this time:

> The unified command should be authorized to conduct military operations without regard to the 38th parallel and should continue the advance northward in order to stabilize and unify as much of the country as is feasible, unless
> (1) Soviet forces occupy North Korea to the 38th parallel.
> (2) Major Soviet or Chinese Communist units engage or indicate their intention of engaging in hostilities against UN forces.
>
> In these cases further UN decisions should be sought. In any event ground operations should be kept away from Manchurian and USSR frontiers.[15]

On September 9 the National Security Council reported to the President:

> The United Nations forces have a legal basis for conducting operations north of the 38th parallel to compel the withdrawal of the North Korean forces behind this line or to defeat these forces.

MacArthur was directed to start planning for a possible occupation of North Korea, but he was told not to execute such plans without the President's approval.[16]

In the tripartite talks, the British expressed doubt whether crossing the 38th parallel could be justified under the June 27 resolution, and the French also opposed crossing that line without a Security Council decision to do so.[17] No clear tripartite decision resulted, but the British government informed India of its perception that it had been agreed that there would be no advance beyond the 38th parallel until the UN had again considered the matter.

Both the Secretary of State and the President continued to say that what to do when the 38th parallel was reached should be a UN decision. On September 11, Acheson told the Senate Foreign Relations Committee, "This must be a United Nations decision... You can't get it in the Security Council [with the Russians present], and therefore the matter has got to be put into the General Assembly, where there is no veto . . ." And as late as September 21 President Truman told his press conference that he had made no decision in the matter because "That is a United Nations force, and we are one of the many who are interested in that situation. It will be worked out by the United Nations and I will abide by the decision that the United Nations makes."[18]

But in fact the decision was made by the United States and not by the United Nations. MacArthur's victory at Inchon changed the psychological climate. Seoul was taken on the September 28th, with the enemy in full flight. There was every likelihood that the conflict could be ended where it began, at the 38th parallel, if the United States and its allies were willing to accept that limited solution. But the Russians and the Chinese had given no clear indication of any intention to intervene. MacArthur was eager to follow up his victory, and his prestige was now very high. The Joint Chiefs of Staff, who had doubted the wisdom of the Inchon operations and had tried to talk MacArthur out of it, were now reluctant to challenge his judgment. Moreover, with the mid-term election approaching, any seeming hesitancy would enable the Republicans to make political capital out of anything that might be construed as "appeasement of communism." The risk of Chinese or Russian intervention began to appear slight in proportion to the tempting prospect of successful unification of Korea under UN auspices.

On September 27th new instructions were approved by the President and sent to MacArthur:

> Your military objective is the destruction of the North Korean armed forces. . . . You are authorized to conduct military operations north of the 38th parallel in Korea, provided . . . that at the time of such operation there has been no entry into North Korea by major Soviet or Chinese Communist forces . . .

On September 29th, the Joint Chiefs of Staff approved MacArthur's plan for an advance up the west coast and a landing on the east coast of North Korea. South Korean forces moved into North Korea on September 29th, and by October 10 they had captured Wonson, 150 miles to the north. U.S. and UN forces moved north of the parallel on October 7th.[19]

American decision-makers had not waited for approval by the UN of the drive to the north. With the Russians in attendance, there was no prospect of getting it from the Security Council. Nor had the General Assembly any authority to take over the direction of military operations.[20] Plans had been made, however, to ask the General Assembly to approve a resolution which merely noted that United Nations forces were "at present operating in Korea in accordance with the recommendation of the Security Council," and then went on to recommend measures to give effect to previous Assembly resolutions concerning the holding of elections to establish a unified Korean government. The British had drafted this resolution, and when they first proposed it, it provided for the establishment of a UN interim commission which would conduct discussions with North Korean representatives regarding the political future of Korea, informing them that the UN intended to hold new national elections to establish a unified government, and assuring them that "any United Nations forces entering North Korea" would do so only for the purpose of maintaining law and order while the elections were held and a new government established.[21] By September 25, however, the British draft had been modified to eliminate the provision for discussions with the North Koreans. The British had evidently decided to accept the American decision to continue the military advance without any suggestion that negotiation was necessary.

The government of India strenuously objected to continuation of the UN offensive beyond the 38th parallel. India was an important factor by virtue of its size, of the prestige of Prime Minister Nehru, and of the fact that it was a leader of Asian opinion, and it was also the non-communist government which had the best channel of communication with the Chinese government in Peking. As the Indian government had been told by the British that UN forces would not go north of the 38th parallel without prior UN direction, Nehru protested when Foreign Secretary Bevin communicated the text of the proposed resolution to him on Sept. 27th. He urged that the Security Council had only authorized military action to procure a return to the 38th parallel and that there was no authority in law for the use of force to alter the *status quo* north of that line or to give effect to the General Assembly's political recommendations. He concluded that the military operation should end when that border was reached, and negotiations should be opened with the North Koreans on the subject of a UN plebiscite for all Korea. The Indian ambassador in Peking was reporting increasing indications that China would intervene if UN forces advanced into North Korea.[22] The British and Americans made no change in plans. They suspected that the Chinese might be bluffing in the hope of influencing the General Assembly.

On Sept. 29th eight delegations joined in submitting the British draft resolution. It said:

> *Mindful* of the fact that the objectives set forth in the [previous General Assembly] resolutions . . . have not been fully accomplished and, in particular, that the unification of Korea has not yet been achieved, and that an attempt has been made by an armed attack from North Korea to extinguish by force the Government of the Republic of Korea . . .
>
> *Having in mind* that United Nations armed forces are at present operating in Korea in accordance with the recommendations of the Security Council . . .
>
> [The General Assembly] *Recommends that*
>
> (a) All appropriate steps be taken to ensure conditions of stability throughout Korea;
>
> (b) All constituent acts be taken, including the holding of elections, under the auspices of the United Nations, for the establishment of a unified, independent and democratic government in the sovereign State of Korea;
>
> (c) United Nations forces should not remain in any part of Korea otherwise than so far as necessary for achieving the objectives specified in paragraphs (a) and (b) above; . . .

U.S. officials lobbied in favor of the resolution. Only the Indian and Yugoslav representatives argued that the UN forces had no authority to change the preexisting *status quo*. The resolution was adopted on October 7th, with the Soviet bloc voting in the negative and with India, Yugoslavia, and five Arab governments abstaining. The closeness of the real division of opinion may be more accurately indicated by the 32 to 24 vote which defeated an Indian proposal to set up a sub-committee to seek a compromise between this resolution and one offered by the Soviet Union, which would have provided for cessation of hostilities, withdrawal of foreign troops and all-Korean elections, in that order, the elections to be supervised by a joint commission of representatives of the Assemblies of North and South Korea and observed by a United Nations committee which would include representatives of the USSR and Communist China. Since the resolution of October 7th assumed rather than decided that the UN forces would pacify North Korea, the most that can be said is that, by adopting the resolution, the majority showed that it did not *disapprove* of the United States' intention to carry the campaign into North Korea.

Richard Neustadt has pointed out that at this point the UN connection produced an element of self-deception in Washington:

> In White House memoranda and in papers for the National Security Council, in intelligence evaluations and the like, repeated use of such terms as 'the UN objective,' 'the decision of the UN,' 'the UN's purpose to unify,' soon dulled awareness that the new war aim [unification of Korea] was nothing but a target of opportunity chosen rather casually (and at first provisionally) by the very men who read these words.... By the middle of October ... Truman and the rest were thinking of the UN aim not as a mere convenience but as a cause.[23]

Soon after the decision to advance north of the 38th parallel had been made in Washington, there came a series of explicit warnings that China would intervene. On October 1, in a speech on the Red Chinese anniversary, Chou En-lai announced: "[The Chinese people] will not tolerate foreign aggression and will not stand aside should the imperialists wantonly invade the territory of their neighbor." On October 3 a second warning was conveyed to the Indian ambassador at Peking. As reported from India, the Chinese Communist government made a distinction in legal terms between crossing of the 38th parallel by South Koreans and crossing by UN forces:

> There was argumentation to effect that crossing of 38th parallel from south would constitute aggression unless Korean conflict from beginning should be considered as civil war.... Peiping officials had made clear that entry of South Korean armed forces into North Korea would not be considered as aggression and that therefore crossing 38th parallel by South Koreans would not necessitate Chinese intervention. Entry of forces other than South Korean into North Korea would be met, however, by Chinese intervention.

On October 7, at Bevin's urging, Nehru appealed to Chou En-lai "to hold his hand." Chou replied that China "had no intention of taking any action if American forces did not cross the 38th parallel, but was determined to do so if American troops moved into North Korea."[24]

General MacArthur had a very great influence on United States decisions concerning the war at this point. This is evident in the report of the conference between President Truman and the general at Wake Island on October 15. The general was there ahead of time to greet the President. They talked privately for an hour, and MacArthur then met for an hour and a half with the President's military and civilian advisers. He exuded confidence. He said that he expected the end of North Korean resistance by Thanksgiving. Asked by the President what the chances were for Chinese or Soviet interference, he answered,

> Very little.... We are no longer fearful of their intervention.... Now that we have bases for our Air Force in Korea, if the Chinese tried to get down to Pyongyang there would be the greatest slaughter.

The question of how far north American troops should go was not brought up.[25]

The first reliable reports of Chinese troops in North Korea came in on October 13th. By the middle of October, U.S. forces had occupied Pyongyang and Wonsan. They could have taken up secure defensive positions there, at the "narrow waist" of Korea, leaving it to the South Koreans to probe further northward or proposing a demilitarized zone between there and the northern border. The British and other allies clearly preferred such a plan, and many officials in Washington, including the Joint Chiefs of Staff, were worried when the evidence of Chinese intervention came in. The directive that had been sent to MacArthur at the end of September had said that no non-Korean ground forces should be used in the areas near the Soviet and Manchurian borders. Yet when MacArthur, on October 24th, announced a plan to have UN forces advance all the way to the northern frontiers of Korea, and when he persisted in that plan even after clashes with considerable Chinese forces, neither the Joint Chiefs nor the President's civilian advisers challenged his judgment. Acheson later conceded that they should have recommended withdrawal to a defensive position on the Pyongyang-Wonsan line.[26]

The Chinese offensive at the end of November found MacArthur's forces widely dispersed. They suffered heavy losses and were forced to retreat into South Korea. The American decision-makers now sought ways to limit the war. It was agreed that anything likely to produce general war with China, such as attack on Chinese bases in Manchuria, must be avoided. All now agreed that a cease-fire and return to the 38th parallel would accomplish the UN mission.[27] But the new conflict in which China was the main opponent was to continue for two and a half years before it was possible to end it close to the 38th parallel.

4. FORMOSA (TAIWAN)

Even before the crossing of the 38th parallel, one part of the initial American response to the North Korean attack had already widened the area of conflict. This was President Truman's order of June 27th which directed the U.S. Navy to prevent any attack by the Chinese Communists against the island of Formosa, the last Chinese territory under control of the Chinese Nationalists, and to prevent any further air and sea operations by the Nationalists against the mainland. The presidential announcement said:

> The attack upon Korea makes it plain beyond all doubt that communism has passed beyond the use of subversion to conquer independent nations and will now use armed invasion and war. It has defied the orders of the Security Council of the United Nations issued to preserve international peace and security. In these circumstances the occupation of Formosa by Communist forces would be a direct threat to the security of the Pacific area and to United States forces performing their lawful and necessary functions in that area.
>
> Accordingly, I have ordered the Seventh Fleet to prevent any attack on Formosa. As a corollary of this action, I am calling upon the Chinese Government on Formosa to cease all air and sea operations against the mainland. The Seventh Fleet will see that this is done. The determination of the future status of Formosa must await the restoration of security in the Pacific, a peace settlement with Japan or consideration by the United Nations. . . .
>
> I have instructed Ambassador Austin, as the representative of the United States to the Security Council, to report these steps to the Council.

Despite the effort to present it as a peace-keeping measure, this was an American intervention in China's civil war. It depended on the United States' own *fiat*. The action was reported to the UN Security Council, but no UN authorization was requested. Communist China was not at that point a belligerent in Korea, and it was clear that the rest of the UN membership would not think that intervention in Chinese politics was justified by the UN principles.

The President's announcement concerning Formosa was a complete reversal of the administration's previous position concerning that island. Arguments that the United States should take the island under its protection had been rejected in a previous policy statement issued by the President on January 5, 1950. That announcement had said:

> Traditional United States policy toward China, as exemplified in the open-door policy, called for international respect for the territorial integrity of China. This principle was recently reaffirmed in the United Nations General Assembly resolution of December 8, 1949. . . .
>
> A specific application of the foregoing principles is seen in the present situation with respect to Formosa. In the joint declaration at Cairo on December 1, 1943, the President of the United States, the British Prime Minister, and the President of China stated that it was their purpose that territories Japan had stolen from China, such as Formosa, should be restored to the Republic of China. The United States was a signatory to the Potsdam declaration of July 26, 1945, which declared that the terms of the Cairo declaration should be carried out. The provisions of this declaration were accepted by Japan at the time of its surrender. In keeping with these declarations, Formosa was surrendered to Generalissimo Chiang Kai-shek, and for the past 4 years, the United States and the other Allied Powers have accepted the exercise of Chinese authority over the Island.
>
> The United States has no predatory designs on Formosa or on any other Chinese territory. The United States has no desire to obtain special rights or privileges or to establish military bases on Formosa at this time. Nor does it have any intention of utilizing its armed forces to interfere in the present situation. The United States Government will not pursue a course which will lead to involvement in the civil conflict in China. . . .[28]

We must consider why this reversal occurred.

While it was not the reason for the decision of June 27th, American policy-makers found that decision easier to take because they were conscious of a possible legal argument that Formosa would not be fully Chinese until completion of a formal peace treaty with Japan.

Formosa (or Taiwan, as the Chinese called it) had been taken from China by Japan in 1895 and it was governed by Japan until 1945. The Cairo Declaration of Dec. 1, 1943 had announced the decision of the United States, the United Kingdom, and China that "all the territories Japan has stolen from the Chinese, such as Manchuria, Formosa, and the Pescadores, shall be restored to the Republic of China." In the Potsdam Declaration of July 26, 1945, those governments reaffirmed that "the terms of the Cairo Declaration shall be carried out and Japanese sovereignty shall be limited to the islands of Honshu, Hokkaido, Kyushu, Shikoku, and such minor islands as we determine." These terms were accepted by Japan in the Instrument of Surrender of Sept. 2, 1945. Japanese forces on Formosa surrendered to Generalissimo Chiang Kai-shek and the Chinese took over the island's administration. That action assumed that the island had become Chinese territory, and the legal opinion that Japan had lost sovereignty over Formosa and that Formosa had been restored to China was stated in an instruction from the Department of State to the commanding general of U.S. forces in the China theater in March, 1946. It contained only a brief caveat that "this transfer may eventually have to be formalized by appropriate treaty arrangements."[29]

Questioning whether it had been wise to treat Formosa as part of China began to be expressed about a year later, in February-March, 1947, when a rebellion of the islanders was harshly repressed by Chinese military force, followed by summary executions of many Formosans. American Ambassador to China John Leighton Stuart now reported that the people of the island would much prefer UN trusteeship or U.S. guardianship to the Chinese government's rule, and he raised for the first time the question whether intervention might not be justified "under present Japanese *de jure* sovereignty."[30]

In 1948 and 1949 much thought was given to possible expedients to save Formosa in view of the disintegration of Kuomintang authority on the mainland. Ambassador Stuart wrote (Dec. 17, 1948):

Problem of Taiwan presents . . . certain differences from other peripheral areas. Inhabitants, after more than generation of Japanese rule and their geographic detachment from the mainland, have developed political sense of autonomy which, if anything, has been strengthened since war by Chinese maladministration. Despite commitment of Cairo declaration, Taiwan is still legally part of Japanese empire and occupied territory. It could therefore be given somewhat different treatment from peripheral areas on mainland. Further, it is more directly related to American security and strategic plans. In event of political and military developments on Chinese mainland involving establishment of regime hostile to it, it is probable we should be loath to see island remain under authority new Chinese Government. Proper course would probably lie in holding

Taiwan in trust for people of China under UN with U.S. as administering trustee until ratification Japanese peace treaty.[31]

These ideas were expressed in Britain as well as the United States. The *Economist* published an article on May 21, 1949 which said,

> If the American Government still wishes to save anything from the wreck of its China policy, the unsettled status of Formosa in international law would afford a ground for treating the island as a separate entity, even if recognition were given to a Communist regime as the Government of China . . .[32]

In Washington, the National Security Council wrestled with the problem. They noted (Jan. 19) that "the present legal status of Formosa and the Pescadores is that they are a portion of the Japanese Empire awaiting final disposition by a treaty of peace." They agreed that it would be desirable to prevent Communist domination of Formosa if that could be accomplished without unacceptable cost. They considered the possibility of asking for a special session of the UN General Assembly to consider the Formosa problem, invoking "special responsibility" of the United States "by reason of the part it played in the liberation of the island." The thought was that the United States would ask for a plebiscite on their future by the people of the island, and would argue that the Chinese government, by misrule, had "forfeited the right to a perfunctory confirmation of sovereignty at the time of concluding a peace settlement with Japan."[33] But there were formidable obstacles in the way of such a plan. The Chinese Nationalist government had on the island 300,000 troops and was not likely to give up its control.

The strongest opponent of any U.S. attempt to detach Formosa from China was Secretary of State Acheson. He focused his attention on the overall objective of "preventing China from becoming an adjunct of Soviet power." To this end, he counselled the National Security Council in February 1949 against trying to isolate a Chinese Communist regime from the western world and urged the restoration of ordinary trade relations between China under the Communists and the United States and Japan. On March 3 he warned the NSC that any U.S. attempt to detach Formosa from China "would raise the spectre of an American-created irredentist issue just at the time we shall be seeking to exploit the genuinely Soviet-created issue in Manchuria and Sinkiang," and at the end of the year he argued against a program of military aid to the Nationalists that had been proposed by the Joint Chiefs of Staff:

> In all this we must take the long view. . . . I said that in the Soviet effort to detach the northern tier of provinces in China exists the seed of inevitable conflict between China and the Soviet Union. Mao is not a true satellite in that he came to power by his own efforts and was not installed in office by the Soviet Army. This situation, I pointed out, is our one important asset in China and it would have to be for a very important strategic purpose that we should take an action which would substitute ourselves for the Soviets as the imperialist menace to China.[34]

President Truman accepted Acheson's view. To set the matter at rest, he issued the public announcement of January 5, 1950. Holding a press conference on the same day, Acheson specifically rejected arguments based on technical flaws in China's title to Formosa:

> When Formosa was made a province of China nobody raised any lawyers' doubts about that. That was regarded as in accordance with the commitments. . . . We did not wait for a treaty on Korea. We did not wait for a treaty on the Kuriles. We did not wait for a treaty on the islands over which we have trusteeship.[35]

Yet on June 25 Acheson recommended the naval intervention between Formosa and the mainland. The reason given for this measure was the new situation created by the attack upon Korea, and Acheson insisted that that was the only reason. It was recalled that at his press conference of January 5 Acheson had taken the opportunity to explain the meaning of the words, "at this time," in the President's statement. He said that this was "a recognition of the fact that, in the unlikely and unhappy event that our forces might be attacked in the Far East, the United States must be completely free to take whatever action in whatever area is necessary for its own security." The attack upon Korea made it possible to argue that this was the kind of situation envisaged by those words. The presidential announcement also spoke of "Communism" as the aggressor in Korea. This implied that Communist China could be assumed to be associated with the Korean conflict despite the lack of any involvement of the Chinese in the Korean fighting.

It is also necessary to note the intense domestic political pressure the administration was under. This appeared first in the matter of possible diplomatic recognition of the Chinese Communist regime.

The collapse of resistance by the Nationalists had become evident when the Communist armies crossed the Yangtze River in April 1949 and occupied the Nationalist capital of Nanking without opposition. The Nationalist government retired to Canton. It abandoned that city and fled to Formosa on December 7. The question of recognition was not formally posed until the formation of the Central People's Government of the People's Republic of China was proclaimed in Peking on October 1, 1949. In the spring of 1949, however, the United States, Britain, and other nations began discussions in an effort to coordinate their policies on recognition. U.S. Ambassador Stuart remained in Nanking, with the other ambassadors, when the Nationalists fled from that capital. The foreign diplomats, awaiting developments, then had no official dealings with the Communists. Stuart asked the State Department for guidance on the recognition question, and Acheson replied (May 13) stating the "general approved position of the Department" that recognition of any new government should be based on three factors:

> a) *De facto* control of the territory and administrative machinery of the state, including maintenance of public order;
>
> b) Ability and willingness of the government to discharge its international obligations; and
>
> c) General acquiescence of the people of the country in the government in power.

He added: "Furthermore, recognition by US should not be withheld as political weapon except in extreme cases when US national interest [is] served thereby." He said the Department was opposed to hasty recognition and favored continued efforts to present a common front with the other concerned foreign powers, particularly the British.[36]

Given Acheson's belief that the wisest course was to accept the victory of the Chinese Communists as something not within the power of the United States to prevent, and to work patiently to encourage their independence from the Russians, there seems little doubt that he would have eventually favored recognition of the new regime. But Republicans in Congress, and the Chinese Communists themselves, complicated his task and no practical opportunity for recognition presented itself during the tenure of the Truman administration.

There were indications of ambivalence in the attitude of the Chinese Communists towards the United States at this time.[37] A critical juncture came in the months of May and June, while Ambassador Stuart remained in Nanking. Because he was well known and respected in China as the founder of Yenching University and its president from 1919 to 1946, Stuart was uniquely qualified for his position. Informal contact between the Communist leadership and Stuart was opened through Philip Fugh (Fu),[38] Stuart's personal secretary who had been a Yenching classmate of Huang Hua, the head of the Communist Party's "Alien Affairs Office" in Nanking. Stuart and Huang then held three informal meetings. Huang spoke of the needs of China for commercial and other relations and repeated Mao's statement "that CCP was willing to recognize any nation on terms of equality, mutual benefit and respect for each other's territorial and other sovereign rights." Stuart said that in the U.S. view "question of national government was internal; . . . that it was customary to recognize whatever government clearly had support of people of country and was able and willing to perform international obligations; that therefore USA and other countries could do nothing but await developments in China." Huang asked what action the United States would take if the Kuomintang government moved to Taiwan, and Stuart replied "that in all probability we would not follow it there with diplomatic mission and that I felt that was position of other foreign countries concerned." At their third meeting Huang conveyed a message from Mao Tse-tung and Chou En-lai that Stuart would be welcome to visit Yenching University (in the city of Peking). It was understood to be a veiled invitation to talk with Mao and Chou. Stuart outlined the "pros" and "cons" of accepting the invitation in a message to Washington:

> To accept would undoubtedly be gratifying to them, would give me chance to describe American policy; its anxieties regarding Communism and world revolution; its desires for China's future; and would enable me to carry to Washington most authoritative information regarding CCP intentions. Such trip would be step toward better mutual understanding and should strengthen more liberal anti-Soviet element in CCP. It would provide unique opportunity for American official to talk to top Chinese Communists in informal manner which may not again present itself. It would be imaginative, adventurous indication of US open-minded attitude towards changing political trends in China and would probably have beneficial effect on future Sino-American relations.

On negative side, trip to Peiping before my return to US on consultation would undoubtedly start rumors and speculations in China and might conceivably embarrass Department because of American criticism.... [It] would enhance greatly prestige, national and international, of Chinese Communists and Mao himself and in a sense would be second step on our part (first having been my remaining Nanking) toward recognition Communist regime.

On July 1 Acheson replied: "Following highest level consideration ... you are instructed under no circumstances to make visit Peiping."

The idea of a visit by Stuart to Yenching University had originated in a "casual" question put to Huang by Philip Fugh, and Stuart later concluded "that Mao and Chou have lost face, are chagrined at my rejection of their 'invitation' to visit Peiping and consider it clear indication of American policy."[39] Soon after this, Stuart departed from Nanking for Washington. He did not return.

It is not at all surprising that Truman and Acheson did not permit Stuart to visit Peking. The difference between the freedom of action enjoyed by the British cabinet in responding to developments in China, and the severe restriction imposed on the American President by the independent power of Congress was very apparent. Republicans were threatening to make China policy a major partisan issue. They attracted enough Democratic support to form a potent coalition and to jeopardize the bipartisan support which had made possible the administration's policies towards Europe. As criticism of the administration's policy of detachment from Chinese politics mounted, the administration made concessions that narrowed its freedom of action. On July 1, 1949, in a letter to its chairman, Tom Connally, Acheson assured the Senate Committee on Foreign Relations that the committee would be consulted before any decision on recognition was made. With the President's concurrence, Acheson decided on an effort to educate public opinion through the publication of a documentary record of American relations with China from 1944 to 1949. This became the "China White Paper" of August 1, 1949. It included confidential reports of American emissaries to China and it detailed the extent of American aid to the Chinese national government and the causes of the collapse of the national government. The main conclusion drawn by the administration was stated in Acheson's letter of transmittal:

The unfortunate but inescapable fact is that the ominous result of the civil war in China was beyond the control of the government of the United States. Nothing that this country did or could have done within the reasonable limits of its capabilities could have changed that result; nothing that was left undone by this country has contributed to it. It was the product of internal Chinese forces, forces which this country tried to influence but could not. A decision was arrived at within China, if only a decision by default.[40]

But Acheson also made a seemingly unnecessary concession to his critics. His letter said, "The Communist leaders have foresworn their Chinese heritage and have publicly announced their subservience to a foreign power, Russia . . ." It was a statement that seemed to belie the arguments Acheson had been making that the United States should avoid making itself a target of Chinese national resentment because the natural operation of national interests would eventually separate the Chinese Communists from the Russians.

The recognition question became pressing after the formation of the Central People's Government of the People's Republic of China was proclaimed in Peking on October 1, 1949. The announcement contained an expression of willingness to establish diplomatic relations "with any foreign government which is willing to observe the principles of equality, mutual benefit and mutual respect of territorial integrity and sovereignty." Recognition by the Soviet Union came the next day. A letter from Premier and Foreign Minister Chou En-lai transmitted the proclamation to Edmund Clubb (U.S. consul general at Peking) and to the other foreign representatives. Washington authorized Clubb to reply, saying the letter had been forwarded to his government, and the reply took the opportunity to call Chou's attention to the situation of Angus Ward, former American consul general at Mukden, who had been isolated in the consular compound there since November 1948 and who had not been permitted to leave, despite the U.S. decision in May to close that office. Clubb wrote, "The US Government is deeply concerned with this situation, which is contrary to established principles of international comity . . . , and it is hoped that action will be taken by the concerned authorities promptly to rectify that situation."[41]

The United States and the other principal interested governments had agreed that it would be desirable to concert their policies on the recognition question, and they tried to do so. The British led the group favoring recognition. Their position was expressed in a Foreign Office memorandum of November 1:

> The communists are now the rulers of most of China.... Moreover the fall of Canton has brought them to the frontier of Hongkong.... The United Kingdom has also to consider its own trading interests in China, which are considerable and of long standing. His Majesty's Government have advocated a policy of keeping a foot in the door, and if this policy is to bear fruit it can only be as a result of recognition of the Chinese communist government.... It can be asserted that the resistance of the Nationalist Government in China is now ostensibly hopeless and its control over any portion of Chinese territory on the mainland hardly more than nominal, and in these circumstances Mr. Bevin is advised that *de jure* recognition of the communist government is legally justifiable.[42]

On December 8, Acheson gave the British ambassador the reasons why the United States was opposed to hasty recognition:

> It was important to have evidence of how they proposed to conduct themselves with respect to the outer world: whether it would be in conformity with international law and usage as a civilized power.... [Also] as respects the U.S., it was important for us to bring Congress into our deliberations so that, at any rate, the problem would be fully talked out and the issues clarified.

India recognized the Peking government at the beginning of the year, and Britain did so on January 6, 1950. Canada, Norway, Sweden, the Netherlands, and Denmark all followed the British lead.

The Chinese Communists themselves did much to stimulate American opposition to recognition of their regime. When they occupied Mukden in November 1948 they alleged that the American consulate there had served as a center of espionage for the Kuomintang.[43] A number of alleged Chinese agents were arrested and Consul General Ward and his staff were confined to the consular compound. U.S. attempts to secure their departure from China produced no result. This was the case with Clubb's letter of Oct. 8, 1949 to Chou En-lai following Chou's bid for recognition. Then, on October 25, the incident was magnified by highly publicized and evidently trumped-up charges that Ward had mistreated and assaulted a Chinese worker. Ward and several of his staff were jailed and tried by a people's court. In efforts to secure their release, the U.S. government gave thought to forcible measures but concluded they would be impractical, and asked for representations to the Chinese authorities by other governments. It was not until December that Ward and his staff were permitted to leave China. There were other respects also in which the United States saw Chinese violations of international legal obligations (among them the seizure of American consular premises in Peking, originally a military barracks but converted to office use and acknowledged as American property by treaty in 1943, when the United States relinquished extraterritorial rights).[44] These incidents hardened American determination not to recognize the Communist regime until it showed more respect for international obligations.

By the spring of 1950, communication between the United States and the Chinese Communist regime had reached an impasse. Just before the closing of the American consulate in Peking in April, Consul General Clubb was directed to try to arrange an informal interview with Chou or some other high official to discuss points of friction. This approach was rebuffed. The only official who would speak with Clubb said that there could be no improvement in the general situation so long as the United States continued to support Chiang Kai-shek.[45]

In the United States, attention shifted to the question of Formosa. The January 5 announcement showed that the President and the Secretary of State still held out against American action to separate the island from China. It provoked a vigorous Congressional debate. Senator Knowland accused the administration of defeatism and inconsistency. It had stood up to communism, he said, in Europe, taking risks of war in Greece, Turkey, and Berlin. But in the Far East it seemed to be abandoning the defense of freedom. Senator Taft urged use of the navy to protect Formosa. If the United States had any consistent foreign policy, he said, its basis was "to contain communism where it is and prevent any single step of advance." He could not see why the United States should be less firm respecting Formosa than it had been with respect to Berlin, especially in view of the fact that to prevent the Communists from taking Formosa would be comparatively easy.[46] Although the Democrats were almost unanimous in their support of the non-intervention policy, their speeches stressed the practical dangers of military involvement. Only Senator Lehman of New York argued that the United States was bound by past commitments and had no right to send the navy to separate Formosa from China. No effective answer was made to Knowland's statement that, if the United States would not help Formosa to resist a

Communist attack, no one could tell whether it would help South Korea, Burma, or Thailand, in the event they were attacked.[47] No one pointed out that an attack on one of those countries, in contrast to an attack on Formosa, would be clearly international in character and would therefore violate the UN Charter.

Besides the clamor the Republicans were raising on this issue, a significant group within the administration was also working to secure reconsideration of the January decision. It included General MacArthur and Secretary of Defense Louis Johnson, and within the Department of State it included Dean Rusk, who was made assistant secretary for Far Eastern Affairs on March 28, 1950, and John Foster Dulles, who was brought into the Department as a consultant in April to improve relations with the Republicans in Congress.[48] Rusk agreed with a memorandum prepared by Dulles on May 18 which argued that the loss of China had tipped the balance of world power in favor of Russia, that other peoples' view of American power and position were affected, and that there was an urgent need to counteract an impression that the United States would continue to retreat. Dulles' memorandum argued that Formosa had superior advantages as a place to make "a dramatic and strong stand" to show American confidence and resolution. The advantages were that it was close to U.S. naval and air power, that its status was "undetermined by any international act" (he ignored the Cairo and Potsdam Declarations and the delivery of the island to China), and that the Unied States had "at least some moral responsibility for the native inhabitants." Dulles recommended that the United States should announce "that it would neutralize Formosa, not permitting it to be taken by Communists or to be used as a base of military operations against the mainland."[49] When Rusk discussed this proposal with Ambassador at Large Philip Jessup and other officials on May 30th, he was persuaded to alter the approach so as to involve the UN. The idea was that the United States should attempt to persuade Chiang Kai-shek to request a UN trusteeship for the island which would consider the wishes of its inhabitants, and that the United States might then support his request by providing naval protection while the move for trusteeship was pending. Such action seemed somewhat more defensible in terms of legality than any purely unilateral action by the United States.[50] These ideas were still under consideration when the Korean aggression occurred.

Faced with all of these pressures from Congress and from other presidential advisers, Secretary of State Acheson abandoned his previous stand against intervention and recommended to the President that he should now use the fleet to protect Formosa. The memorandum of the conversation between the President and his advisers which took place at Blair House on June 25 shows that they had in mind the supposed legal indeterminacy of the title to Formosa: "[Mr. Acheson] said that the United States should not tie itself up with the Generalisimo [Chiang Kai-shek]. He thought that the future status of Formosa might be determined by the UN. The President interposed 'or by the Japanese Peace Treaty.' " At their next meeting (June 26th) the President issued the order to the Seventh Fleet and also said that "he wished consideration given to taking Formosa back as part of Japan." It was decided to reserve that question for further study.[51]

While the possibilities for legal justification made the Formosa action easier, it is clear that the basic reasons for the reversal of the January 5 decision were political and strategic. As stated in the President's announcement, he and his advisers saw the Korean aggression as assumption of the offensive by "international communism." They thought that this was a change in the situation which justified reexamination of the previous policy. General war might result from the Korean fighting and in that event the island would be useful as a base. Its defense would be easier than the defense of South Korea. Had American politics not stood in the way, it might also have been a bargaining asset in peace negotiations. Perhaps most important of all was the fact that the prospect of at least partial mobilization, brought on by the Korean crisis, removed the reason which had originally led the Joint Chiefs of Staff to oppose the use of any of the United States' limited forces for this purpose. Finally, the administration wanted the wholehearted support of Congress, and this was assured by coupling the action taken in Korea with the defense of Formosa.

When it became necessary to defend the Formosa action in the United Nations, American representative Ernest Gross used the argument about Japanese sovereignty:

> The actual status of the island is that it is territory taken from Japan by the victory of the Allied forces in the Pacific. Like other such territories, its legal status cannot be fixed until there is international action to determine

its future. The Chinese Government was asked by the Allies to take the surrender of the Japanese forces on that island. That is the reason the Chinese are there now.[52]

It was an argument that was rejected both by the Chinese Nationalists and by the Chinese Communists. The Nationalists' representative in the Security Council declared on June 27th:

> I should like to say, for the information of this Council that before 1895 Formosa was one of the provinces of China and was again made one of our provinces after the surrender of Japan. The Chinese people expect their Government to utilize the human and material resources of Formosa to recover the territorial integrity and the political independence and freedom of China.[53]

And on behalf of the Chinese Communist government, Chou En-lai declared the following day:

> Truman's statement of June 27, and the actions of the American Navy, constitute aggression against the territory of China, and a total violation of the United Nations Charter . . . The fact that Taiwan is part of China will remain unchanged forever . . . All the people of our country will certainly fight to the end single-mindedly to liberate Taiwan from the grasp of the American aggressors.[54]

British Foreign Secretary Bevin voiced his concern to Acheson:

> [If the Russians] show a readiness to co-operate in re-establishing the *status quo* in Korea, they will almost certainly raise the question of Formosa . . . [and] the question of Chinese representation in the United Nations would be raised and become acute, the Russians arguing that they could not play their part in the Security Council with China not represented. . . .
>
> The United States have the whole-hearted backing of world opinion in the courageous initiative they took to deal with the aggression in Korea. I do not believe they could rely on the same support for their declared policy in connexion with Formosa. Not only would many powers, particularly Asian powers, dislike the prospect of an extension of the dispute which might follow if the Central People's Government were to attempt an attack on Formosa, but some undoubtedly feel that, now that the Central People's Government are in control of all Chinese territory, it would not be justifiable, in view of the pledge under the Cairo Declaration, to take steps which might prejudice the ultimate handing over of the territory to China. India especially . . . is very sensitive on this aspect of United States policy.

Acheson's reply made it clear that he regarded the Chinese Communists as being involved in the Korean aggression. The question of China's UN seat should not be dealt with, he said, until that aggression was resolved.[55]

After the Chinese intervention in the Korean War, the Truman administration changed its position again. Where Truman had said in July: "The present military neutralization of Formosa is without prejudice to political questions affecting that island,"[56] at December meetings between President Truman and Prime Minister Atlee it was made clear that the Americans thought that the situation had been changed by China's action in Korea and that Formosa should now be kept permanently out of Communist hands. When Atlee brought up the Cairo Declaration, Acheson responded:

> ... this was more of a problem for the UK than for the United States. The United States says it does belong to China and that the Chinese actually have it and are in possession of it. He recalled that the Cairo Declaration also talked about Korea. The Russians and the Chinese were violating the Cairo undertakings about Korea. In effect, they were saying that all their promises mean nothing but that we must give full performance on ours. He recalled that the doctrine of failure of consideration was an old legal proposition. At Cairo we had been talking about another Chinese Government not one equipped with Soviet planes and pilots. This is a very different situation.[57]

The pretense that sovereignty over Taiwan remained in limbo was later dropped when the United States and most of its allies concluded the 1951 treaty of peace with Japan, in which Japan "renounced" all right, title and claim to Formosa and the Pescadores. Neither Chinese government had been invited to sign the Japanese peace treaty, because the allies were hopelessly split as to which government to invite, but on April 28, 1952, the same day as that multilateral peace treaty came into force, a separate treaty of peace was signed between Japan and the Republic of China (Chiang's regime). It was applicable by its terms to "all the territories which are now or which may hereafter be" under that government's control. The United States had taken an active role in bringing that treaty about. It was now clearly treating Taiwan as Chinese territory.

5. NON-RECOGNITION AS A DIPLOMATIC WEAPON

The practice of recognition or non-recognition on political grounds apart from the issue of a government's factual control of population and territory has been more widely resorted to by the United States than by any other major state and has been employed as a means of evading legal restraints concerning the use of force in international relations. To understand this development of American policy, and its significance, we need to trace its origins.

Recognition refers to the action whereby an already-established state commits itself to treat as a state and as a subject of international law a new entity which possesses the attributes of a state (territory, permanent population, central authority, independence) or, in the case of recognition of a new government resulting from revolution in an old state, commits itself to treat the new authority as the government of that state. Recognition is a key institution in the application of international law, for it brings into play the international rules applicable to relations between states and governments. By the same token, refusal to recognize the existence of states or governments has sometimes been used as an excuse for evading legal obligation.

The first need for the United States to formulate a recognition policy occurred when the French monarchy was declared abolished in September 1792, and when that was followed by the execution of Louis XVI and the French declaration of war on England and Holland. It was necessary to decide whether to accept a minister from the French revolutionary government and whether the treaty of alliance and commerce which the United States had made in 1778 with King Louis remained in effect. Jefferson, as Secretary of State, instructed the American minister in Paris: "It accords with our principles to acknowledge any Government to be rightful which is formed by the will of the nation substantially declared.... With such a Government every kind of business may be done . . ." His opinion, written for President Washington on the treaty question, said:

> I consider the people who constitute a society or nation as the source of all authority in that nation; as free to transact their common concerns by any agents they think proper; to change these agents... or the organization of them ... whenever they please.... All the acts done by these agents under the authority of the nation, are the acts of the nation ... and can in no way be annulled or affected by any change in the form of government, ... consequently the treaties between the United States and France, were not treaties between the United States and Louis Capet, but between the two nations of America and France; and the nations remaining in existence, though both of them have since changed their forms of government, the treaties are not annulled by these changes.[58]

The United States, newly independent, also naturally claimed that new states had a right to be recognized by the international community, once they had in fact established their independence. A request for U.S. recognition for a new government in Buenos Aires was turned down by Secretary of State John Quincy Adams in 1818. He gave the reason that the military struggle between Spain and its colonies was still continuing. That being so, he wrote,

> [Their independence] can scarcely be considered in a condition to claim the recognition of neutral powers. But there is a stage in such contests when the parties struggling for independence have, as I conceive, a right to demand its acknowledgment by neutral parties, and when the acknowledgment may be granted without departure from the obligations of neutrality. It is the stage when independence is established as a matter of fact. . . .[59]

The United States recognized the first of the new Latin American states in 1822.

After the Napoleonic Wars, Great Britain followed a similar policy, granting recognition wherever a new government appeared to be in clear control of a country as a matter of fact. Despite the defense of monarchical legitimacy by the conservative continental powers, the British-American criteria for recognition became the prevalent ones. But as late as 1825 Spain still contended that for foreign governments to recognize the *de facto* governments which had become established in Spanish America would violate the rights of the King of Spain. Replying to a Spanish protest against Britain's recognition of the new states of Mexico, Colombia, and Buenos Aires, Foreign Secretary Canning wrote a strong statement of the reasons why recognition should follow conditions of fact:

> To continue to call that a possession of Spain, in which all Spanish occupation and power had been actually extinguished and effaced, could render no practical service to the Mother Country; — but it would have risked the peace of the World. For all political communities, are responsible to other political communities for their conduct . . .
>
> Now, either the Mother Country must have continued responsibility for acts over which it could no longer exercise the shadow of a control; or the Inhabitants of those countries, whose independent political existence was, in fact, established, but to whom the acknowledgment of that independence was denied, must have been placed in a situation in which they were either wholly irresponsible for their actions, or were to be visited

for such of those actions as might furnish ground of complaint to other Nations, with the punishment due to Pirates and Outlaws.

If the former of these alternatives, the total irresponsibility of unrecognized States, — be too absurd to be maintained; and if the latter, — the treatment of their Inhabitants as Pirates and Outlaws be too monstrous to be applied, for any indefinite length of time, to a large portion of the habitable Globe: — no other choice remained for Gt. Britain, or for any other Country having intercourse with the Spanish American Provinces but to recognize, in due time, their political existence as States, and thus to bring them within the pale of those rights and duties, which civilized Nations are bound mutually to respect, and are entitled reciprocally to claim from each other.[60]

In 1913 Assistant Secretary of State Adee summarized U.S. recognition policy in a memorandum for Secretary Bryan:

Ever since the American Revolution entrance upon diplomatic intercourse with foreign states has been *de facto*, dependent upon the existence of three conditions of fact: the control of the administrative machinery of the state; the general acquiescence of its people; and the ability and willingness of their government to discharge international and conventional obligations. The form of government has not been a conditional factor in such recognition; in other words, the *de jure* element of legitimacy of title has been left aside.[61]

While Britain and the United States sometimes delayed recognition for moderate periods to extract commitments with respect to governmental obligations, there was no disposition to deny that a state which had gone through a change of government was still a subject of international law.

This policy and practice with respect to recognition was adjunct to a policy of neutrality. Until 1919 there was no question about the right of any state to go to war, and, as a belligerent, to side with one party or the other in a civil conflict, but foreign states wishing to remain at peace were obligated not to take sides. "Premature recognition" of a rebel government would be regarded as an unfriendly act by the government whose authority was challenged.

The Anglo-American criteria for recognition became accepted by the other members of the Society of Nations. In 1913, however, the United States began to depart from them. The change was inaugurated by President Wilson and reflected his belief that the United States should play a more active role for the purpose of reforming other nations and the international system. He at first confined his intercession to the Americas, but after April, 1917, he extended it to the world.

As we noted in the chapter on world organization, Wilson was shocked into action by the brutal unconstitutional overthrow of the elected government of Mexico. He decided to withhold recognition of the Huerta regime and by that and other pressures to force Huerta's resignation and the restoration of constitutional rule. He also announced his intention to withhold recognition of other Latin American regimes resulting from violent overthrow of constitutional processes. This policy was viewed with consternation by the professionals in the State Department. It was the cause of Bryan's request for the memorandum on the subject from Adee which we quoted earlier. Most unhappy was John Bassett Moore, the international lawyer whom Wilson had appointed as Counselor of the Department and its senior official next to the inexperienced Bryan. Moore tried to dissuade Wilson from his non-recognition policy, and he resigned in 1914 because of his dissatisfaction with it, though loyalty to the administration kept him from criticizing it publicly at that time.

The United States persisted until 1933 in refusing to recognize the Soviet government which was established in Russia in 1917. Here, as in the case of Mexico, American policy differed from that of the European governments. Britain extended *de facto* recognition to the Soviet government by the conclusion of the Anglo-Russian commercial agreement of 1921. It provided for the exchange of official agents, and it was accompanied by a declaration stating the parties' intention to negotiate a settlement of claims. The establishment of regular diplomatic relations was deferred until 1924.[62] Most of the other European governments also established diplomatic relations with the Soviet Union in 1924 (Germany had done so in 1922, in the Treaty of Rapallo).

American policy on the subject was first outlined by Secretary of State Colby on Aug. 10, 1920. Noting that the Bolsheviks had not permitted popular elections, he alleged that they did not rule by the will or consent of the Russian people. He also noted that they had declared their intent to foment revolutions in other countries, and concluded:

> We cannot recognize, hold official relations with, or give friendly reception to the agents of a government which is determined and bound to

conspire against our institutions; whose diplomats will be the agitators of dangerous revolt; whose spokesmen say that they sign agreements with no intention of keeping them.[63]

To this objection on ground of principle later Republican administrations added pecuniary complaints. In his annual message to Congress on December 6, 1923, President Coolidge said, "Our Government does not propose . . . to enter into relations with another regime which refuses to recognize the sanctity of international obligations." In 1933 President Roosevelt decided upon recognition. He sent a letter to the Soviet President calling for negotiations "to end the present abnormal relations." This led to the exchange of notes of Nov. 16, 1933 in which diplomatic relations were established.

In the 1930s John Bassett Moore belatedly criticized the use of non-recognition by American policy-makers. He had served as a judge of the Permanent Court of International Justice from 1921 to 1928, and despite his dislike of Wilson's policies he did not speak out until his resignation from the court. His first criticism was contained in an address to the New York City Bar Association in December 1930. It was occasioned by an incident in American relations with Brazil. A revolt had taken place there against the established government. Secretary of State Stimson had applied an embargo against the shipment of any arms from the United States to the revolutionaries, and at the same time permitted and encouraged the sale of arms to the Brazilian government. The rebellion nevertheless succeeded, despite this action by the United States. Moore attacked the arms sale policy. He evidently thought that a state of belligerency should have been recognized, bringing into play the obligation of neutrality. He also assailed Wilson's departure from the recognition policy laid down by Jefferson, saying:

> Not only does [this] departure keep us in an attitude of intervention in the domestic affairs of other countries, but it has indoctrinated our people in the preposterous and mischievous supposition that the recognition of a government implies approval of its constitution, its economic system, its attitude towards religion, and its general course of conduct.

He also criticized American refusal to recognize the Soviet government. It was a fallacy, he said, to suppose "that recognition and the establishment of diplomatic relations imply the relinquishment of claims. . . . The maintenance of such relations does not involve the abandonment of any claim or difference but only keeps open the channel of discussion."⁶⁴

In another article Moore expressed his own view that international law made recognition of *de facto* governments a legal duty:

> In a general sense international law does impose upon nations the duty in time of peace to recognize one another's governments and to practice commercial and diplomatic interchange. . . . The nations of the West even used force to compel the nations of the East to do this. It is not easy to conjecture how international law and the amenities of international life could be preserved if the governments of the world refused to recognize or to talk with one another.⁶⁵

Despite misjudgment of the situation in Brazil in 1930, Secretary Stimson was in basic agreement with Moore on the desirability of returning to the Jeffersonian policy of recognition of *de facto* governments without inquiring into their constitutional legitimacy. This accorded with his intention to end the practice of American intervention in the affairs of the Latin American countries. But if Stimson was non-interventionist with respect to the domestic affairs of other nations, he was interventionist with respect to international control of aggressive war. Although he had favored moderate reservations to the League of Nations Covenant, he considered the rejection of the League to be "the gravest error made by the United States in the twentieth century."⁶⁶ Therefore, when Japan embarked on the military conquest of Chinese Manchuria in the fall of 1931, in violation not only of the Kellogg-Briand Pact, but also of the Nine Power Treaty of 1922 which pledged respect for the territorial integrity of China, he sought in some way to uphold the treaty commitment to refrain from forcible conquest. He could not take any action, such as an embargo or sanctions, which might risk war with Japan. President Hoover had flatly ruled that out.⁶⁷ The President and the Secretary agreed that non-recognition was left as the only way to make a moral statement and, hopefully, to mobilize world opinion in support of the principle.

Stimson accordingly denied recognition to the nominally independent state (Manchukuo) which Japan created out of Manchuria. He informed China, Japan and the world, on Jan. 7, 1932, that the United States would not recognize any situation, treaty, or agreement which may be brought about contrary to the covenants and obligations of the Pact of Paris of August 27, 1928, to which treaty both China and Japan, as well as the United States, are parties.[68]

Cooperating with the League of Nations, the United States accepted membership on the commission named by the Council of the League to study and report on the Sino-Japanese dispute, and the Assembly of the League adopted a non-recognition resolution, following the American example, which said that it was "incumbent upon the Members of the League of Nations not to recognize any situation ... brought about by means contrary to the Covenant of the League of Nations or to the Pact of Paris."

We should note that this use of non-recognition was qualitatively different from Wilson's use of it on constitutional grounds, which implied intervention in the internal politics of a foreign state. Stimson's declaration was a form of pressure and of protest against foreign action violative of American treaty rights and a refusal to accept an infringement of those rights. It also related to the emerging rule against the use of force in international relations and to the organization of collective action to enforce it. That rule took on vastly greater authority as a principle of international law by its incorporation in the UN Charter, and the United States become committed to it by becoming a member of that organization. Non-recognition by decision of the international organization was now a form of action to thwart aggression which was among the options open to the Security Council.

The past instances in which the United States withheld recognition of governments which were established in fact, were precedents which affected public attitudes towards recognition and encouraged pressure on Truman and Acheson to withhold recognition of the Communist government of China. France, which had been reported to be on the verge of recognizing Communist China, also postponed recognition when Peking gave premature recognition to Ho Chi Minh's insurrectionary government. Non-recognition by these two permanent members of the UN Security Council at once created very serious problems for the world organization.

In November 1949 and in January 1950, the Communist Chinese government informed the Secretary-General, the General Assembly, and the Security Council that the Nationalist delegation headed by Dr.

T.F. Tsiang no longer had the right to speak for China. On January 20, Foreign Minister Chou En-lai of the People's Republic named a new ambassador to represent China in the UN. The Soviet delegate asked the Security Council to expel the Nationalist Chinese delegate, and when his proposal failed to receive majority support, he announced that the Soviet Union would not participate in any further Council meetings so long as the Nationalist delegate was accredited.

Although he disapproved of Russia's boycott tactics, Secretary-General Trygve Lie thought it essential for the UN that China's seat should be held by the government in actual power there. Without the effective governments of China and the Soviet Union, the UN would no longer be a world organization. There would be only two competing alliances. The UN would no longer serve as a meeting place and moderator between East and West.

While the rules of procedure allowed a member of the Security Council whose credentials were challenged to continue to participate in Council proceedings until the Council decided the matter, the United States had conceded that the issue was a procedural one, not subject to veto. With the ten members of the Council other than China evenly divided on the recognition question, Lie tried hard to change two votes so as to provide the needed majority to seat the Communist Chinese representative. At his request, the Secretariat's Legal Department prepared a memorandum which tried to separate the question of representation in the UN from national recognition policies. It argued that even though states persisted in treating recognition as a unilateral act which could be granted or withheld for political reasons, the collective decision of a UN organ which had to choose between two governments claiming to represent a member state should address the question "which of these two governments in fact is in a position to employ the resources and direct the people of the State in fulfillment of the obligations of membership." Citing past cases where members had cast votes in favor of admission to membership of entities they had not recognized as states, the memorandum concluded:

> (1) A Member could properly vote to accept a representative of a Government which it did not recognize, or which it had no diplomatic relations, and (2) Such a vote did not imply recognition or a readiness to assume diplomatic relations.[69]

The Secretariat was really urging the UN membership to apply at least in UN matters the *de facto* recognition policy that they had departed from in their diplomatic practice.

But the Secretary-General failed to change any votes. The Truman administration, under pressure from its Congressional opponents, remained inflexible, and Lie was disappointed to find the United States using its influence to hold the other anti-communist votes in line.[70]

So the matter stood when the Korean conflict erupted. In September, 1950, when the Chinese Communist government sought to send a delegation to represent China in the General Assembly, the United States opposed it, arguing that the Chinese Communists were "co-conspirators" in the aggression in Korea and were supporting the North Koreans, and that the Chinese representation issue should be taken up only after the Korean crisis was settled. Acheson outlined the problem to President Truman in August:

> I reviewed with the President the difficult situation in which we found ourselves with our allies and in the Security Council by reason of the Russian ability to play on the Korean situation, Formosa and the Chinese Communists....
>
> I pointed out the great need for circumspection in regard to Formosa and the importance of not having the Communists seating issue arise for a vote on the merits. To seat the Chinese over our objection would whip up opinion here against our Allies. We could not meet the views of our allies as long as the fighting in Korea continued.
>
> ... It seemed to me that the best chance [to preserve our unity] was by ... trying to have the whole thing referred to the General Assembly for discussion, first, on the general criteria to be applied in such cases ... The discussion of criteria would undoubtedly involve acceptance of the principles of the Charter and the decisions of the Security Council. Here we were in a strong position.[71]

On the criteria to be applied, the Truman administration did make concessions to the Secretariat's position. It agreed that the question of representation of members in an international organization should be kept separate from the question of diplomatic recognition, and that it was essential to the effectiveness of international organizations that the member states should be represented by the authorities in actual control of those states. It also adhered to the position that a simple majority vote in the General Assembly would decide it, reasoning that:

Although this question is obviously important, it is not one of the important questions listed in Article 18 of the Charter. As a matter of sound organizational procedure, it is necessary to facilitate decisions of the Assembly on questions which are essentially organizational in nature and it would be an unfortunate practice to permit a minority group of one-third of the Assembly to prevent its proper functioning.[72]

But it succeeded in postponing UN consideration of the specific issue of China's representation for so long as the Korean conflict continued.

The ways in which a recognition policy based on political considerations rather than conditions of fact could be used to justify national uses of force that were contrary to the essential intent of the UN Charter were demonstrated in the next administration, and will be considered in the next chapter.

CHAPTER V

THE POLICIES OF EISENHOWER AND DULLES

1. THE ATTEMPT TO SAVE INDOCHINA FROM
"INTERNATIONAL COMMUNISM"

After 1917 an exaggerated fear of communism, tending to inhibit rational policy-making, was never far below the surface of American thinking about world affairs. When he decided upon recognition of the Soviet government, Franklin Roosevelt had to move cautiously, taking particular pains to win over religious groups that had been opposed to recognition.[1] During the Second World War the fear of communism was submerged beneath a greater fear of the fascist aggressors, but after the war it again became a powerful factor. It particularly affected American attitudes towards the anti-imperialist revolutions taking place in the Asian nations. The traditional American response to such revolutions was sympathy for the desire of colonial peoples to gain independence, but wherever the new leaders were thought to be communists the counter-tendency came into play. As a consequence, the United States followed an inconsistent course. In China, the Truman administration vacillated between the attempt to bring about a coalition government, by mediating between Chiang and the Communists in North China, and the alternative of limited intervention in Chiang's behalf which was evidenced in the airlift of Chiang's armies into Manchuria and the coastal provinces so as to get there ahead of the Communists. The Truman administration desisted from support of Chiang only when it became clear that the effort to save his regime would be ineffectual. With respect to Dutch Indonesia, the anti-colonial impulse prevailed because Sukarno and Hatta, the Indonesian leaders who proclaimed the independence of the Indonesian Republic in August 1945, were opposed by the local Communist party as well as by the Dutch. When negotiations between the Dutch and the Republican leaders produced the agreement of Nov. 15, 1946 by which the Netherlands recognized the *de facto* authority of the Republic and the two sides agreed to cooperate in establishing a Netherlands-Indonesian union, the United States and other powers also extended *de facto* recognition to the Republic. When further negotiations broke down and the Dutch resorted to military action, India and Australia took the case to the UN Security Council. The United States backed the UN peacekeeping effort and applied continuous pressure which finally induced the Netherlands to abandon the attempt to reimpose control by military means.[2] The settlement which conceded sovereignty to Indonesia came about late in 1949 and was not affected by the furor in United States politics over the "loss" of China.

In Indochina, on the other hand, initial American sympathy for the independence movement evaporated because of the fact that its leadership was communist. During the Second World War President Roosevelt had been opposed to restoration of French rule in Indochina, and he at first thought to establish a UN trusteeship instead, but strong resistance of Churchill and de Gaulle to any interference with their pre-war empires made him modify that position. He decided to leave specific decisions about Indochina to be dealt with after the war, and he approved a statement by Secretary of State Stettinius on April 3, 1945 that said the trusteeship structure planned for the United Nations organization should only apply to the prewar League of Nations mandates, to certain territories taken from the enemy, and to "such other territories as might be voluntarily placed under trusteeship."[3] In May 1945, at the San Francisco Conference, France's foreign minister asked for, and was given, assurance that the United States did not question French sovereignty over Indochina.[4] At Potsdam, in July 1945, Truman and Churchill agreed that military operations in Indochina south of the 16th parallel would be assigned to Lord Mountbatten's Southeast Asia Command. This had the effect that the British took the Japanese surrender in southern Indochina, and without American objection they returned control to the French.

A detachment of French commandos was with the British force which entered Saigon on September 13th, and the British rearmed French soldiers they found there who had been prisoners of the Japanese. The British and French found a Vietnamese government already in control in Saigon. This was the local administration of the Democratic Republic of Vietnam, which Ho Chi Minh, the leader of the Vietnamese nationalists, had proclaimed in Hanoi on Sept. 2, 1945.

Ho was also the leader of the Vietnamese Communists. As a young man, he had left Vietnam as a seaman, visited England and America, and been a student in Paris. At the Versailles Peace Conference he addressed a petition for the rights of the peoples of Indochina to the Allied leaders. It was quite natural that a Vietnamese nationalist dedicated to ending colonialism should study Marxism. He participated in the founding Congress of the French Communist Party. In 1923 he went to Moscow and studied revolutionary tactics at the school operated by the Comintern. In 1925 he went to Canton as an assistant to the Soviet envoy, Michael Borodin. When Chiang Kai-shek turned on the Chinese Communists, Ho returned to Russia with Borodin. He would have been imprisoned by the French if he had gone to Indochina. In Hong Kong in 1930 he was the principal founder of the Indochinese Communist Party. In the course of World War II he did return to Indochina to organize resistance to the Japanese. In 1945 he emerged as the popular leader of the "League for the Independence of Vietnam" (Viet Minh), a coalition of nationalist groups. When Ho proclaimed the Democratic Republic, Bao Dai, the former emperor of Annam under the French protectorate, abdicated and announced his support for the Republic. In conversations with American representatives at the end of 1945, Ho minimized his Communist convictions, saying that "he now realized that [Communist] ideals were impractical for his country, and that his policy now was one of republican nationalism, in which decision rested with the people. If they wanted an imperial house, without power such as that in England, he and his party had no objections . . ."[5]

Conflict between the French and the Vietnamese began in Saigon on September 23rd, when the French troops seized the town hall and public buildings by force. The Vietnamese counterattacked and the British came to the aid of the French. More French troops arrived in October, and fighting spread, between them and the nationalists. In the north, where Chinese troops were in occupation, Ho Chi Minh's government continued to function in Hanoi. In the hope of extending their control to the north, and of pacifying the country, the French opened negotiations both with the Chinese and with Ho's government.

The United States originally assumed a hands-off attitude. This policy was defined by Acting Secretary of State Dean Acheson on August 30, 1945:

US has no thought of opposing the reestablishment of French control in Indochina . . . However, it is not the policy of this Govt to assist the French to reestablish their control over Indochina by force and the willingness of the US to see French control reestablished assumes that French claim to have the support of the population of Indochina is borne out by future events.[6]

Ho Chi Minh entertained some hopes for American support. He modeled his Declaration of Independence of Vietnam, of September 2, 1945, on the American Declaration of 1776, quoting at length from that document, and invoking also the French Revolution's Declaration of the Rights of Man and the UN principle of self-determination.[7] And in February 1946 he sent letters to the governments of the United States, China, Russia and Britain, requesting their mediation to bring about an end to the war and a fair settlement. He also asked them to bring the Indochinese issue before the United Nations. No action was taken on his appeal.[8]

The French secured Chinese agreement to the arrival of French troops at Haiphong and Hanoi at the beginning of March 1946, in return for renunciation of French extraterritorial rights in China and other concessions to Chinese interests. An agreement between Ho Chi Minh and France's negotiator, Sainteny, also facilitated French occupation of the north. Signed at Hanoi on March 6, it provided that, effective immediately, "The French Government recognizes the Vietnamese Republic as a Free State having its own Government, its own Parliament, its own Army and its own finances, forming part of the Indochinese Federation and of the French Union." In return the Vietnamese government declared that it would "welcome amicably the French Army when . . . it relieves the Chinese Troops." There were to be an end to hostilities and further negotiations to deal with diplomatic relations of Vietnam with foreign states, the future law of Indochina, and French interests in Vietnam. In the matter of reuniting the three regions of Cochin-China, Annam, and Tonkin, the French government pledged itself "to ratify the decisions taken by the populations consulted by referendum."[9] After this agreement was announced, the Vietnamese Republic requested that the United States and other governments recognize it, as France had done, as a free state within the French Union. The British government replied that it could not recognize because Vietnam's actual status was still the subject of continuing negotiations. We have no evidence of any reply by the United States.[10]

Further negotiations between the French and the Vietnamese were unproductive. A major problem was French determination to separate Cochin-China (Saigon and the south) from the rest of Vietnam. In December 1946 war broke out between the two sides, and as their conflict intensified, the French emphasized the fact that its leaders were communist, and American officials readily adopted the habit of referring to Ho Chi Minh as "a Moscow-trained communist" or "an agent of international communism." Those labels were true in part, but they diverted attention from another very important part of the truth — that Ho remained first and foremost a Vietnamese and a dedicated patriot.

In 1946 and 1947 France and the United States were both concerned that the Vietnamese question might be raised in the UN Security Council. One can only speculate as to why the USSR did not ask for UN support of Ho Chi Minh's regime.[11] The State Department told the French the United States would oppose any outside interference, but it urged them to make concessions so as to settle the question quickly. "If some country should bring matter before Security Council," it cabled Paris in February 1947, "we would find it difficult to oppose an investigation Indochinese problem unless negotiations between parties were going on."[12] The French then turned to an effort to persuade Bao Dai to head a Vietnamese government to take the place of Ho Chi Minh's regime, and the United States welcomed that alternative. Finally, on March 8, 1949, the French president and Bao Dai concluded an agreement which stated that Vietnam, under Bao Dai's government, was an independent associated state within the French Union, and that it should include Cochin-China as well as Annam and Tonkin. The new state would lack complete independence, however, since France reserved control over its army and foreign relations.

Up to this point, the United States had remained officially neutral in the French-Vietnamese war. Its policy was summed up as follows:

> The immediate objective . . . is to assist in a solution of the present impasse which will be mutually satisfactory to the French and Vietnamese . . . We should continue to press the French to accommodate the basic aspirations of the Vietnamese . . . We have recognized French sovereignty over Indochina but have maintained that such recognition does not imply any

commitment on our part to assist France to exert its authority over the Indochinese peoples. . . . [We have] declined to permit the export to the French in Indochina of arms and munitions for the prosecution of the war against the Vietnamese.[13]

The victory of the Communists in the Chinese Civil War then produced a policy change. It was decided at the end of 1949 to support the French with American weapons and funds for the war as soon as the French Parliament completed ratification of the March 8 agreement (to which there had been considerable French opposition). Parliament ratified the agreement in January, following which the United States recognized the Bao Dai regime and the associated governments of Laos and Cambodia. China and the Soviet Union had recognized Ho's government a short time before. Acheson said that by these actions the issue in Indochina had become "more clearly defined as an anti-communist versus communist effort."[14] U.S. military aid for the French Union forces was approved, and its level was increased when the Korean war began. The Truman administration did not, however, contemplate any American military intervention, except in the event that Communist China should send its army into Indochina. (In that case, they would support a French request for immediate UN action, and would send air and naval forces to help the French.)

The Eisenhower administration recognized fewer restraints. Eisenhower and Dulles assumed that the Communist leadership of the Viet Minh were servants of the Moscow-Peking alliance, and that the Communists would use any means, regardless of legal or moral considerations, to advance the cause of world revolution. Eisenhower and Dulles drew the conclusion that the United States should be equally unfettered in its choice of means. Illegal or otherwise immoral actions would be justified, they thought, in order to bring about the defeat of communism. By now the search for culprits for "the loss of China" had driven out of the State Department its most competent Chinese experts. No official any longer dared to question the prevailing assumptions.

In the spring of 1954 the new administration seriously contemplated the overt use of American military force in Indochina, where it was by then apparent that the Viet Minh were winning their war with France. Alternatives facing Eisenhower and his advisers were whether to seek an international settlement in Indochina that would respect the interests of the world powers, or to join the French in military action.

There had been some important new developments since President Eisenhower took office. The Korean War had ended in an armistice reflecting the stalemate there, and there were some indications of change in Soviet foreign policy since the death of Stalin. The new Soviet leaders had resumed diplomatic relations with Yugoslavia and Greece, abandoned claims against Turkey, and helped to end the Korean War, evidently pressing the Chinese to accept the neutral plan for exchange of prisoners which made the armistice possible. They also took the lead in proposing that an international conference should be held at Geneva at the end of April 1954 to discuss the problems of Korea and Indochina. There were two ways to regard these initiatives. One was to assume that the Soviet drive for world domination was unchanging and that these were mere tactical shifts, though they might reflect consciousness of weakness. With communists there could be no real agreement. Only strong counter-pressure could be effective. This was the old rationale for the containment policy, and this was the position of John Foster Dulles. The other approach, to which the British inclined, was to exploit the possibility that time and circumstances had produced a real change in Soviet policy, a willingness to compromise, and a chance for the West to move beyond containment to settlement of some of the issues of the cold war. After eight years of fighting in Indochina, the French were tired of the costly and unsuccessful struggle, and they welcomed the Soviet proposal to discuss Indochina and Korea at a conference at Geneva. Communist China was to participate, along with the United States, the Soviet Union, Britain, France, the Viet Minh, and the Indochinese governments dependent on France. With the other powers all supporting the idea, the United States had to agree to the conference, although Eisenhower and Dulles were unenthusiastic about the prospect.

Before the conference opened, the French military situation became desperate. An important part of the French army in Indochina had been placed in the mountain outpost of Dien Bien Phu, inviting battle with the Viet Minh. Now it was besieged and facing defeat. A visit to Washington by the French chief of staff, General Paul Ely, March 20 to 26, described the seriousness of the situation. Ely reported that the prospects for the French holding out at Dien Bien Phu were no better than 50% and asked whether the United States would send its air force into action if the Chinese Communists sent jet fighters to aid the Viet

Minh. The Chairman of the Joint Chiefs of Staff, Admiral Radford, personally favored American action in support of the Dien Bien Phu garrison, even in the absence of Chinese intervention, and did not hide this opinion from Ely, thus encouraging a French request for U.S. naval air support at Dien Bien Phu, which was sent to Washington on the night of April 4. To justify it, the French claimed that Communist China had already intervened by providing technical advisers and one Chinese general to the force besieging the french fortress, as well as Chinese-manned anti-aircraft guns and supply trucks, artillery and ammunition. The reports of the presence of a Chinese general and anti-aircraft gunners were doubted by the American intelligence community, but they agreed that the Viet Minh had Chinese advisers.[15]

Eisenhower regretted Radford's indiscretion, and Dulles hastened to inform the French that "full political understanding" with other countries, as well as approval by Congress, would be required before the United States could take belligerent action.[16]

Radford's conviction that air attacks alone could remedy the situation was not shared by the other members of the JCS. General Ridgeway, in particular, strongly opposed intervention on the ground that air and naval power would not be enough, and that American ground forces would have to follow and would fight under the most adverse conditions.[17] The Intelligence Advisory Committee estimated that "if the United States intervened in such force as to contrive the defeat of the Vietminh, there would be very great danger of overt Chinese Communist intervention."[18] President Eisenhower, himself, began with a strong aversion to any American ground force commitment. Nevertheless, he and his associates attached very great importance to preventing the Communists from winning in Indochina, and he accepted Dulles' view that sufficient legal justification for intervention could be found. He instructed Dulles to get the views of Congressional leaders and to prepare an authorizing resolution for possible submission to Congress. Dulles would also begin discussions with the British, the French, the Australians, and other nations close to Indochina, to see if they would agree to intervene together with the United States.

Dulles began to test the degree of public support for intervention in a speech on "the threat of a Red Asia" which he delivered on March 29. He repeated an earlier warning that "if Red China sent its own army into Indochina, that would result in grave consequences which might not be confined to Indochina." He said that they had not done so thus far, but were supporting the Indochinese Communists "by all means short of open invasion." He then proposed "united action" by "the whole free community" to save Southeast Asia. He did not specify what kind of action might be required.[19]

Dulles prepared a draft resolution, for possible submission to Congress, which would authorize the use of U.S. forces in Indochina. This draft indicates the legal argument Dulles was prepared to make. It began with an assertion that "the Chinese Communist regime and its agents in Indochina are engaging in armed attack against Vietnam." It then invoked the right of collective self-defense in the face of an armed attack (Art. 51):

> Whereas peace and order may be restored and this aggression ended if it is known that the United States is prepared, in pursuance of a decision or recommendation of the United Nations, or by united action with other free nations or in the exercise of the inherent right of individual or collective self-defense recognized by Article 51 of the United Nations Charter, to restrain and retaliate against such armed attack; . . .

The draft concluded with language to authorize the President to employ U.S. naval and air forces to defeat aggression in Southeast Asia.[20]

There was no expectation that either the UN Security Council or the General Assembly would authorize any such intervention. The Department of State's Office of UN Affairs had been asked for an appraisal of the prospects of UN action. It estimated that a complaint of aggression against the French-sponsored associated states in Indochina would not receive more than 36 affirmative votes in the Assembly, well short of the necessary two-thirds majority, and that any discussion of the Indochina problem would produce strong pressure for a cease-fire and negotiations with Ho Chi Minh, or a plebiscite, which Ho would be likely to win.[21]

As instructed by Eisenhower, Dulles discussed the question of intervention with Congressional leaders on April 3, without showing them his draft resolution. It was the unanimous reaction of the Congressional leaders that while a resolution to authorize military action could probably be passed if definite commitments to participate were obtained from the United Kingdom and America's other allies, there must be "no more Koreas with the United States furnishing 90% of the manpower." While Dulles and Radford said the administration did not then envisage the use of American land forces, "the Congressmen replied that once the flag was committed the use of land forces would inevitably follow."[22]

The next step was to take the matter up with the allies, and Dulles held conversations with the British, the French, the Australians and the New Zealanders. With all of them, he argued in favor of joint military intervention. None were willing to give the commitments he wanted. The French were focusing their hopes on a negotiated settlement at the forthcoming conference and wanted to form a coalition to provide useful leverage in obtaining a negotiated solution rather than to seek a military solution. They were unwilling to promise to continue the war. The Australian government was unwilling to make any commitment in advance of elections which were scheduled for the end of May.

Despite the President's aversion to participating in a ground war in Indochina, he agreed to Dulles' suggestion that he should send a personal message to Prime Minister Churchill urging the formation of a coalition to save Indochina. His message was not free from ambiguity as to what action was intended, but it said the coalition "must be willing to join the fight if necessary." With respect to the conference at Geneva, Eisenhower said his administration had concluded "there is no negotiated solution of the Indochina problem which in its essence would not be either a face-saving device to cover a French surrender or a face-saving device to cover a Communist retreat. . . . Somehow we must contrive to bring about the second alternative."[23] To follow up this initiative, Dulles went to London to meet with Foreign Secretary Eden.

Eden's memoirs describe the American proposal in more specific terms:

> [It] was to the effect that all the countries concerned should issue, before Geneva, a solemn declaration of their readiness to take concerted action under Article 51 of the United Nations Charter against continued interference by China in the Indo-China war. We were informed that the proposed warning would carry with it the threat of naval and air action against the Chinese coast and of active intervention in Indo-China itself. This *ad hoc* coalition, comprising the United States, France, the United Kingdom, Australia, New Zealand, Thailand, the Philippines and the three Associated States of Indo-China, would simultaneously set about organizing the collective defence of South-East Asia.[24]

The British were unwilling to make any such commitment. Their chiefs of staff estimated that intervention would require land forces and might result in all-out war with China, including possible use of atomic weapons (Admiral Radford had this thought also in mind), and Eden wanted no action before Geneva which might prejudice the negotiation there. He was much more sensitive than the Americans to the interest of India in an Indochina settlement. On that subject he wrote:

> I knew that China would be reluctant, at this stage at any rate, to align India against her, and would make considerable efforts to conciliate Asian opinion in general. India had an abiding interest in the outcome of the conference and could play a considerable part at Geneva behind the scenes. Nobody could tell what the future would hold, but it was essential not to alienate India by our actions in a part of the world which concerned her closely.[25]

On April 27 Prime Minister Churchill assured the House of Commons that there would be no British commitment to military action in Indochina before the conclusion of the Geneva Conference, though he added that "if settlements are reached there Her Majesty's Government will be ready to play their full part in supporting them in order to promote a stable peace in the Far East."[26]

Before settling on the effort to persuade the British and other allies to join in overt intervention, Eisenhower and his advisers had considered covert intervention, by such means as sending unmarked U.S. planes to bomb the Viet Minh or allowing French pilots to fly B 29s based at U.S. installations in the Philippines.[27] Such proposals were rejected only because it was concluded they would not be effective. Dulles also urged that if the French were thrown out of Indochina and the Viet Minh formed a new government, the United States should then promote guerilla operations against it. "We can raise hell and the Communists will find it just as expensive to resist as we are now finding it." President Eisenhower responded "that he wished we could have done something like this after the victory of the Communists in China," and Dulles agreed.[28]

A final review of the question of possible U.S. military intervention took place in the National Security Council on April 29. Three days before, Eisenhower had met with Republican legislative leaders and told them that he would support intervention if it were done jointly by the free countries. But it was clear by then that Britain, Australia and

New Zealand were unwilling to make any immediate commitment of that kind. The April 29 meeting was addressed to the question whether the United States should intervene without participation by its major allies. At the beginning of the meeting Admiral Radford reported that a renewed request for American intervention had been made to him by the French chief of staff, who said he was acting for Prime Minister Pleven and Foreign Minister Bidault. Several of the President's advisers urged intervention even without allies. Governor Stassen, director of the foreign aid program, argued for it vehemently. But Eisenhower firmly stated his opposition to such a course. "A collective policy with our allies," he said, was the only wise course. To act alone in such cases would be to try "to police the entire world," and would draw accusations of imperialism. Moreover it would be a fatal mistake, in his opinion, to "fritter away our resources in local engagements." Before he would commit U.S. ground forces to such a conflict, he said repeatedly,

> he would want to ask himself and all his wisest advisers whether the right decision was not rather to launch a world war. If our allies were going to fall away in any case, it might be better for the United States to leap over the smaller obstacles and hit the biggest one with all the power we had.[29]

Eisenhower had been able to turn away pressure from those within the Administration who wanted to enter the war by making the proposal for joint intervention by a coalition of allies. The failure of that effort, which he may have foreseen, ended the pressure on him. Now he and Dulles took advantage of the opportunity to blame the British, the French, and the Australians for the failure to act, thus absolving the administration from imputations of weakness.[30]

With military intervention excluded, it was necessary to go through with the conference that had been agreed to. Consideration of the Indochina problem at Geneva began on May 8, the day after the French position at Dien Bien Phu fell to the Viet Minh. The other major powers all approached the conference in the hope that it might achieve a real settlement of the Indochinese problem. The compromise they were working towards included two elements:

1) An agreed end to the war between France and the Viet Minh, through a cease-fire and separation of the opposing forces. This would be followed after a short interval by an internationally supervised national election.

2) Cambodia, Laos, and Vietnam would each be treated as independent

and sovereign states. French troops would be withdrawn and the three states would be committed not to participate in any military alliance. The carrying out of the settlement and the provisions for neutralization of Cambodia, Laos, and Vietnam would be guaranteed by the powers participating in the conference.

But the Eisenhower administration did not share the willingness of the other outside governments to guarantee such a settlement. It had no confidence that any settlement made with Communists would be any more than temporary. It apparently feared the domestic political consequences of any concessions as much as it did the possibility of future communist aggression. This was especially true with respect to the proposed guarantee of the settlement by the U.S., Britain, France, Russia, and Communist China. Dulles told Prime Minister Mendes-France and Foreign Secretary Eden on July 13: "The US Government could not be in a position of seeming to approve the sale of Cambodia, Laos, and Vietnam into Communist captivity. . . . The US Government cannot be associated with a settlement which would be portrayed in the US as a second Yalta." To Bedell Smith, who was representing the United States at the conference, he said, "You will avoid participation in the negotiations in any way which would imply, or give the Communists a plausible case for contending, that the United States was so responsible for the result that it is in honor bound to guarantee that result to the Communists." The United States should not even "become cosignatory with the Communists" in any declaration. And on July 18 Smith was instructed "to bear in mind that Executive has no Constitutional power to give 'guarantee.' That can only be done by treaty, ratification of which would surely be rejected."[31]

A role for the UN in guaranteeing a settlement was made impossible by the U.S. insistence on continuing to exclude the *de facto* Chinese government from participating in the UN. Finally, Eisenhower and Dulles were sure that any Vietnamese elections in the near future would be won by the Viet Minh. They therefore ended by trying to make the part of the settlement which provided for a temporary division of Vietnam, in order to separate the opposing forces, into a permanent partition of the country which would save as much of it as possible from Communist control.

There was hard bargaining at the conference on the location of the temporary demarcation line. The Chinese helped to persuade the Viet

Minh to accept a division near the 17th parallel, considerably further to the north than Ho's government had wanted. While the powers other than the United States were all treating the conflict in Vietnam as civil war, rather than communist aggression, the British and French agreed with the United States in regarding the Viet Minh incursions into Laos and Cambodia as international in nature, and China's Chou En-lai also agreed that the Viet Minh must withdraw its forces from the territory of those states.

Although the United States had actually abandoned the thought of military intervention before the Indochinese negotiations began, rumors of imminent American intervention repeatedly circulated at Geneva.[32] This seemed to be a purposeful tactic by the French and the Americans to strengthen France's bargaining position. Randle, whose study of the Geneva Conference is sympathetic to Dulles' tactics, thought Dulles did not actually favor intervention, but that he "always was ready to threaten the use of military force."[33] His frequent discussion of military alternatives, coupled with Eden's inability to pin him down as to what action was contemplated, left confusion in Eden's mind.[34] It contributed to misunderstandings two years later about how the United States would regard British use of force against Egypt at Suez. Arrival at a compromise agreement at Geneva may have been assisted by awareness on the part of the Chinese and the Viet Minh of the danger of war with the United States, and the Viet Minh's further knowledge that that would bring Chinese military intervention.[35] There was a traditional fear of the Chinese in Vietnam and the presence of large numbers of Chinese troops would be more disturbing than welcome.

Pressed by the USSR and China, the Viet Minh accepted the agreements of July 21, 1954. The agreement on the cessation of hostilities was concluded between the commanders of the French Union Forces and the People's Army of Vietnam. It provided for the temporary partition into two "regrouping zones," and stated:

> Pending the general elections which will bring about the unification of Viet Nam, the conduct of civil administration in each regrouping zone shall be in the hands of the party whose forces are to be regrouped there.

An international commission, composed of representatives of Canada, India, and Poland was created to supervise the carrying out of the agreements.

The Final Declaration of the Conference referred to Vietnam as one nation, saying,

> The Conference recognizes . . . that the military demarcation line is provisional and should not in any way be interpreted as constituting a political or territorial boundary.

It declared that the settlement of political problems in Vietnam should be based on respect for the principles of independence, unity and territorial integrity, and on free general elections by secret ballot. The elections were to be held in July 1956 under the supervision of the international commission.

The Final Declaration also provided (para. 12):

> In their relations with Cambodia, Laos and Viet Nam, each member of the Geneva Conference undertakes to respect the sovereignty, the independence, the unity and the territorial integrity of the above-mentioned states, and to refrain from any interference in their internal affairs.

Finally, it pledged the members of the conference (other than the United States, which did not join in the declaration) to consult on any question referred to them by the international commission "in order to study such measures as may prove necessary to ensure that the agreements . . . are respected."[36]

Despite British and French urging that the United States should join in sponsoring the settlement, Eisenhower and Dulles held out to the end against any U.S. assumption of responsibility. American representative Bedell Smith refused to join in the Final Declaration, and made a separate unilateral declaration of the U.S. position. It said that the United States would not resort to force to disturb the agreements reached, and that it "would view any renewal of the aggression in violation of the . . . Agreements with grave concern and as seriously threatening international peace and security."[37]

Also disassociating itself from the settlement was the Saigon regime associated with France which called itself the government of the State of Vietnam (under Bao Dai as chief of state). Its views had been ignored by the French high command which entered into the cease-fire agreement. On July 19, the Saigon government protested against the solution the conference was about to adopt, saying:

Although this partition is only provisional in theory, it would not fail to produce in Vietnam the same effects as in Germany, Austria, and Korea. It would not bring the peace which is sought for.

The Saigon government proposed instead a cease-fire with minimum regroupment of troops, and administration of the entire country by the UN until general elections could be held. In a final statement of its own, this government said that it reserved to itself complete freedom of action to protect the territorial unity, national independence and freedom of the Vietnamese people. It denied the right of the signatories of the agreements to fix the date of future elections without securing its concurrence.[38]

Neutralization of the three states of Indochina through U.S. backing for the Geneva settlement would have seemed a practical political solution from the standpoint of the United States if it had been able to reconcile itself to communist leadership of Vietnam by Ho Chi Minh. As Eisenhower conceded, Ho was clearly the national leader preferred by the Vietnamese people in 1954.[39] The policy of neutralization would have relied on an assumption that a Ho Chi Minh regime would want to protect Vietnam's security and independence by steering clear of the conflicts of the great powers. But Eisenhower and Dulles were unable to make that assumption. They assumed that communist leadership would make certain the subjection of Vietnam to Russian and Chinese control. Where the other powers and the Final Declaration of the Geneva Conference regarded North and South Vietnam as parts of a single nation, the United States henceforth treated South Vietnam as a separate sovereign state. Spurning collective responsibility for enforcing the settlement, the Eisenhower administration assumed unilateral responsibility instead. They set out to replace French influence in South Vietnam with American influence, sent in American military and economic aid, supported the Saigon government in its repudiation of the plan for elections, and sent sabotage and psychological warfare teams to Hanoi to harass the communist government there.[40] Close American identification with South Vietnam's government began the process which later eventuated in the American Vietnamese War of 1965-1973.

2. NON-RECOGNITION AS AN EXCUSE FOR INTERVENTION IN THE CHINESE CIVIL WAR

In the spring of 1953, when it appeared that an armistice would finally be achieved in Korea, the question of China's representation in the UN could no longer be avoided by the formula of postponing it until the Korean conflict was over. The "China bloc" in Congress was more than ever determined to keep the Chinese Communists out. They attached a rider to a UN appropriations bill which would have cut off all U.S. funds for the UN if the Communist government got China's seat. President Eisenhower met with Congressional leaders on June 2, 1953 and persuaded them to withdraw that provision, but only by assuring them, as he told Dulles,

> that so long as Red China was constituted on its present basis, under its present rulers, and so obviously serving the ends of Soviet Russia, . . . I would *never* be a party to its recognition and its acceptance in the United Nations.[41]

This went beyond the policy of the previous administration that recognition could not be considered until the Chinese Communist regime gave indications that it would respect the obligations of international law and the UN Charter. Dulles defended the new policy of permanent non-recognition in the following terms:

> One country has no right to demand recognition by another. Generally, it is useful that there should be diplomatic intercourse between those who exercise *de facto* governmental authority . . . [But] in relation to Communist China, we are forced to take account of the fact that the Chinese Communist regime has been consistently and viciously hostile to the United States. . . .
>
> [We] must ask . . .: "Will it help our country if, by recognition, we give increased prestige and influence to a regime that actively attacks our vital interests?"[42]

He also took a more adamant position against changing the representation of China in the UN. "As far as the General Assembly is concerned," he said on July 8, 1954, "this certainly is an important matter which would require a two-thirds vote . . . I believe that in the Security Council it is a matter which is properly subject to veto.[43]

In October 1950, Dulles had said in a letter to Ambassador Tsiang, "The Chinese Nationalist Government must see the disadvantage of the United States adopting the position that Formosa was part of China which would mean that neither the United States nor the United Nations could do anything in what would be a purely civil war." But in April of 1952, when it sponsored the treaty of peace between Japan and the Republic of China (Chiang's regime), the United States did decide to treat Taiwan as Chinese territory. Now Dulles resorted to non-recognition of the actual government of China, and continued recognition of the exile regime, as a substitute device to permit the United States to engage in forcible intervention between the two Chinese factions without conceding that it was violating the UN Charter.

The Eisenhower administration moved beyond Truman's imposition of a cease-fire in the Formosa Strait, to alliance with Chiang's regime. The first step was an announcement in Eisenhower's inaugural address that restrictions against Formosa-based military operations against the mainland would be removed. "We certainly have no obligation," Eisenhower said, "to protect a nation fighting us in Korea." When peace returned to Korea the restrictions were not reimposed. Chiang's operations against the mainland were launched from bases in some small Nationalist-held islands close to the coast, and those operations were being secretly supported by the CIA.[45] It is probable that the Communist government in Peking was alarmed by U.S. support for those operations and by a report that the United States intended to conclude a defense treaty with Chiang's government similar to the one it had concluded with the South Korean government after the armistice in Korea. It decided to take counter-action to preserve its claim to Taiwan. Chou En-lai proclaimed anew Communist China's determination to "liberate" Taiwan, and on September 3, 1954 the Chinese Communists began artillery bombardment of Chiang's forces on Quemoy Island, which was only two miles from the mainland. Eisenhower then decided to give Chiang the mutual defense treaty that he had been pressing for, guaranteeing U.S. protection to Formosa and the Pescadores, but exacting in return a pledge that Chiang would not undertake any more military operations against the Communist mainland without American approval.[46]

The result was the mutual defense treaty of December 2, 1954, between the United States and "the Republic of China."[47] It specified that the territories guaranteed against armed attack should mean "in respect of the Republic of China, Taiwan and the Pescadores." An accompanying exchange of notes formalized the understanding between the two governments that, although the Republic of China controlled "other territory" (i.e. the off-shore islands) and possessed with respect to all territory under its control the right of self-defense, it would not launch any use of force from either area except by joint agreement with the United States. Unfortunately, although the treaty was published, the exchange of notes was kept secret until February 7, 1955, which left the Chinese Communists in the dark for that long as to the restraints placed on the Nationalist forces. In the meantime, mounting Communist attacks on the offshore island garrisons led to Eisenhower's request for Congressional authority to employ U.S. forces to protect Formosa, as well as "related territories . . . now in friendly hands" if he thought that to be necessary to assure the defense of Formosa. Congress gave him that authority in the "Formosa Resolution" of January 28, 1955. Both Dulles and Eisenhower suggested that tactical atomic weapons might be used if the United States went to the aid of the Nationalists, with Eisenhower saying:

> In any combat where these things can be used on strictly military targets and for strictly military purposes, I see no reason why they shouldn't be used just exactly as you would use a bullet or anything else.[48]

The mutual defense treaty with the Taiwan-based government, which claimed to be the government of all of China, and which the United States continued to recognize as the government of all of China, placed the United States in an anomalous legal position. It was compared to the treaty made previously with "the Republic of Korea," to defend a part of that divided country against the other part. But the situations were dissimilar. While everyone agreed that Korea ought to be reunited, it had never been under one government since its long occupation by Japan. The United Nations had clearly declared the illegitimacy of the effort by North Korea to unify Korea by force. By contrast, the UN had never been asked to interfere in the Chinese civil war. The United States' defense treaty with Chiang's regime was clearly an intervention in Chinese affairs for which there was no justification under the UN Charter.

Dulles did his best to muddy the waters. He often talked about the government on Taiwan as a separate nation, ignoring the fact that it claimed to be the government of China. At other times he seemed to be asserting a right to intervene in the Chinese civil war on a theory that prior experience, including Soviet aid to the Chinese Communists, had so clearly demonstrated the aggressive nature of "international communism" that rules against the use of force did not apply to the struggle against it. Neither the theory that the Republic of China on Taiwan was a separate nation-state, nor the theory that forcible intervention in civil wars should be considered self-defense under Article 51 so long as it was against Communists, had much support at the United Nations.

The issue of hostilities between the Nationalist and Communist Chinese forces and the threatened participation by the United States in defense of Chiang's off-shore island positions was taken to the Security Council in January 1955 by New Zealand and the Soviet Union. The representative of New Zealand made no attempt to assess blame, but emphasized the international danger from increasing military activity in a situation in which "two governing authorities were involved, each claiming the same territory and in control of part of that territory, each disposing of powerful military forces and each in alliance with one of the most powerful countries in the world." New Zealand urged the Council to concentrate on the sole objective of stopping the fighting and preventing its extension.[49] The Soviet Union, on the other hand, charged that the mutual defense treaty was aggressive intervention by the United States in China's domestic affairs:

> When the Korean war ended, the Government of the United States was deprived of the opportunity of using that war as an excuse for the further occupation of Taiwan. It therefore attempted with the help of this treaty to consolidate its occupation of the Chinese territory of Taiwan . . .[50]

Consideration of these items by the Security Council was prevented when the People's Republic of China rejected an invitation to participate because it was denied representation as the government of China.

It would be a long time before the United States could extricate itself from the contradictory legal situation it got itself into by its treaty with the "Republic of China." In the Shanghai Communique of 1972, issued jointly with the Communist Chinese leaders, President Nixon acknowledged "that all Chinese on either side of the Taiwan Strait maintain there is but one China and that Taiwan is a part of China." He affirmed that "The United States Government does not challenge that position."[51] Yet it was not until December 1978 that relations between the United States and China were "normalized" by American recognition of the Communist government in Peking as the national government of China. As a necessary element in that recognition, the United States terminated diplomatic relations with the Republic of China and gave notice of termination of the mutual defense treaty of 1954.[52]

3. SECRET ILLEGAL OPERATIONS

The readiness of Eisenhower and John Foster Dulles to use illegal force in the anti-Communist cause was most clearly demonstrated in a greatly expanded program of CIA covert operations. Allen Dulles, an enthusiastic supporter of "operations," as distinct from the more mundane "intelligence" function of the agency, had been promoted from Deputy Director to Director of the CIA, and worked closely with his brother, the Secretary of State.

The history of the Central Intelligence Agency which was prepared by the staff of the Senate's Select Committee on Intelligence Activities details the process by which a modest proposal made in 1948 for a small contingency force capable of operations on a limited basis and subject to policy guidance by the State Department grew into a large program of ongoing operations that came to overshadow the intelligence-collection function of the CIA.[53] Covert operations had been initiated with a program of propaganda activity, food shipments, and funding of anti-Communist parties, to prevent Communists from winning elections in Italy in 1948. It was the Eisenhower administration which promoted the operations branch of the CIA to a central place in policy execution. Before it went out of office proposals for covert action were being constantly generated.

The first major covert intervention was in Iran in August, 1953 —the operation by which Mohammed Mossadegh was overthrown and the shah restored to power. Mossadegh was not a Communist, but the administration considered him to be allied with Iranian Communists, putting the country on a "downhill course toward Communist-supported dictatorship."[54] Truman and Acheson had been opposed to any attempt to oust Mossadegh, but the Eisenhower administration enthusiastically embraced the scheme to overthrow him.[55] That operation began the identification of the United States with the shah's regime, and had adverse long-term consequences, but the coup was regarded in Washington as a brilliant success, and it encouraged the administration to try to duplicate it in Guatemala.

In that Central American country the radical reformist regime of President Jacobo Arbenz Guzman had embraced agrarian reform and expropriated lands of the United Fruit Company, as well as giving official positions to a number of Communists and legalizing the local Communist party. While it never accused Arbenz, himself, of being a Communist, the administration decided that to eliminate the danger that Guatemala might later come under Communist control Arbenz must be ousted.[56] To accomplish that, two action plans were embarked on simultaneously. One was the plan for a covert military operation. The other was an effort to persuade the Organization of American States to decide upon common action to prevent Communist control of any American state. On March 6, 1954 Dulles proposed to the Tenth Inter-American Conference what became the "Declaration of Caracas." As drafted by the United States, it would condemn "the activities of the international communist movement as constituting intervention in American affairs," and declare "that the domination or control of the political institutions of any American State by the international communist movement . . . would constitute a threat to the sovereignty and independence of the American States, endangering the peace of America, and would call for appropriate action in accordance with existing treaties." Opposing any such declaration, the Guatemalan foreign minister asked, "What is communism?," and protested that the United States' purpose was to intervene illegally in Guatemalan affairs. Dulles replied:

> I thought that by now every Foreign Minister of the world knew what international communism is. . . . International communism is that farflung clandestine political organization which is operated by the leaders of the Communist Party of the Soviet Union . . . It has a hard core of agents in practically every country of the world. The total constitutes not a theory, not a doctrine, but an aggressive, tough, political force, backed by great resources, and serving the most ruthless empire of modern times.[57]

The Declaration was approved by the conference, against the opposition of Guatemala and with Mexico and Argentina abstaining, but only after it was amended to specify that communist control in any American State would call for "a meeting of consultation," instead of "appropriate action," as the United States had proposed. It was clear that the other American States were a long way from authorizing actual armed intervention in Guatemala.

Without waiting further for OAS action, Washington therefore proceeded with its covert action plan. A small force of Guatemalan exiles headed by Colonel Castillo-Armas had been assembled by the CIA in Honduras, trained by U.S. instructors, and equipped with American weapons and a small CIA air force. On June 14th, this force crossed the border into Guatemala. When the invasion faltered, and the Guatemalan army failed to defect, Allen Dulles recommended that the United States send two U.S. Air Force fighter-bombers, in addition to the CIA planes already provided, to help Castillo-Armas. Eisenhower approved that action, when he was told that the bombers were Castillo-Armas' only hope of success, despite argument by Assistant Secretary of State Henry Holland that such action was clearly illegal and that, if it became known, it would be condemned by the other Latin American republics. The bombing planes attacked Guatemalan towns, and the threat of heavier bombing was exploited, with other techniques of psychological warfare by radio, to pressure Arbenz into resigning so as to prevent further damage to his country. The American ambassador negotiated directly with the Guatemalan army chiefs to bring Castillo-Armas to power.[58]

In the week before the fall of Arbenz, Guatemala had requested urgent UN Security Council consideration of the situation. The Guatemalan representative told the Security Council that his country was undergoing "an international invasion masked as a movement of exiles." He asked the Security Council to send an observation mission to investigate. He rejected consideration by the Organization of American States.

Lodge, the United States representative, asserted that there was only "a revolt of Guatemalans against Guatemalans" and said, "the United States has no connection whatever with what is taking place." As President of the Security Council for the month of June, he took the position that the matter *must* be referred in the first instance to the regional organization of the American States, and Brazil and Colombia supported the call to refer it to the OAS. The representative of France drily recalled a statement Lodge had made just two days previously, when Thailand requested a UN observation mission because of fighting along its border with Indochina. Lodge had said:

> I hope that I will never live to see the day when a small country comes to the United Nations and asks for protection against war and is simply greeted with the question: What is the hurry?

Nevertheless, France supported the resolution to refer the Guatemalan complaint to the OAS, after adding a paragraph by which the Security Council would call for "the immediate termination of any action likely to cause further bloodshed." When the Soviet Union vetoed referral, the Council adopted the French amendment as a separate resolution.[59] The Council then suspended discussion while the OAS Peace Committee took up the matter. On the 22nd the Guatemalan foreign minister complained to the Secretary-General that the resolution was not being complied with, and again requested a Council meeting, but although the Secretary-General urged that the Council should meet without delay, Lodge refused to call another meeting until June 25 and then opposed adoption of the agenda. He succeeded by a 5 to 4 vote, with France and Great Britain abstaining. This prevented any action by the Security Council while the OAS organs discussed "the international communist threat to the Americas" and the overthrow of Arbenz proceeded according to plan. However, Lodge's argument that Articles 34, 35 and 52 of the Charter should be interpreted as meaning that only the regional organization had jurisdiction to deal with disputes within the region was clearly not accepted by the other Council members, and Secretary-General Hammarskjold told Sir Pierson Dixon that he considered Lodge's attack on the Council's jurisdiction so serious a blow that if it were pressed he would consider resigning.[60]

At several points in the administration's campaign against Guatemala, it had met objections from the British and French. Before the invasion began, an American plan to search and seize ships transporting arms bought by the Guatemalan government was protested by the British. The plan had been adopted despite an opinion by the State Department Legal Adviser's Office that it would be contrary to international law.[61] The British government was induced to cooperate in preventing such shipments, while maintaining their objection in principle. At a later stage, the British and French governments favored sending UN observers to Guatemala, rather than referring the matter to the OAS. Lodge strongly asserted preeminent United States interest in the matter, and told their representatives, on instructions from the President:

> If Great Britain and France felt that they must take an independent line backing the present government of Guatemala, we would feel free to take an equally independent line concerning such matters as Egypt and North Africa in which we had hitherto tried to exercise the greatest forbearance...

The European allies were persuaded, reluctantly, to abstain on the Security Council vote of June 25.[62] The memory of these events contributed to Eden's expectation of American neutrality two years later, when Britain decided upon military action at Suez.

Before leaving the subject of the American intervention in Guatemala, we must note its long-term consequences for that country. The urgently needed reform of Guatemalan society which was begun in 1944 under Juan José Arevalo, and continued and expanded after 1951 under the presidency of Jacobo Arbenz Guzman, redistributed agricultural land to landless campesinos, began a massive literacy campaign, extended the right to vote to the bulk of the population which had been denied it, and gave workers for the first time the right to organize and strike. The American intervention aborted those reforms and turned the clock back. Agricultural land was returned to the ownership of the few, including United Fruit Company, the country's largest landowner. The military dictatorships which have ruled since then have held on to power by vote fraud and by calculated extermination of their opponents. The Guatemalan revolution of the early 1950s bore resemblance to the Mexico of the 1930s. Without American intervention it might have evolved in a similar way. When it was repressed, it was only to reemerge in the spreading guerilla insurgency that threatens Guatemala's right-wing dictatorship of today.

Still other covert operations of the Eisenhower administration included support for a rebellion against Sukarno in Indonesia in 1958 (it failed, and an American bomber pilot was captured by the Indonesian government) and raids into China by Tibetan exiles.[63] The most ambitious of the Eisenhower CIA's plans for covert operations was the one against Cuba which is discussed in the next chapter. In his administration, the CIA also conspired to bring about the assassination of two foreign national leaders considered to be pro-Soviet —Congolese Premier Patrice Lumumba, and Cuba's Fidel Castro. These covert operations were just as much policy measures as were overt uses of force, and their consequences were the more serious for the fact that the American public was the party principally deceived.

4. SUEZ: THE UNITED STATES SUPPORTS THE RULES OF THE CHARTER

President Eisenhower was hardly consistent in his attitude towards the UN rules, for, despite his readiness to consider forcible intervention in Iran, Guatemala, Cuba, Indochina and China, he reacted with severe disapproval when Britain, France, and Israel used force against Egypt without American consent in 1956.

In this crisis there was a basic difference in perspective between the British and American governments. From the British viewpoint Nasser's nationalization of the Suez canal company posed a vital political threat, while for Eisenhower and Dulles the canal issue was of secondary importance. Their concern was to prevent a British response that might have spreading and dangerous consequences. From the start, it was apparent that Prime Minister Eden was contemplating resort to force. He recalled the occasions on which the United States had been willing to consider the use of force — in the Far East and to topple Arbenz and Mossadegh, and while he did not expect any direct American participation, he assumed that the United States would at least remain benevolently neutral.[64] While Eisenhower's communications to Eden after canal nationalization and before the landing at Suez left no doubt that he considered the use of force by Britain in this instance would be unwise and unjustifiable, he did not go so far as to say that offensive force must never be employed. His warnings included qualifying phrases, to the effect that every peaceful means of resolving the controversy must first be exhausted (letter to Eden, July 31, 1956), or, "There should be no thought of military action before the influences of the UN are fully explored" (letter to Eden, Sept. 2, 1956).[65] Perhaps Eden's ear was tuned to hear what he wanted to hear, but he interpreted Eisenhower's July 31 letter as meaning that the President was "emphatic about the importance of negotiation," but "did not rule out the use of force."[66] The one step that might have been taken to disabuse Eden of any doubts would have been to warn him that if the threats to use force were carried out the matter would be taken at once to the United Nations by the United States. But in the light of previous American conduct such a warning would have seemed unmannerly. Thus Eden was permitted to continue in his belief that Eisenhower would in the last analysis acquiesce, or simply stand aside, when Britain and France took forcible action.

Until the military attacks on Egypt at the end of October, when Eisenhower took direct control of the American response, the conduct of negotiations in London was left to Dulles, whose maneuvers contributed to British exasperation and uncertainty about American intentions. He could have taken the position that Egypt's right to nationalize the property of the canal company, an Egyptian company, with compensation to the shareholders, was legally unassailable. Instead, he accepted the British argument that the canal company was "an international agency" and nationalization was therefore not permissible.[67] To deflect the British and French from forcible action, he proposed the convocation of an international conference at London to consider new international protection for the canal. The procedures of this conference blurred the basic choice between a negotiated solution, needing Egypt's consent, and a solution imposed on Egypt, which could only be obtained by the exercise of coercion.

The invitations to the conference were issued by the Western big three, and Egypt was in effect summoned to appear. Normal negotiating procedure, had Egypt been treated as an equal, would have called for preliminary consultations leading to agreement on the calling of a conference in which Egypt would be one of the inviting powers. The Egyptian government, not unexpectedly, declined the invitation to attend because that procedure had not been followed.[68] Without the principal party in interest, the London Conference was not a genuine negotiation. It produced an eighteen-power proposal calling for operation of the canal by an international authority. Egypt rejected that proposal, which left the negotiations where they had started. Eden, concerned with laying a foundation for the use of force, knew that Nasser could not accept the proposal for an international authority which would operate the canal. President Eisenhower had noted that this was likely to be a stumbling block for Nasser, and had given his opinion that the international board should have "a *supervisory* rather then an *operating* role, similar to that of a corporate Board of Directors, with day-to-day operating responsibility in an executive appointed by Nasser, subject to the Board's agreement."[69] A proposal close to Eisenhower's suggestion had in fact been submitted to the conference by the Indian government, which had the confidence of President Nasser. It included provisions for equitable tolls and proper maintenance of the canal, and the "association of international user interests with the 'Egyptian Corporation for the Suez Canal,'" and annual reports to the United Nations. It probably represented the maximum concessions that Egypt could have been prevailed upon freely to accept.[70] The President should have insisted on his point, but instead he allowed Dulles to talk him out of it when Dulles cabled that "it would be very difficult and perhaps impossible from the standpoint of the British and French to get agreement now" to such a change.[71] If Eisenhower had been handling these negotiations directly instead of through Dulles, perhaps the Anglo-French military adventure at Suez might have been avoided.

Dulles never having made it clear to the British and French that the United States absolutely rejected the legitimacy of the use of force against Egypt, even "in the last resort," the British were stunned by the American reaction to Israel's Oct. 29 invasion of the Sinai and the British-French ultimatum and military action which followed. Dulles having undergone an emergency operation for cancer on November 3, the President now took personal charge, calling for an immediate meeting of the UN Security Council, and reminding Prime Minister Eden of the 1950 Tripartite Declaration in which Britain, France and the United States undertook to take joint action to prevent violation of frontiers or armistice lines in the Middle East. He regarded the failure to consult the United States before taking action as a violation of that commitment as well as the UN Charter. Pressing in the Security Council, and then in the General Assembly, for an immediate cease fire and withdrawal of British, French and Israeli forces, he backed this demand with uncompromising economic pressure against both Britain and Israel, which left them no alternative to unconditional withdrawal. When the Israeli government balked at complete withdrawal without a firm guarantee that Egypt would respect the right of free passage into the Gulf of Aqaba and concession of Israeli administrative control over the Gaza Strip, Eisenhower threatened to support a UN call to cut off all private as well as public assistance to Israel if it did not withdraw. He was not deterred by objections voiced by Congressional leaders and he took the case to the public in a televised address on Feb. 20, 1957. "This raises a basic question of principle," he said. "Should a nation which attacks and occupies foreign territory in the face of United Nations disapproval be allowed to impose conditions on its own withdrawal?" Answering his own question in the negative, he continued:

> If the United Nations once admits that international disputes can be settled by using force, then we will have destroyed the very foundation of the organization. . . . The United Nations has no choice but to exert pressure upon Israel to comply with the withdrawal resolutions. . . .[72]

Eisenhower thus showed that he could be firm, despite domestic political opposition, on what he characterized as a matter of principle. But it must be recognized that more was involved, in his eyes, than the law of the Charter. The case was distinguished from those which had arisen in the Far East where the contemplated use of force had been to block the success of Communists. Secondly, a major factor throughout the crisis was his political judgment that the attack on Egypt, if not firmly countered by the United States and the United Nations, would unite the Arab world and many other countries against the West, play into the hands of the Russians, and lead to endless guerrilla warfare such as France had encountered in Algeria.[73] Finally, he was affected by his judgment that American public opinion would not approve the use of force. On July 31 he had written to Eden:

> [If force were used] I personally feel sure that the American reaction would be severe.

On September 2:

> I must tell you frankly that American public opinion flatly rejects the thought of using force, particularly where it does not seem that every possible peaceful means of protecting our vital interests has been exhausted . . .

And on September 8:

> I must say frankly that there is as yet no public opinion in this country which is prepared to support [the use of force against Egypt], and the most significant public opinion that there is seems to think that the United Nations was formed to prevent this very thing.[74]

The American attitude might have been different if the case had been seen as one involving a communist threat. In his messages to Eisenhower following nationalization of the Suez Canal, Eden had raised the specter of increasing Russian influence in the region, but he was not a true believer in the international communist menace, and he did not take full advantage of that American obsession.

CHAPTER VI

VIETNAM: THE AMERICAN MILITARY INTERVENTION

President Eisenhower's decision to extend American protection to an anti-communist regime in South Vietnam, rejecting the Geneva alternative of a unified Vietnam, probably communist but neutralized by a multilateral agreement, led finally, under President Johnson, to full American military intervention.

Whether the United States had legal justification for its intervention to defend the government in Saigon has been a hotly debated question. Proponents and opponents of the war both argued in terms of legal right.[1] As we have noted with respect to international law generally, it was impossible to settle such an argument in the absence of any international authority with compulsory jurisdiction.

The U.S. government's legal defense of its intervention claimed that South Vietnam, an independent state, was resisting an attack on its independence and integrity by North Vietnam, a separate state, and that the United States had the legal right to join in the defense of South Vietnam against external attack. The alternate perception, that the conflict was essentially a Vietnamese civil war, was widely held in countries not closely associated with the United States. France, which had fought so long against the Viet Minh, now took that view of the matter. Its representative in the General Assembly in 1966 called for revival of the Geneva Agreements.

> This means agreeing to evacuate all foreign troops and to prohibit their return and forbidding any outside interference whatsoever in the affairs of Viet-Nam, which must undertake to maintain in future a policy of strict neutrality. These directives would be embodied in an international treaty which would be signed by — and hence would be binding upon — all the great Powers and other countries directly involved. . . . The question of reunification would be recognized as a purely Viet-Namese problem, to be settled, when the time comes, in full independence between the parties concerned.[2]

French experts thought Ho Chi Minh would keep Vietnam independent of both the USSR and China, and de Gaulle advised President Kennedy to accept a unified, neutralized Vietnam even though it be communist.[3] He stated his opinion, and his recollection of the advice he gave to Kennedy, in his memoirs:

You will find . . . that intervention in this area will be an endless entanglement. Once a nation has been aroused, no foreign power, however strong, can impose its will upon it. . . . The ideology which you invoke will make no difference . . . The more you become involved out there against Communism, the more the Communists will appear as the champions of national independence, and the more support they will receive, if only from despair.[4]

There was a significant difference from the situation in Korea when the North Koreans attacked the South. There, geopolitical considerations counseling an American military response had been strongly reinforced by the perception, in all countries except the Communist bloc, that a deliberate invasion had taken place across an internationally established legal border, in violation of the law of the UN Charter. In the case of America's Vietnam adventure, by contrast, the perceptions which brought about intervention were not legal but geopolitical. The conflict did not originate as an invasion from the North. Although it was stimulated by the North Vietnamese regime, it developed gradually as an internal revolt in South Vietnam. North Vietnamese military intervention came later and kept pace with the growing American intervention. After the United States directly entered the fighting in 1965, the legal arguments based on the theory of collective defense against North Vietnamese invasion were issued as a standard response to criticism of the American role, but they are more accurately seen as justification after the fact than as a factor in the calculations which brought the intervention.

The United States acted unilaterally. It reported its military measures to the Security Council, but it did not ask the Security Council to consider the situation until the end of January 1966.[5] It then asked the Security Council to help arrange discussions that might lead to a cessation of hostilities. But the Security Council was incapacitated from dealing with the problem because neither Communist China, a major interested party, nor the rival Vietnamese governments, were represented at the UN, and because China was adamantly opposed to appearing before the UN Security Council on any *ad hoc* basis. For this reason the only international forum capable of dealing with the issue would have been a revived Geneva Conference. But the United States had turned its back on that authority in 1954, preferring to play a unilateral role. The North Vietnamese now refused to return to the negotiating table without prior American acceptance of their conditions.

The American intervention failed to achieve its objective of preventing communist control and was enormously costly. It was a failure that resulted from a chain of false perceptions.

The first was a misperception of the nature of the Vietnamese Communist leaders. Officials in Washington considered that the fact that Ho Chi Minh and his associates were Communists meant that they were nothing more than subservient agents of an international conspiracy. That perception caused American policy-makers to neglect the nationalist character of those leaders of North Vietnam, and their dedication to Vietnamese independence. The single fact that Washington concentrated on was that, unless the United States could prevent it, South Vietnam was likely to be taken over by Communist leadership, and the example would encourage Communists in neighboring countries. In no other terms was this small and distant country of any real interest to the United States. Today we have ample evidence that Communist Vietnam is as determinedly independent as any other nation, and has bitter conflicts with Communist China. Had that been appreciated in 1954, when Dulles and Eisenhower turned their backs on the diplomatic settlement worked out at Geneva, or in 1961 when Kennedy endorsed a plan for counter-insurgency assistance to Diem's government, or in 1965 when Johnson ordered American air and ground forces to enter the war, the deepening American involvement might have been avoided or aborted before it reached costly proportions.

A second misperception had to do with the readiness of the Vietnamese for Western-style democracy. Along with the belief that Vietnamese Communists were agents of an international conspiracy went the belief that the Vietnamese people, if they had a choice, would recognize the superiority of democracy over communism. Senator John F. Kennedy expressed that attitude when he told an organization called American Friends of Vietnam, in a 1956 speech, "We must offer them ... a revolution — a political, economic and social revolution far superior to anything the Communists can offer."[6]

The belief that we were qualified to make a revolution for the Vietnamese, or that institutions which had evolved in the American context could be transplanted to Vietnam had no informed basis. Not until Frances Fitzgerald's *Fire in the Lake*,[7] which was published near the end of the long American military intervention, was there any penetrating study by any American of the Vietnamese revolution and

American intervention in terms of an understanding of the Vietnamese social context. Her study shows that to the peasant villagers of South Vietnam, who comprised 85% of the population at the beginning of the war, "democracy vs. communism" was an unreal issue. The village was the country's essential social and political unit, the center of a way of life based on family, the land, and ancestor worship. In the Vietnamese villager European-American concepts of individual liberty and private property struck no responsive chord. So far as there was a sense of national identity, it was a recent creation, dating from the struggle waged by Ho Chi Minh against the French. Apart from the Viet Minh, there existed no legitimate national leadership. The governments in Saigon, from Ngo Dinh Diem to Nguyen Van Thieu, could hold office only so long as they were propped up by the United States. Their supporters, aside from the minority of Catholics from North Vietnam who were brought as refugees to South Vietnam by the U.S. fleet during the Geneva armistice, included administrators from the French colonial regime, profiteers, refugee landlords, army officers, and other dependents of the French or Americans. The American attempt to win the loyalty of the Vietnamese villagers never made headway, and it was largely abandoned in 1965 when regular American troops entered the war with a new strategy which entailed the destruction of the many villages in which the Viet Cong were found.

The villagers of Vietnam were not aroused by talk about freedom and democracy. The real issue for them was simply the collapse of political order that was destroying their established way of life (and which ultimately made five million villagers into homeless refugees, deprived of their former identity). Their response to the collapse of order and their old way of life was to await "the will of heaven" and to give their support to whatever authority seemed most capable of establishing a viable new order. Consensus was what they wanted, rather than free political competition. An understanding of Vietnamese history and society rather than our own preconceptions and traditions should have led us to the conclusion that foreigners were utterly unqualified to make Vietnam's revolution or to guide its modernization.

The third of the misperceptions that led to American intervention was failure to appreciate the limits of American military power. It was thought that the United States, with unlimited firepower, could not possibly lose a contest with NLF guerrillas or a North Vietnamese army equipped only with small arms. Despite the ultimate abandonment of the American military effort, this belief lingers on in the view of some military chiefs that a more intensive use of American firepower might have produced victory. That view neglects the rational limits to escalation of the conflict by the United States. While the conflict was held within the old borders of Indochina, with the Soviet Union limiting its assistance to North Vietnam to the supply of arms and equipment, and there was no nuclear confrontation of the superpowers, there was in fact very significant escalation. With the failure of expectations that the Saigon government could compete politically with the NLF, increasing amounts of American military power were applied, from President Kennedy's decision to greatly increase the numbers of American military advisers and "Special Forces," to President Johnson's commitment of American combat troops and initiation of air attacks on North Vietnam. In 1968, with more than half a million American troops in Vietnam and General Westmoreland asking for 200,000 more, it became apparent that one practical limit on escalation had been reached. The American public had had enough. Johnson, recognizing that it was not politically feasible to increase further the commitment of American manpower, decided to de-escalate and seek a political settlement. He would not run for re-election. Opinion polls, and the New Hampshire primary, confirmed that a majority of the public now believed that it had been a mistake to send American troops to fight in Vietnam. The NLF, and their allies in North Vietnam, having indeed far greater interests at stake in the conflict, and consequently a far greater political commitment to the struggle, had more than compensated with staying power for the greater American military capability. President Nixon, unwilling to accept defeat in Vietnam, neutralized part of the American opposition to the war by promising to win it without American ground troops, by "Vietnamization." This meant substituting a kind of push-button war for American troops on the ground. He would fight by using a Saigon army lavishly equipped with superior American firepower, with massive, long-distance bombing of North Vietnam, and by carrying the war into Cambodia and Laos, which had hitherto preserved a precarious neutrality although they were powerless to prevent North Vietnamese use of routes through their thinly-populated border districts. Nixon was able to continue the American military effort for five more years, ending in a "peace agreement" which proved to be only a truce covering American withdrawal. The Vietnamese parties resumed the conflict, which ended two years later with the defeat of the Saigon government. Despite the United States' superior military capabilities, practical limits to the use of those capabilities had asserted themselves. The war had serious economic consequences and the business community turned against it. Finally Congress moved to cut off funds. It was impossible for President Ford to contemplate re-intervention. Much earlier, another limiting factor had been the danger that China would intervene, as it had in Korea. The Chinese government later made it known that, in addition to weapons and ammunition, 300,000 Chinese army personnel were in fact sent to aid the North Vietnamese government between 1964 and 1971 (probably not more than 40,000 to 50,000 at any one time). They served only within North Vietnam, and were limited to anti-aircraft artillery, engineers, road and railway workers, and others involved in logistic support.[8] The Korean experience strongly suggests that Chinese forces would have entered the fighting if U.S. ground forces had entered North Vietnam. There were few in the United States who wanted to take the risk of expanding the war beyond Indochina. Even expanding it to Cambodia provoked a strong negative reaction. And it was apparent that there was nothing to be gained by resort to nuclear weapons. The United States had the capacity, it was true, to bomb Vietnam so intensively as to convert it into a desert, but what meaningful victory would there be in that? Already, from 1965 on, the United States had been employing military tactics that were counter-productive in terms of the political objective of winning the support of the Vietnamese people. When the American army entered the war, it carried out a strategy of destroying the villages and the countryside where the NLF had operated, forcing villagers who did not join the NLF to become refugees. These tactics accelerated the destruction of traditional Vietnamese society. With Vietnamization, reliance on air power and long-distance bombardment took the place of American troops, but this was even more destructive of civilian life and livelihood. A more humane and politically effective strategy aimed at pacifying the country might have called for saturating it with an American occupation force of several million men, but that was politically impossible.

The costs of the unsuccessful attempt to impose an American solution on Vietnam by military means were very high. This American policy ultimately exerted its own kind of domino effect, when President Nixon's incursion into Cambodia undermined the neutrality which the Cambodian government of Prince Sihanouk had managed to maintain, and brought the revolutionary destruction of that peaceful country as well as Vietnam. The war also weakened the United States at home. Compelled to fight in a distant country in a struggle without any convincing relationship to the defense of the United States, it was small wonder that the American army became demoralized. The war contributed to drug addiction in the United States and probably to the propensity to violent crime; it increased government deficits and stimulated inflation; and it resulted in the practice of official deceit against the public and against Congress.[9] Even had military "victory" been won, and a non-communist government established in power throughout Vietnam, its existence would have remained precarious, a continuing military liability for the United States.

CHAPTER VII

COMBATTING REVOLUTIONS IN LATIN AMERICA

1. THE UNITED STATES AND THE CUBAN REVOLUTION

The Cuban Revolution brought about by Fidel Castro posed a continuing challenge to American thinking about foreign policy that is comparable to the challenge of the Chinese Revolution. The Chinese crisis lasted thirty years before it was solved by the revision of American thinking about China which was symbolized by American recognition of the People's Republic. More than twenty years since Castro's advent to power have not yet sufficed to bring an equivalent recognition that the new Cuba is its own master rather than a Soviet puppet, or a comparable readjustment of American policy to accommodate changes in Latin America that cannot be permanently blocked by a paramilitary policy.

The conflict between Fidel Castro and the United States under Eisenhower developed rapidly following Castro's victorious entry into Havana on January 1, 1959. It would be hard to say which side was more responsible. Castro expected U.S. hostility to his revolution and was determined to free Cuba entirely from its past experience of dominant American influence — economic, social, and political. Washington, while it recognized the new government within a week, suspiciously watched for evidence of Russian leanings or participation of Communists in the new regime. Suspicion was whetted when Castro sent arms to anti-government rebels in neighboring countries, conducted summary trials and executions, and began the expropriation of American-owned sugar plantations in his land reform program. Castro's fears seemed confirmed by sporadic raids by planes from Florida.[1] He increased his denunciations of the United States and predicted it would invade Cuba. In February 1960 came Soviet Vice Premier Mikoyan's visit to Cuba, and the signing of a Cuban-Russian trade agreement, including a Russian commitment to buy Cuban sugar and a $100 million credit for Cuban purchase of Soviet goods. It was at this point that Eisenhower abandoned attempts to settle differences with Castro's government and approved a new policy which had as its objective the overthrow of Castro by every means available short of the use of U.S. armed forces in Cuba. On March 17, 1960 the CIA was directed to recruit and train Cuban exiles for military service in the anti-Castro struggle. The American ambassador was not informed of the planning to overthrow Castro (and disapproved of it when he found out). The new policy found expression in two U.S. moves in June and July, 1960. The Secretary of the Treasury urged the Esso, Texaco, and Shell oil companies to refuse to handle in their refineries crude oil which the Cuban government was buying from Russia. That resulted in the Cuban government taking possession of the refineries. Then came President Eisenhower's 700,000 ton reduction of the Cuban sugar quota, under which, since the Spanish-American War, the United States had imported a large part of the Cuban crop at higher prices than obtained on the world market. Ambassador Bonsal saw these actions as nullifying what he thought were the benefits of previous policies of restraint and non-intervention. The sugar quota had been "the keystone in the arch of Cuban-American relations." He agreed with Ernest Hemingway's warning that to terminate the quota would "make Cuba a gift to the Russians."[2] Wholesale Cuban nationalization of American properties, an American embargo on exports to Cuba, and severance of diplomatic relations followed. American moves against Castro impelled the USSR to come to his rescue economically, and Soviet arms shipments then began.[3]

One of the last foreign policy initiatives of the Eisenhower administration was the plan to mount an exile invasion of Cuba. The plan was so far advanced when President Kennedy took office that he found it not politically practicable to call it off. The exile force, situated at a base in Guatemala, had already been trained by U.S. army instructors and completely equipped with U.S. army stores. Doomed to disaster, this invasion plan stands as the classic example of the disadvantages of secret para-military operations.

Originally, the plan was to infiltrate the Cuban exiles into Cuba in small groups to join resistance forces. From this beginning it expanded into an operation so large and visible that it would not be possible to maintain the fiction that the United States was not involved. Before the 1960 election the CIA had abandoned the infiltration idea in favor of a sizeable beachhead assault supported by a CIA fleet of B-26 bombers flying from Nicaragua. 500 U.S. army instructors were brought to the Guatemalan coffee plantation where the Cuban Brigade was in training. Realizing that secret support would be inadequate after the attack began, the planners envisaged a patent legal manipulation — they would fly in a provisional government which would be immediately recognized by the United States and would request overt American aid to the new "legitimate" government of Cuba.[4]

One of the disadvantages of secret operations is that they receive inadequate discussion. During the interregnum between Kennedy's election and his inauguration on January 20, 1961, preparations for the assault went forward. Kennedy received a detailed briefing on November 29, and deferred his own decision. The fact that the succeeding administration would make the ultimate decision became an excuse for deferring any top-level review of the plan within the Eisenhower administration. After Kennedy's inauguration, the secrecy requirement meant that only a limited number of high officials attended the series of meetings at which the plan was discussed. They included Secretary of State Rusk, Thomas Mann (the assistant secretary for Latin American Affairs), Secretary of Defense McNamara, Allen Dulles and Richard Bissell of the CIA, Adolf Berle (chairman of Kennedy's pre-inauguration Latin American task force), and the Joint Chiefs of Staff. Arthur Schlesinger was asked for his opinion, and one meeting was attended by Senator Fulbright. Surprisingly, only Schlesinger and Fulbright argued against the plan, urging that the operation was out of proportion to the threat from Castro, that it would revive Latin American memory of American imperialism, that it contravened treaty obligations and would compromise America's moral position, and that it was unlikely to succeed and would lead to pressure to send in U.S. forces. Rusk had private doubts but took a passive role. The CIA itself had lost its objectivity. Dulles and Bissell were such ardent advocates of the plan that they concealed its negative features. Kennedy, seeking to limit the risks, rejected the first proposed landing site at the port of Trinidad as too visible, and clearly specified that, whatever happened, there would be no intervention by regular U.S. forces. Neither the CIA nor the JCS told him of their opinion that success could not be assured under those circumstances. When the new landing site at the "Bay of Pigs" was substituted, he was not told that this site was one from which there was no possibility of the invaders escaping to the mountains in the event of failure, as had been part of the original plan. He was told that the landing would trigger an uprising in Cuba, but he was not told that the CIA had no way of alerting the Cuban underground resistance. The inadequacy was not so much in the limited number of advisers who were in on the decison as it was in the fact that secrecy prevented any input from the knowledgeable experts at lower bureaucratic levels, who would otherwise have brought the negative features of the plan out into the open. Under Secretary of State Chester Bowles learned that a decision was soon to be made on the proposed invasion when he was left in charge during an overseas trip by Secretary Rusk, and Bowles gave Rusk, on his return, a memorandum urging that the plan be cancelled. His reasons were the same as Schlesinger's and Fulbright's — violation of the non-intervention commitments which were the basis of the OAS system, the very adverse effect that the operation would have on world opinion, and the very dubious prospect that the operation would succeed without direct American military support.[5] Bowles urged Rusk to advise the President against the plan, and to give Bowles a chance to take his objections to the President personally if the plan was still operative. Rusk apparently did not convey Bowles' objections to the President. Roger Hilsman, director of the State Department's Bureau of Intelligence and Research, also got wind of the plan, was disturbed by it, and asked Rusk for permission to put his analysts to work on the question of the validity of the CIA assumption that the landing would trigger a popular uprising. He was told not to do so as "this is being too tightly held."[6] Even the CIA's own intelligence branch was kept in the dark about the plan, although it might have been expected to have answers to the critical question whether any uprising was likely.[7] The very cursory evaluation of the plan by the Joint Chiefs of Staff may also have been affected by the fact that very few officers were told about it. Public discussion would unquestionably have stimulated criticism, but President Kennedy had successfully interceded with publishers to prevent their following through with stories on what was afoot that they were about to print.[8]

While secrecy contributed to over-optimism about the chances of the operation succeeding, Bowles felt that the basic flaw which made such a mistake possible was the prevailing pragmatism of officials who lacked any basic convictions about right and wrong.

> ... When CIA chief Allen Dulles proposed to the President of the United States that our govenment finance and sponsor an invasion of Cuba by one thousand Cuban expatriates in clear violation of previous treaty

commitments, there was no need, in my opinion, for a series of endless White House meetings to examine the proposal from a hundred different angles. The answer to Mr. Dulles' proposal should have been promptly and finally negative.[9]

And he had written soon after the event:

> The question which concerns me most about the new Administration is whether it lacks a genuine sense of conviction about what is right and what is wrong! . . . Anyone in public life who has strong convictions about the rights and wrongs of public morality, both domestic and international, has a very great advantage in times of strain, since his instincts on what to do are clear and immediate.[10]

Since the State Department's Legal Adviser had not been informed or asked for his advice on the legal implications of invasion by an American-trained exile force, Kennedy may not have been aware of the clear illegality of the operation. He seemed to think that only the use of United States armed forces would be "intervention" precluded by the principles of the OAS.[11] Richard Nixon, invited to the White House for consultation, advised outright U.S. invasion. "I would find a proper legal cover and I would go in," he told Kennedy. "There are several justifications that could be used, like protecting American citizens living in Cuba and defending our base at Guantanamo."[12]

Though Kennedy decided against any open U.S. intervention to reinforce the exile brigade, he continued through covert operations the attempt to overthrow Castro by force. These operations were made the first priority of the counter-insurgency group that was set up under the chairmanship of General Maxwell Taylor in July 1961 and of the "Special Group" which supervised "Operation Mongoose," in which the CIA organized raids from the sea and sabotage attacks on sugar refineries and oil depots, and tried to build a resistance movement in Cuba. Besides General Taylor, Robert Kennedy was an active member of these committees, and the presence on their membership of other trusted presidential advisers such as Richard Goodwin, McGeorge Bundy and U. Alexis Johnson, as well as Director McCone and Richard Bissell of the CIA, is an indication of their importance.[13] General Edward Lansdale, considered the best counter-insurgency expert, was named to run Mongoose, and the CIA station in Miami which controlled these operations became a very large one with a fleet of speed boats, hundreds of case officers and several thousand Cuban agents.[14] Kennedy's CIA also revived earlier plots to get rid of Castro by assassination, and employed underworld agents in that effort.[15] Outside of Cuba Kennedy focused on efforts to prevent the expansion of communist influence from Cuba to other Latin-American countries. The Kennedy administration seemed to be making with respect to Cuba the same misjudgment as Eisenhower and Dulles had made with respect to China — assuming that communism in Cuba meant that Castro had given up Cuba's independence to the Soviet Union. Secretary of the Treasury Douglas Dillon told the Inter-American conference at Punta del Este in August 1961:

> ... Day by day we saw the Government of Cuba betray the aims of the revolution which had brought it to power and give over the people of Cuba to the domination of a foreign power.... We await the day when the people of Cuba have once more regained their freedom from that foreign domination.[16]

Under United States urging, the OAS foreign ministers resolved on January 31, 1962 "that adherence by any member of the Organization of American States to Marxism-Leninism is incompatible with the inter-American system." They excluded the Castro government from further participation in the system.[17]

The missile crisis of October 1962 grew out of the previous American campaign to overthrow Castro. The first thing to note about it is that the crisis was unnecessary. It was the fear of another invasion, with American forces this time involved, that induced Castro to seek military alliance with the Soviet Union. If the United States had adhered to its non-intervention commitments it is unlikely that it would have been faced with Soviet missiles in Cuba.

Kennedy's determination to obtain removal of the Soviet missiles whatever the cost, was, we have already noted, political.[18] Law seemed to favor the Soviet Union rather than the United States. No legal consideration seemed to stand in the way of Russia's sending the missiles, with the Cuban government's consent, and there had been no "armed attack" such as would entitle the United States to exercise the right of self-defense referred to in Article 51 of the UN Charter. Legal considerations did play a modest part, however, in the deliberations on the choice of an appropriate American response. Kennedy and his committee of advisers were debating the relative advantages of an air strike against the missile sites, as against a blockade or quarantine (with the air strike held in reserve if other means should fail). Ambassador Llewellyn Thompson observed that Russian decision-makers were influenced by legalistic considerations and this brought a request for advice from legal advisers from the Justice Department (called in by Attorney General Robert Kennedy) and the State Department. Nicholas Katzenbach, deputy attorney general, gave his opinion that the United States could argue that the use of force to eliminate the missiles would be an act of self-defense justified by Article 51. Leonard Meeker, the State Department's acting Legal Adviser, disagreed, since there had been no "armed attack." To invoke Article 51 in such circumstances would, he thought, set a dangerous legal precedent. It was his advice that action taken by the OAS as a regional organization provided for by Chapter VIII of the UN Charter would give the best legal basis for action. Under Article 6 of the Rio Treaty the OAS might authorize measures to maintain the peace and security of the continent in the face of a "situation that might endanger the peace of America."[19] Former Secretary Acheson, one of those participating in the discussion, favored the air strike option and sided with Katzenbach. He thought that in "questions of ultimate power," such as the case before them, law was essentially irrelevant. For the purpose of the customary legal argument after action was taken it would be sufficient to make the claim of self-defense.[20] Consensus settled, however, on the blockade option and the request for OAS action. The desire to present a stronger legal case thus had an influence on strategy.

Adlai Stevenson, the U.S. ambassador to the UN, brought the UN perspective into the discussions. He assumed that the issue would come before the Security Council (the existence of the United Nations ensured that) and he argued the importance of calling for an emergency meeting and seizing the initiative rather than appearing as defendant against Russian or Cuban charges. He thought the United States should go into the Security Council with a proposed resolution which would state the willingness of the United States to guarantee the territorial integrity of Cuba and call for dismantling the Soviet missile sites and withdrawal of Soviet military personnel so as to ensure the security of the hemisphere. He thought the United States should also be ready to negotiate, offering to give up its base in Cuba at Guantanamo and to dismantle its missile bases in Turkey and Italy in return for Russia's withdrawal of its missiles from Cuba. Stevenson was alone in his willingness to give up the Guantanamo base and to couple Russian missiles in Cuba with American missiles in Turkey and Italy, but in the final resolution of the crisis President Kennedy did pledge respect for Cuba's territorial integrity and assured Khrushchev unofficially, through his brother Robert, that the President was going to remove the American missiles from Turkey and Italy. Stevenson endorsed the move to get OAS backing so as to strengthen the United States' case. He was successful in seizing the initiative at the UN. His request for a Security Council meeting "to deal with the dangerous threat to the peace and security of the world which had been caused by the secret establishment in Cuba by the USSR of launching bases and long-range ballistic missiles capable of carrying thermonuclear warheads to most of North and South America" preceded counter-requests by Cuba and the Soviet Union that the Council consider aggressive acts committed by the United States. The Council took up the three complaints simultaneously. Stevenson's opening speech characterized the situation as an assault on the principle of the territorial integrity of the Western Hemisphere. His proposed resolution called for the dismantling and withdrawal of Russian offensive weapons and authority for the Secretary-General to send to Cuba a UN observer corps to report on compliance, to be followed by termination of the American quarantine. Before completing the speech, Stevenson received and read to the Council the resolution just adopted by the OAS, in which the OAS took a common stand with the United States. This was followed by notes from many Latin American countries offering military and logistical support to carry out the collective action taken under the inter-American treaty. In a later speech Stevenson's manner was almost that of a cross-examiner as he questioned Soviet ambassador Zorin about the missiles with the aid of aerial photographs, so that Zorin protested that he was not "in an American court of law."[21] If the Soviet Government had been confident of the legality of their aid to Cuba, they were no doubt rudely surprised by this turn of events. The efforts of their Ambassador and of the Cuban representative to focus attention on the use of force by the United States fell on largely deaf ears, as the United States' allies closed ranks and the neutrals and the Secretary-General sought ways to end the confrontation peacefully rather than trying to assess blame.

Further American military action to prevent completion of the missile bases was averted by Khrushchev's decision to dismantle the bases and remove the missiles in return for Kennedy's promise to end the quarantine and give assurances that there would be no United

States invasion of Cuba.[22] The United States had now returned, on the level of acknowledged policy, to the position of non-intervention in Cuba. Secretly, however, through the CIA, Kennedy continued his efforts to remove Castro. The outcome of the Missile Crisis was not entirely happy, for the humiliating retreat forced on the Soviet government led it to a sustained military catch-up effort which by the late 1970s made possible Soviet interventions in Africa and caused new feelings of insecurity in the United States and Europe.

2. PREVENTING "ANOTHER CUBA"

The Dominican intervention. After Kennedy's assurance to Khrushchev that the United States would not invade Cuba, U.S. attention focused on preventing any other Latin American country from following Cuba's course. This was the purpose of President Johnson's decision to send 20,000 United States troops to the Dominican Republic in April 1965.

Following the 1961 assassination of Trujillo, who had held power for thirty-one years, the Dominican Republic had experienced several military coups. Juan Bosch became the elected president on Dec. 20, 1962, but was ousted nine months later. The military leaders who had overthrown him entrusted the administration to a civilian junta headed by Reid Cabral. On April 24, 1965 there was a revolt by supporters of Bosch. Reid Cabral had neither the support of the military chiefs, who now wanted a new military junta, nor that of the rebels who had begun the insurrection, and he resigned on April 25. This left the country without an established government. The capital city was in the hands of the pro-Bosch rebels, but they were under attack by the military chiefs, and the latter asked for United States military intervention.

When President Johnson announced, on April 28, that he had ordered U.S. troops ashore, the justification he gave was that "military authorities" in the Dominican Republic had informed the United States that American lives were in danger and that they were no longer able to guarantee their safety. He said 400 Marines had already landed, to protect the Americans and other foreigners who asked for help, and to "escort them safely back to this country." He said the United States had appealed repeatedly for a cease-fire between the contending forces of the Dominican Republic. The next day Ambassador Stevenson informed the president of the UN Security Council to the same effect, and said the United States had requested the OAS to consider the situation.[23]

In those first statements there was no mention of the purpose to guard against the defection of the Dominican Republic to communism. It is clear, however, that the more basic reason for the presidential decision was apprehension that victory for the pro-Bosch rebels, and the return of Bosch under rebel sponsorship, might result in the establishment of a communist regime on the Cuban model.[24] From the beginning of the revolt, the President had expressed privately his determination not to accept "another Cuba." That purpose was also evident in the decision he made on the same day that the first Marine detachment was sent, to send after it much larger forces so as to make sure that the United States could completely control the situation.[25] Within ten days of the first landing, the U.S. occupying force had increased to 23,000. The intent to prevent the establishment of a communist regime was soon made official. On May 2 President Johnson declared in a nationwide address:

> The American nations cannot, must not, and will not permit the establishment of another Communist government in the Western Hemisphere. This was the unanimous view of all the American nations when, in January 1962, they declared . . . "The principles of Communism are incompatible with the principles of the Inter-American system."[26]

Ambassador Stevenson repeated that declaration to the UN Security Council.

The administration had quickly realized the importance of associating the other members of the Organization of American States with its intervention. At the OAS Meeting of Consultation which convened on April 30th, U.S. ambassador Bunker described the Dominican situation as anarchy, with the fighting in progress endangering U.S. and other foreign nationals and "no authority able to accept responsibility for primary law and order." In that situation, the United States had exercised "its right to protect its own citizens and officials from violence," and was also protecting other foreigners. Despite this, he said that the United States "wholeheartedly subscribed" to the inter-American obligations of nonintervention and self-determination. Calling upon the OAS "to assist the Dominican people to constitute a government which reflects their wishes," he said the United States was prepared to transfer its responsibility to the OAS as soon as possible.[27] A United States draft resolution called for a cease-fire and the establishment of a neutral zone in the center of the city of Santo Domingo. It was adopted by the meeting but with Chile, Mexico, Uruguay, and Venezuela abstaining, to show their concern to maintain the principle of nonintervention. Later, in the UN Security Council, that concern was strongly voiced by the representative of Uruguay:

> My country opposed the request to convene the [OAS] Meeting of Consultation, on the ground that the regional organization was not authorized to take action in respect of the civil conflict taking place in the Dominican Republic . . .
>
> . . . The very heart of that whole system of [OAS] guarantees was to be the principle of non-intervention. . . . The American States agreed that the only situation in which the principle of non-intervention might not be rigidly applied . . . relates to measures which . . . are adopted multi-laterally through the Organ of Consultation convened previously and in due form . . .
>
> . . . This Johnson doctrine — as it is now being called — . . . that while revolutions are *prima facie* the internal affair of countries and for them alone to deal with, they cease to be so and become matters calling for hemispheric action when their object is to establish a communist dictatorship — seems to go beyond the body of norms existing in the inter-American system and constitutes, in its spirit and letter, a notion which my delegation cannot regard as consistent with the principle of self-determination of peoples. . . .[29]

With only Venezuela abstaining, the OAS voted on May 6th to establish an inter-American force, of contingents from such OAS member states as were willing and able to provide them. It would assume responsibility for restoring in the Dominican Republic "normal conditions" and "an atmosphere . . . that will permit the functioning of democratic institutions."[30] In the UN Security Council, while several members were critical of the American intervention, most were content to leave primary responsibility to the regional organization. The Council did adopt a unanimous resolution which called for a strict cease-fire and asked the Secretary-General to send a representative to the Dominican Republic for the purpose of reporting on the situation to the Security Council.

An effective cease-fire between the forces of the two opposing self-constituted "governments" of the Dominican Republic, and between the original rebel faction and the U.S. forces, took effect on May 21. On that day also Brazil agreed to contribute a 1250-man contingent to the inter-American force, and a Brazilian general became its nominal commander. The American commanding general then became deputy commander. Token contingents came from Costa Rica, Nicaragua, and Honduras, but the great bulk of the force remained the United States contingent.

Efforts of the ad hoc committee of the OAS to resolve the crisis reached a successful conclusion on August 31, when the opposing sides agreed to an "Act of Dominican Reconciliation." It provided for a general amnesty and the creation of a provisional government. The provisional government then announced that national elections would be held on June 1, 1966, and it transferred to diplomatic posts abroad the leaders of the opposing factions who had been engaged in the civil war. The OAS sent 28 prominent Latin Americans to observe the elections, and the provisional government took extraordinary precautions to prevent interference with the electoral campaign. All the Dominican armed forces were confined to barracks for the two weeks preceding the election. Juan Bosch returned to the Dominican Republic to participate in the campaign. Ten parties contested the election, and Joaquin Balaguer defeated Bosch by a vote of 769,265 to 525,230. While some irregularities were claimed, Bosch conceded that they did not significantly affect the result, and he announced that his party would function as "a democratic and honest opposition." The OAS then decided to withdraw its peace force over a three month period. The withdrawal was completed in September, and on October 22, 1966 the United Nations mission, which had cooperated in the peace-making efforts of the OAS committee and had sent regular reports to the UN Secretary-General, was also withdrawn.[31]

Six weeks after the landing of American troops, the State Department's Legal Adviser, Leonard Meeker, presented a legal brief in justification of the intervention. There had been, he said, a complete breakdown of order in the Dominican Republic, following the resignation, first of Reid Cabral, and then of the leader of the pro-Bosch party who had succeeded him, the latter having taken refuge in a foreign embassy when the rebel regime was attacked by elements of the armed forces. This left a condition of anarchy, with armed mobs shooting indiscriminately and attacking foreign embassies. Furthermore, "with the withdrawal of a number of moderate political leaders from the rebel movement, it appeared that the Communists were in a fair way to take over." In this situation, Meeker argued, President Johnson's decision to intervene was justified:

> We landed troops . . . in order to preserve the lives of foreign nationals . . . We continued our military presence [after the foreign civilians had been evacuated] for the additional purpose of preserving the capacity of the OAS to function . . .

Arguing that there was an external threat in view of the proximity of Cuba and "the announced drive of the Communists to expand their control in this hemisphere," Meeker claimed that the American intervention had even contributed in a constructive way to the development of international law:

> . . . International law which cannot deal with facts such as these . . . is not the kind of law I believe in. . . . We see from the action of [the United Nations and the OAS] that they have worked together toward common purposes. The United Nations has supported the cease-fire appeals and peacemaking proposals of the OAS. The latter, in its own region, has been operating to give effect to charter purposes and principles — to restore peace and to afford to the Dominican people the chance to decide freely their own future.

He compared what was done in this instance to the action taken by the United States and the OAS in the Cuban Missile Crisis. Both, he said, were examples of the law-creating process.

> [In the Missile Crisis] the United States Government did not resort to any absolutes in theoretical analysis. . . . We recognized that, regardless of any fundamentalist view of international law, the situation then existing required us to take action to remove the threat . . . In the tradition of the common law we did not pursue some particular legal analysis or code, but instead sought a practical and satisfactory solution to a pressing problem.[32]

That national spokesmen would claim legality for the actions their government had taken was only to be expected. There was also no doubt that such actions had an effect on the development of international law. What was important, however, was whether the effect would promote the interests of the United States and other nations or would be harmful. As far as the immediate situation in the Dominican Republic was concerned, the outcome was a relatively happy one, thanks to the rescue of the United States in this instance by the OAS. The administration deserved credit for its successful diplomatic effort to transform United States intervention into OAS action, but if the other Latin-American States had joined Uruguay in refusal to cooperate, the United States would have been in a very difficult position. It is not even clear that intervention was necessary to save the country from communism. If President Johnson had decided not to intervene, or to undertake only a limited mission to evacuate foreign nationals, the rebels would evidently have succeeded in the restoration of Bosch to which they were committed. There is no good evidence that the United States would not have been able to establish good relations with a Bosch government.

Nixon's interference in Chile. The problem of how the United States should respond to social revolution in Latin America continued to confront succeeding U.S. administrations. The most extreme response was President Nixon's campaign to subvert constitutional democracy in Chile after the 1970 electoral victory of Salvador Allende.

Allende, 62 years old when he was elected president, had helped found the Chilean Socialist Party in 1933 and had long been a member of the Chilean Senate. He had been a candidate for president three times previously. In the 1970 election he was the presidential candidate of the Popular Unity coalition, which included the Socialist and Communist parties and smaller groups of Social Democrats, Radicals and dissident Christian Democrats. Their electoral program promised "to bring to an end the rule of the imperialists, the monopolists, and the landed oligarchy and to initiate the construction of socialism in Chile." Basic industries and large landholdings were to be nationalized. With respect to foreign policy, the program denounced "American aggression in Vietnam" and called for solidarity with the Cuban Revolution.[33] The program denounced the OAS as a tool of American imperialism, but Allende later declared his intention to retain Chilean membership.

In the presidential election of Sept. 4, 1970, there were three candidates and Allende received only a plurality of the vote. Millions of dollars funnelled secretly by the CIA to his opponents had failed to prevent his election. According to the Chilean Constitution, a joint session of Congress, to be held on October 24, 1970, was to decide between the first- and second-place candidates. To win the support of the Christian Democrats, Allende accepted a "Statute of Democratic Guarantees," pledging adherence to democracy, the rule of law, and civil liberties, and he stressed the commitment, contained in the Popular Unity program, to maintain a multiparty system. With these assurances, it appeared a foregone conclusion that he would be named president by the Congress. American Ambassador Korry reported:

> Chile voted calmly to have a Marxist-Leninist state, the first nation in the world to make this choice freely and knowingly.... [It] has taken the path to communism ... It will have the most profound effect on Latin America and beyond; we have suffered a grievous defeat ... [34]

As Kissinger has described it, "Nixon was beside himself" at the prospect of an Allende regime.

> For over a decade he had lambasted Democratic administrations for permitting the establishment of Communist power in Cuba. And now what he perceived ... as another Cuba had come into being during his own Administration without his having been given the opportunity to make a decision.[35]

He decided on an all-out effort, first to prevent Allende's election by the Congress, and failing that, to bring about his overthrow.

Two lines of action were initiated, later referred to as Track I and Track II. Track I was a political maneuver, managed by the U.S. ambassador — a plan whereby the supporters of the other two candidates would vote in Congress for Jorge Alessandri, the right-wing candidate, with agreement that Alessandri should resign after he took office. A contributing factor in Allende's victory in the general election had been a provision of the Chilean Constitution that precluded the incumbent President (Eduardo Frei, leader of the Christian Democrats) from immediately succeeding himself. He would be eligible again, however, after another presidency, no matter how brief that one might be. It was thought that he would win a new election, following Alessandri's resignation. This strategem for evading the Constitution failed because Frei would not agree to it.

The other line of action which Nixon pursued, Track II, was a directive to the CIA to use any and all covert means to prevent Allende from becoming President. That directive was given to Richard Helms, the CIA Director, at a meeting on September 15, 1970 between Nixon, Helms, National Security Adviser Kissinger, and Attorney General Mitchell. Helms later testified,

> ... the President came down very hard that he wanted something done, and he didn't much care how.... This was a pretty all-inclusive order.... If I ever carried a marshall's baton in my knapsack out of the Oval Office, it was that day.[36]

Assassination was one of the options considered as a result.[37] Another was promotion of a Chilean military coup d'etat. Helms was assured of unlimited funds for these operations, but the actions taken under this directive were to be kept strictly secret, even from Ambassador Korry and from the Departments of State and Defense. The matter was not put before "the 40 Committee" which had the responsibility of reviewing more "normal" covert action proposals and which included deputy secretaries of State and Defense and the Chairman of the Joint Chiefs of Staff.

One of the actions pursued by the CIA was participation in a plot to kidnap General René Schneider, the commander-in-chief of the Chilean army and an officer who was firmly committed to the Chilean military tradition of strict constitutionalism. Without his removal, intervention by Chilean military elements to disrupt the constitutional process was considered impossible. CIA officials later claimed that they did not desire Schneider's death, but only that he be kidnapped, but they admitted that there was a "foreseeable risk" the plan might result in his death.[38] On October 22, 1970 Schneider was in fact shot by the plotters in the attempt to kidnap him.[39] He died three days later.

The effort to bring about a coup to prevent Allende from taking office failed. The shooting of General Schneider resulted in a declaration of martial law, and Allende's installation as President was ensured by the decision of the leaders of the Christian Democratic Party to throw their support to Allende following his agreement to abide by the "Statute of Democratic Guarantees."

The Nixon campaign against Allende did not stop when he was elected by the Chilean Congress. The study conducted by the U.S. Senate's Select Committee to Study Governmental Operations with Respect to Intelligence Activities revealed that the United States spent $8 million, covertly, beteen 1970 and 1973, on propaganda, support for opposition parties and groups, and the promotion of strikes and antigovernment demonstrations. U.S. voting power in the World Bank and other international lending institutions was used to cut off the flow of credit to the Allende regime. This was also a case where American corporations with heavy investment in Chile were urging the Administration to employ its full influence against Allende. But it was more a case of cooperation than of corporate pressure on the U.S. Government, for the administration was fully as concerned about the threat they saw in an Allende government as the corporate executives were about the threat to their Chilean properties. The companies cooperated to create economic problems for Chile by withholding credit, technical help, and spare parts for the American equipment they had brought to Chile.

Whereas international economic aid to Chile was drastically reduced as a result of the policy of the Nixon administration, U.S. military aid to Chile was substantially increased while Allende was President. It went to sustain the forces which represented the administration's hope of reversing the Allende revolution. U.S. military aid went from $.8 million in 1970 to $12.3 million in 1972, and to $15 million in 1973. One aspect of the military assistance program was U.S. training of Chilean military personnel in Panama.

The investigation by the Senate's Select Committee found "no hard evidence of direct U.S. assistance" to the military coup which overthrew Allende on September 11, 1973. Allende's downfall was the product of domestic as well as external causes, which had brought the country close to civil war, and the military might have intervened against him even if the United States had refrained from any interference.[40] However, the Chilean military leadership knew that the United States had favored a coup in 1970 and had no reason to doubt that it still continued to favor such a move. The CIA received advance reports on the planning of the group which carried out the 1973 coup.[41]

Nixon and Kissinger have done their best to cover their tracks. In the light of testimony of other witnesses, one must discount Nixon's response to Senate interrogatories that he was not aware that between Sept. 15 and Oct. 24, 1970 "the CIA was attempting to promote a military coup in Chile."[42] Helms and Kissinger both recalled that Nixon wanted the CIA to get rid of Allende. Helms understood that he was given *carte blanche* as to what action to take. His assumption that a military solution was authorized was not at all illogical. Kissinger reports that "Nixon was briefed at various times on Track II by Tom Karamessines, head of CIA's covert operations, always pessimistically."[43] Those briefings certainly dealt with the CIA's efforts to promote a coup. Kissinger claims that he called off Track II on October 15, but the CIA's record of the meeting between Kissinger and Karamessines on that date only records a decision to advise the chief Chilean conspirator not to take precipitate action, while assuring him of continued U.S. support. Karamessines testified that "As far as I was concerned, Track II was never really ended.... What we were told to do was to continue our efforts." He also testified, "I am sure that the seeds that were laid in that effort in 1970 had their impact in 1973."[44]

In his memoirs Kissinger bases his justification of the U.S. campaign to bring Chilean military intervention against the duly elected constitutional government of Chile on his assumption (shared by others in the Nixon Administration) that the meaning of Allende's presidency was that Chile was being converted into a totalitarian state on the Soviet model. "By definition," he says, "his would be the last democratic election." Citing reports that Allende had received funding and assistance from Cuba and other Communist sources, he concluded: "In these circumstances it was neither morally nor politically unjustified for the United States to support those internal political forces seeking to maintain a democratic [sic] counterweight to radical dominance."[45]

Kissinger's assumptions were not justified by anything that had occurred. The other political parties in Chile remained strong. Allende had committed himself to maintaining the multiparty system. There was no proof that he was not sincerely committed to democratic procedures, as he said he was.[46] The fact that he stood for nationalization of major industry and large landholdings did not in itself imply the renunciation of constitutional guarantees. The armed forces had a long tradition of defense of the constitution, and Chile itself had enjoyed democratic governance during most of its history since independence. There had been no interruptions of democratic rule since 1933. What gave the United States the right to decide for the Chileans that a military takeover was the only way to preserve their liberties?

Nor were the pessimistic assumptions of Nixon and Kissinger shared by the intelligence analysts in the CIA. The Agency's national intelligence estimates backed away from their first prediction, made before the 1970 election, that an Allende administration would be a Chilean version of an East European communist state. The next estimate, issued in August 1971, noted that Allende had taken care to observe constitutional forms, and the 1972 estimate stated that Chile's traditional political system was demonstrating "remarkable resiliency" and that prospects for the continuation of democracy in Chile appeared good. An estimate issued in September 1973 predicted a continued political standoff preventing Allende from consolidating his political power.⁴⁷

But Nixon and Kissinger were not really concerned about preserving democracy in Chile. Their actions tended to the opposite result. What they feared was Chile's rejection of United States leadership. There was no doubt that Allende meant to free Chile from its dependence on the United States. A Chilean-Cuban partnership would exert a strong influence throughout Latin America and threaten the breakup of the United States' traditional sphere of influence.

Nicaragua's Sandinist revolution. The next Latin American crisis was the one that confronted the Carter administration in Nicaragua, when the nation-wide revolt against the Somoza dictatorship reached its climax in 1978-79. President Carter had made a major commitment to the support of human rights and had pledged to end U.S. support of repressive dictatorships, of which the Somoza regime was a prime example. This prevented military support for Somoza. But the Nicaraguan insurrection was led by Marxist Sandinistas, and Washington feared that they might establish a government that would ally itself with Cuba. Faced with an inescapable dilemma, and perhaps with conflicting advice within the administration, Carter avoided the trap of unilateral intervention but made a futile effort to secure intervention by the Organization of American States. Speaking to a meeting of the OAS foreign ministers on June 21, 1979, Secretary of State Vance spoke of the destruction in Nicaragua, widespread abuses of human rights by the government, and "mounting evidence of involvement by Cuba and others." He asked for an OAS decision to insist on a cease-fire within Nicaragua, the formation of "an interim government of national reconciliation," and an OAS peacekeeping force to help restore order "and to assist the interim government in establishing its authority and beginning the task of reconstruction." This would be accompanied by "a major international relief and reconstruction effort." But as a State Department spokesman later told Congress,

> A majority of OAS members clearly and openly sympathize with the opposition now fighting Somoza . . . The member states were plainly not prepared to approve an OAS peace force at the present time . . . This reflected how deeply the American states were sensitized by the Dominican intervention of 1965, and how deeply they fear physical intervention.⁴⁸

In place of the United States proposal, a resolution was adopted which declared "That the solution of the serious problem is exclusively within the jurisdiction of the people of Nicaragua." It expressed the "view" of the meeting that the Somoza regime should be replaced and a democratic government installed "which should include the principal representative groups which oppose the Somoza regime and which would lead to free elections," and it urged on the member states "scrupulous respect" for the principle of non-intervention. Even this mild compromise resolution, which the United States accepted, drew two negative votes and five abstentions.[49]

Less than a month later Somoza resigned and a Sandinista-backed provisional government assumed power. Putting the best face on the situation, the Carter administration recognized the new government and offered economic assistance. Deputy Secretary of State Warren Christopher told the House Subcommittee on Foreign Appropriations on Sept. 11, 1979:

> The government's orientation, as revealed in its initial policies, has been generally moderate and pluralistic and not Marxist or Cuban.[50]

Mexico, Venezuela, West Germany, France, and other European countries extended economic aid to Sandinist Nicaragua, along with the Carter administration, to prevent exclusive Nicaraguan dependence on the Soviet bloc. Despite the revolution, Nicaragua's close relations with Cuba, and the postponement of elections to 1985, that country still had a substantial middle class, a mixed economy with a strong private sector, vocal opposition parties, and independent labor unions.

The situation was worse in neighboring El Salvador, a country polarized between a few powerful families, supported by the army and in possession of most of the land and wealth, and a great mass of landless poor. With the oligarchy determined to hold on to its privileged position, the people were being terrorized by indiscriminate killing by right-wing assassins and by the National Guard as well as by the actions of leftist guerrillas. President Carter, who had criticized the reign of terror and pressed the ruling junta to institute reforms, reinstituted U.S. military aid in January 1981 to combat a guerrilla offensive.

Legally there was an important difference between what the United States might do concerning these two countries. It might be debated whether the interests of the Salvadoran people would be better served by victory of the established government or by an insurgent victory, but the fact that whatever U.S. intervention might be decided upon in the case of El Salvador would be on invitation from the established government made it easier to intervene there than in Nicaragua. Plausible legal justification could be argued to the UN, the OAS, and the American people. A U.S. attack on the established government of Nicaragua would be much harder to justify.

President Reagan rejected the option of working with Mexico (an important neighbor which was as vitally interested in Central America as was the United States), and with other friends such as the European governments and Social Democratic parties which had a measure of influence with Nicaragua and with the Salvadoran opposition. All of these urged the administration to seek a negotiated solution to the conflict in El Salvador. Reagan and Secretary of State Haig were convinced that such a course would lead to communist control of El Salvador and a domino effect in Central America. Minimizing the native aspects of the Salvadoran insurrection, the Reagan State Department called it "a textbook case of indirect armed aggression by Communist powers through Cuba." Strong public sentiment in the United States against any participation by U.S. forces in the Salvadoran conflict limited the available options, but American military advisers were sent to train El Salvador's army in counter-guerrilla tactics, and the supply of weapons and helicopters was stepped up.

Where the Carter administration had sought to encourage Nicaragua's independence and neutrality despite Sandinist leadership, President Reagan treated Nicaragua as a communist state. He quickly terminated the Carter program of economic aid. The new administration also used its voting power, as Nixon had done against Chile, to prevent loans to Nicaragua by international lending institutions. It was unable to convince Mexico, Venezuela, and the European countries of the wisdom of this course, and their aid programs for Nicaragua continued. France, despite U.S. remonstrances, provided Nicaragua with arms valued at $15.8 million to prevent its dependence on the Soviet bloc. Where the previous administration took seriously the U.S. obligation, under the UN Charter and inter-American treaties, not to intervene in the internal affairs of Nicaragua, the Reagan administration seemed to assume it could evade that obligation by accusing Nicaragua, Cuba, and the Soviet Union of advising and supplying the insurgents in El Salvador. It embarked upon covert operations against the Nicaraguan government along the lines of the previous Eisenhower and Kennedy operations against Guatemala and Cuba. By the spring of 1983 a commando force of anti-Sandinista Nicaraguans, assembled and trained in Honduras by U.S. and Argentine instructors, was fighting a guerrilla war inside Nicaragua.[51] Later in the year the CIA launched raids from the sea against fuel storage tanks in Nicaraguan ports, and early in 1984, employing "Latino" mercenaries based on U.S. ships offshore, it began to plant explosive mines in Nicaragua's harbors. The Soviet Union, one of whose tankers suffered damage from a mine, protested this U.S. action, and there were protests also by Britain and France. In the Security Council the United States voted alone to block with its veto a resolution condemning such action as violation of international law and demanding that it be halted. Except for Britain, which abstained on the vote, all the other Security Council members voted against the United States.

On April 9, 1984 Nicaragua filed suit against the United States in the International Court of Justice. Its complaint asked the court to declare that the United States, by organizing, financing, aiding, and directing military and para-military action against Nicaragua, had violated the UN Charter, the Charter of the OAS, and the Montevideo Convention on Rights and Duties of States, as well as illegally infringing the freedom of the seas and interfering with peaceful commerce. It also asked the court to find that the use of force by the United States against Nicaragua was a violation of general and customary international law, and it asked for a court order requiring the United States to cease and desist from these activities. It also asked the court to find that the United States owed reparations to Nicaragua for the damage caused by U.S. violations of law. One of the lawyers who would argue Nicaragua's case before the court was Abram Chayes, who had been Legal Adviser of the Department of State from 1961 to 1964.

In most instances, as we have noted, a great power having the power of veto in the Security Council can avoid an authoritative international ruling on the legality of its conduct. In this instance, however, that would be exceptionally difficult for the United States. This was because both Nicaragua and the United States had previously filed declarations under the "optional clause" of the court's statute, in which they accepted the jurisdiction of the court as *compulsory*, in relation to other states accepting the same obligation. Nicaragua's acceptance, dating from 1929 and never withdrawn, was unconditional. The United States acceptance, filed in 1946, was hedged with several reservations. They provided that it should not apply to "disputes with regard to matters which are essentially within the domestic jurisdiction of the United States of America as determined by the United States of America," and that it should not apply to "disputes arising under a multilateral treaty, unless (1) all parties to the treaty affected by decision are also parties to the case before the Court, or (2) the United States of America specially agrees to jurisdiction."[52] It was hard to see how the alleged U.S. actions against Nicaragua could be said to be within the domestic jurisdiction of the United States, and while they were said to be violations of treaties, the complaint also argued that they were violative of general and customary international law.

The United States' 1946 acceptance of compulsory jurisdiction had stated that it would remain in effect "for a period of five years and thereafter until the expiration of six months after notice may be given to terminate this declaration." When it realized that the United States was about to be sued by Nicaragua, the State Department hastily filed a notice with the court, just three days before Nicaragua filed its complaint, stating that the United States was adding a new reservation, effective immediately, that "the court's compulsory jurisdiction shall not apply to the United States with respect to disputes with any Central American state or any dispute arising out of, or related to, events in Central America, for a period of two years." It argued that Nicaragua's acceptance of compulsory jurisdiction had not been properly filed, and it might argue that Nicaragua, not having set a term on its acceptance of jurisdiction, could terminate it at any time, and the requirement of reciprocity must mean the United States could do the same. Whether the United States could avoid jurisdiction with such arguments would be the first question to be decided by the world court.

The distinction between covert illegality, and overt use of force which was claimed to be legal under the exception of collective defense against armed attack, had now almost disappeared. When undercover operations against foreign governments were begun, under Eisenhower, their proponents had argued that secret illegality was perpetrated by other governments, especially the Soviet Union, and the United States should compete against them using the same means. The Reagan administration still referred to its operation against Nicaragua as "covert," but they openly acknowledged that the United States was organizing and supporting it. They claimed that it was not intended to overthrow the Nicaraguan government, but only to interfere with Nicaragua's capacity to support rebels in El Salvador. On October 19, 1983 President Reagan answered a question about the propriety of the CIA's sponsorship of attacks on Nicaragua by saying, "I do believe in the right of a country, when it believes that its interests are best served, to practice covert activity."[53] And on April 11, 1984 Deputy Secretary of State Kenneth Dam, in testimony before the House Foreign Affairs Committee, said that if the United States participated in mining Nicaraguan harbors it could be justified as collective self-defense. That claim had little or no support outside of the United States. Nicaragua had mounted no "armed attack" on El Salvador which would justify defensive action under the Charter's Article 51. Nicaragua denied that it was sending any supplies to the Salvadoran rebels, and if in fact they were receiving some supplies from Nicaragua, it was far less than the aid going to the Salvadoran government from the United States. The revelations about the CIA's mining operation, and the protests from other countries, caused a strong reaction in Congress, and both the House and the Senate adopted a resolution opposing the mining. The administration then announced that that particular operation had ended.

On April 27, 1983 the President delivered an address in person before a specially-summoned joint session of Congress, in an effort to win greater support for his Central American policy. In that address he described the threat to U.S. interests in Central America as it appeared to him:

> The national security of all the Americas is at stake in Central America. If we cannot defend ourselves there, we cannot expect to prevail elsewhere. Our credibility would collapse, our alliances would crumble and the safety of our homeland would be put it jeopardy.[54]

That description of the magnitude of the threat seemed irreconcilable with his assurance that U.S. combat troops would not be needed in Central America.

Intervention in Grenada. President Reagan did not ask either the UN or the OAS to consider the Grenadian situation, or give any notice to those organizations, before launching a military operation on October 25, 1983 against the government in power on that island. The administration did claim that the action was legally justified. At the time the operation was begun, it said that seven small Caribbean countries, five of them associated with Grenada in the Organization of Eastern Caribbean States, had requested the United States to act, and that intervention was necessary also to protect the safety of some 1000 U.S. citizens who were in Grenada. A week later a third justification was added—that Sir Paul Scoon, Grenada's Governor-General, "had used a confidential channel to transmit an appeal for action by the OECS and other regional states to restore order on the island" (it was said that earlier mention of his appeal for help would have endangered his safety).[55]

Grenada had been in political turmoil. Its Marxist government, headed by Prime Minister Maurice Bishop, had alienated the United States by aligning Grenada closely with Cuba. Bishop had been a popular leader. The train of events leading to the intervention began when he was ousted and placed under house arrest by a more radical faction which considered him a "bourgeois deviationist." On October 19 a crowd of Bishop's supporters freed him from custody and went with him to army headquarters, apparently demanding his restoration to office. Soldiers then opened fire on the crowd, killing many, and Bishop himself and several of his cabinet ministers were executed.

The justification for forcible intervention in Grenada by the United States which was based on the invitation from five members of the Organization of Eastern Caribbean States was legally dubious. That organization had been founded, less than a year before, with the participation of Grenada's Marxist regime. The Charter of the organization authorized collective security arrangements, but only against external aggression and only by unanimous vote. Grenada, of course, did not vote for intervention, nor did two other OECS member communities—Saint Christopher and Nevis, which became independent on September 19, 1983, and Montserrat, still a British possession. In the larger organization of the Caribbean Community (CARICOM), a proposal to intervene had been opposed by Trinidad, Grenada's largest close neighbor. The government of the United Kingdom, whose Queen remained Grenada's constitutional chief of state, had also been consulted and had advised against military action.

The claim that Americans on the island had been in danger was the same excuse for intervention that President Johnson had used in the Dominican civil conflict. In Grenada, however, there was no conflict before the U.S. invasion, and there was no evidence that the Americans could not have been evacuated without military action. What was intended, it was clear, was a permanent change in the government of Grenada, rather than a mere rescue mission.

Grenada and most of the other Caribbean states were members of the OAS, whose Charter firmly forbids foreign intervention in any state. The principal difference between President Reagan's action in this instance and the earlier action by Johnson was that Reagan did not report the matter to the UN Security Council or call for consideration by the OAS. Consequently, the matter was taken to the UN by others, and the United States, appearing as a defendant, found itself isolated. It had the support only of its partners in the intervention (Jamaica, Antigua, Barbados, Dominica, St. Lucia, and St. Vincent). Trinidad stated its regret that the Caribbean Community (CARICOM) had not been permitted to find a peaceful solution to the situation in Grenada. The French government deplored the armed intervention and declared France's support of the principle that "No state or group of states has the right to intervene militarily on the territory of another state without having been expressly invited by the legitimate authorities of the latter or without having the Security Council formally and explicitly authorize it." A Security Council resolution which called the armed intervention "a flagrant violation of international law" received 11 affirmative votes, including those of France and the Netherlands. It was defeated by the exercise of the U.S. veto. Britain's representative abstained. The matter was then taken to the General Assembly, which adopted a similar resolution by a vote of 108 to 9 and called for "immediate withdrawal of the foreign troops."

The best of the justifications of the U.S. intervention was the request for help issued by Grenada's Governor-General Sir Paul Scoon, but this justification was not put forward until after the UN had completed its consideration of the issue. Deputy Secretary of State Kenneth Dam presented it in a statement to the House Committee on Foreign Affairs on November 2, 1983. The intent and circumstances of Scoon's action remained somewhat obscure. It was not clear whether he had wanted a military assault against the revolutionary regime on Grenada, or action of some other kind. The "channel" through which he made the request was not specified, and there remained some doubt whether Scoon acted on his own or on the urging of outsiders. Scoon's constitutional authority was also open to question, but in the anarchical conditions existing on the island after the execution of Bishop it could be argued that he had certain "residual emergency powers."[56] The outcome of the Security Council debate might have been different if the members had been aware of the Governor-General's appeal for help. It appeared, however, that the Reagan administration was not much concerned about UN opinion. When asked by reporters to comment on the General Assembly vote condemning the intervention as a violation of law, the President said "One hundred nations in the United Nations have not agreed with us on just about everything that's come before them where we are involved, and it didn't affect my breakfast at all."[57]

That the Reagan administration was making its decisions whether or not to use force with very little regard for the UN Charter reflected the fact that many of its officials were drawn from the right wing of the political spectrum. Their animus against the UN was expressed in the acid remarks of Charles Lichenstein, deputy U.S. representative to the UN, on Sept. 19, 1983, when he urged UN members dissatisfied with the United States as the host country "to seriously consider removing themselves and this organization from the soil of the United States . . . The members of the U.S. Mission to the United Nations will be down at dockside waving you a fond farewell . . ." The President later expressed approval of Lichenstein's remarks.[58]

3. COUNTER-REVOLUTIONARY INTERVENTION, AS PRACTICED BY THE SOVIET UNION AND THE UNITED STATES

The United States and the Soviet Union have been about equally responsible for the breakdown of the inhibitions against forcible intervention in the internal affairs of other states which were grounded in the law of the UN Charter, with each unilateral decision to use force serving as an added impetus to similar action by the other superpower. Where the United States has acted to preserve the ideological purity of the Western Hemisphere, the Soviet actions showed similar determination to prevent the defection of states within the "socialist community" which it had established in Eastern Europe after the defeat of Germany. U.S. intervention in Guatemala was followed by

Soviet intervention, on a much larger scale, in Hungary in 1956, and U.S. intervention in the Dominican Republic was followed by the intervention of the USSR and Warsaw Pact allies in August, 1968, to overthrow the Dubcek government in Czechoslovakia. UN Secretary-General U Thant, in the introduction to his annual report for 1968, made the explicit comparison:

> It is, certainly, a frightening commentary on the ominous state of world affairs that one super-State or the other can become exercised to the point of resorting to military action because of a liberalization of a regime in a small country like Czechoslovakia or because of an internal upheaval in another small State such as the Dominican Republic.

The Soviet interventions in Hungary and Czechoslovakia were massive and brutal. In both cases the only attempt at legal justification was a claim that some authorities in each country had asked for Soviet assistance. But in both cases the legal governments denied that there had been any invitation. In Hungary, a popular revolt had resulted in the establishment of a new government which ended the one-party system, abolished the hated secret police, and released political prisoners. It was apparent that Hungary was defecting from the Soviet bloc. To prevent that from happening, the Soviet army launched an attack which overthrew the government headed by Imre Nagy and replaced it with a new Communist regime headed by Janos Kadar. In the Czechoslovak case the Soviet intervention was preventive. There had been no revolt, but only a process of change which was gradual and peaceful. The Communist party remained in control, but it was under new leadership which was responding to pressures for liberalization from the society at large. The Dubcek government expressed its continuing commitment to the Soviet alliance, but it had introduced far-reaching reforms—an end to censorship and travel restrictions, new economic policies looking towards a "Socialist market economy" which would trade with the West as well as the Socialist countries, and a general opening of doors to the outside world. The Russians clearly feared that the process would end with the loss of Czechoslovakia to the Soviet bloc, although that had not yet happened. Soviet forces, with some participation by forces from East Germany, Poland, Hungary, and Bulgaria, crossed the frontier and seized control. While the Czechoslovak Government protested against the intervention and denied that they had asked for assistance, they accepted the futility of resistance. Dubcek and other top government officials were then transported to Moscow for negotiations. Within six days they agreed to a settlement which accepted the Soviet occupation and agreed to changes in the party's policies.[59] This collapse of Czech resistance and the government's acceptance of the occupation required the Czech representative to the U.N. Security Council to ask that the matter be withdrawn from the Council's agenda. The result was reminiscent of the way that the quick collapse of the Arbenz government under U.S. pressure had removed the Guatemalan question from the agenda in 1954. Dubcek and his associates were later deprived of their posts and expelled from the Czechoslovak Communist Party, their retreat having saved them from the harsh fate of the Hungarian leaders of 1956.

The assertion that Czechoslovakia had asked for help having been denied by the Czech government, the Soviet leaders seemed to recognize that their intervention could not plausibly be justified as legal, and they turned to an overtly political justification which became known in the West as the "Brezhnev Doctrine." While it was developed more fully in a *Pravda* article, Brezhnev summed it up in an address to the Polish United Workers' Party in October 1968:

> When external and internal forces hostile to socialism try to turn the development of a given socialist country in the direction of restoration of the capitalist system, when a threat arises to the cause of socialism in that country—a threat to the security of the socialist commonwealth as a whole—this is no longer merely a problem for that country's people, but a common problem, the concern of all socialist countries. It is quite clear that an action such as military assistance to a fraternal country to end a threat to the socialist system is an extraordinary measure, dictated by necessity . . .[60]

He seemed to be saying that "necessity knows no law." The theoretician who wrote the *Pravda* article was somewhat less forthright. He denied that the invasion had contradicted the principle of national self-determination, arguing that "the abstract and non-class approach" to such questions must be rejected, where to interpret self-determination as requiring that the other Socialist countries remain neutral would have led to "the dismemberment of the socialist commonwealth."[61] The Soviet author's approach reminds one of Meeker's rejection of "absolutes in theoretical analysis."

Yugoslavia and Albania had gone their separate ways, but Brezhnev had declared that the USSR and its allies would not permit any further defections from "the Socialist commonwealth." Cuba had defected to communism, but President Johnson had declared that the American nations would not permit the establishment of another Communist government in the Western hemisphere. These positions were almost exactly similar. Yet the wisdom of United States counter-revolutionary intervention in Latin America remained a hotly debated issue, and one can guess that the same issue was debated behind closed doors in Eastern Europe.

CHAPTER VIII

DECISIONS CONCERNING AFRICA

1. THE UN INTERVENTION IN THE CONGO

1960 was the decisive year of African independence. That year sixteen black African countries, including Nigeria, the Belgian Congo, and all of French sub-Saharan Africa, gained freedom from colonial rule and were admitted to the United Nations. A steady succession of others were to follow. For these countries the transition to independence was certain to be a difficult period. Their borders having been arbitrarily determined by their former colonial rulers, most of them contained diverse tribes, with national consciousness confined to a small elite.

Previously, African affairs had been treated as a European matter and the United States was historically uninvolved. The region was remote from both of the superpowers. The United Nations, under its activist Secretary-General, Dag Hammarskjold, was available as a source of advice and assistance to its new members. For all of these reasons Africa was the place where the United States had the best chance to make effective use of the United Nations as a policy instrument and as a substitute for direct political or military involvement.

Of all the newly independent countries, the largest in area and tribal diversity and the most poorly prepared for independence was the Belgian Congo, where planning for independence was not even begun until 1959. Turmoil broke out almost immediately following the independence ceremonies of June 30, 1960. The army revolted against its officers, who were Belgians, and the soldiers attacked European civilians. Belgium, which had kept two military bases in the Congo, then intervened. On July 10 Belgian paratroops landed at Elizabethville, the capital of Katanga province, at the request of the provincial president, Moise Tshombe, and the next day Tshombe proclaimed the secession and independence of Katanga. Belgian troops landed also at Luluabourg, where Europeans had been attacked, and occupied the river port of Matadi.

The American consul in Katanga had joined his British and French colleagues in appealing for Belgian military intervention. But that intervention contravened the treaty between Belgium and the Congo, by the terms of which Belgian troops were to return only if requested by the Congolese government. The secession of Katanga was a particularly severe blow to the new nation. It was the country's richest province, and its mining industry was the country's major asset. Predominant control over that industry was held by Belgian and English financial interests, through two corporations, Union Miniere du Haut-Katanga and Tanganyika Concessions, which also had links with Rhodesian and South African mining concerns. Katanga's secession was made possible by the Belgian intervention, for Belgian troops rounded up and disarmed the Congolese army units in the province and Belgian officers were loaned to Tshombe to create a Katanga "gendarmerie" to support his government.[1]

The Congolese central government sought outside military help. According to Andrew Cordier, then executive assistant to UN Secretary-General Hammarskjold, they "began addressing frantic appeals in many directions for troops to help them deal with the Belgian 'aggression'—to the United States, to the Soviet Union, to Ghana and Guinea in Africa, as well as to the United Nations Secretary-General."[2]

Hammarskjold strongly believed that the United Nations must respond to a situation of this kind. He was convinced that the organization would find its most useful role in limiting conflicts growing out of the liquidation of the colonial system. He had foreseen the probability of difficulties in the Congo, and had sent Ralph Bunche to represent him during the transition to independence. Bunche was to be ready to provide assistance if needed. Hammarskjold feared that unless the Belgian intervention ended promptly, other nations would intervene as well and the situation would escape control. Encouraged by the successful precedent of the UN Emergency Force which had been sent to Egypt in 1956 and which had led to the withdrawal of British and French forces from Suez, he saw an opportunity for the UN to play a similar role in the Congo. He therefore responded to the Congo's call for help by calling a meeting of the Security Council on his own initiative, and the Council endorsed his proposal for the introduction of a UN peacekeeping force, while also requesting the withdrawal of the Belgian troops.

The Eisenhower administration welcomed Hammarskjold's initiative, for it had enough troubles elsewhere and did not want to become unilaterally involved. Eisenhower and his advisers saw the need for non-Belgian military help, to keep the Congolese from turning to the Soviet Union, and it appeared that UN intervention would serve the American purpose of keeping the Russians out. Supporting Hammarskjold's plan, the United States provided airlift for the UN force, which came initially from African nations, with smaller contingents from Sweden and Ireland, and it provided funds in support of the UN's non-military aid.

The Congo problem turned out to be more complex than Hammarskjold had anticipated. The major difficulty was the Katanga secession. It confronted Hammarskjold with a dilemma. His interpretation of the mandate given him by the Security Council was that the UN troops should not use force except in self-defense, and should not be used to enforce any specific political solution in internal conflicts. He preferred to assume that once Belgium withdrew its troops the Katanga problem would resolve itself into a constitutional question of the extent of federalism the Congo's provinces should enjoy. When Tshombe adamantly blocked the entry of UN troops into his province, threatening armed resistance, Hammarskjold flew to Katanga to negotiate. He secured Tshombe's consent to the arrival of UN troops in return for concessions. In a memorandum interpreting the Security Council resolution which authorized the UN force, Hammarskjold wrote:

> . . The United Nations force cannot be used on behalf of the Central Government to subdue or to force the provincial government to a specific line of action. It further follows that United Nations facilities cannot be used, for example, to transport civilian or military representatives, under the authority of the Central Government, to Katanga against the decision of the Katanga provincial government. . . . The United Nations, naturally, on the other hand, has no right to forbid the Central Government to take any action which by its own means, in accordance with the purposes and principles of the Charter, it can carry through in relation to Katanga. . . .

Tshombe interpreted this as sufficient acceptance of his conditions, which were that the UN should not interfere in the internal affairs of Katanga, should not hinder Katanga's control of persons entering Katanga, and should not oppose the organization and training of Katanga's own "forces of order," and that "Katanga would remain free to enter in negotiations or refuse to do so with any government of the former Belgian Congo or of a part thereof."[3]

Hammarskjold's compromise brought a bitter attack on him by Congolese Prime Minister Patrice Lumumba. Lumumba was infuriated by the Secretary-General's failure to include the Congolese government in his consultations and by his concessions to Tshombe. Lumumba concluded that the United Nations would not help to end the secession and that the only way to keep it from becoming final was for the Congo itself to reconquer the province. For that he needed foreign help, and only the Russians were willing to provide it. A Soviet aid mission arrived in Leopoldville, and the Russians sent Lumumba 100 trucks and 16 transport planes with crews. These enabled Lumumba to send troops to South Kasai province (which had also tried to secede), preparatory to a move into Katanga. In South Kasai, however, the government troops seized food and vehicles, and became involved in conflict with local tribesmen and in massacres of civilians. By the end of August, Hammarskjold had concluded that Lumumba was "totally irresponsible," and Lumumba had lost all confidence in Hammarskjold.[4]

American officials also quickly soured on Lumumba. He visited Washington in July, 1960, and met with Secretary of State Christian Herter and Under Secretary C. Douglas Dillon. Lumumba's personality—passionate, impatient, inflexible—made a very bad impression on the American officials, and it is apparent that no real communication took place. As Dillon later testified:

> He would never look you in the eye. He looked up at the sky. And a tremendous flow of words came out. He spoke in French. . . . and his words didn't ever have any relation to the particular things we wanted to discuss. . . . You had a feeling that he was a person that was gripped by this fervor that I can only characterize as messianic . . . he was just not a rational being.[5]

The American decision-makers concluded that there was no possibility of reaching an understanding with Lumumba.

The fervor which possessed Lumumba was nationalist or Pan-Africanist.[6] In a country as underdeveloped as the Congo there were no educated Marxists. Yet Lumumba's impatience, and his distrust of Hammarskjold and other UN officials, had clearly presented the Soviet Union with an opportunity to meddle. This seemed to confirm

U.S. fears of an impending communist takeover. On the same day that the clash between Hammarskjold and Lumumba took place in Leopoldville, the new CIA "station officer" there cabled to Washington:

> Embassy and station believe Congo experiencing classic Communist effort takeover government. . . . Whether or not Lumumba actually Commie or just playing Commie game to assist his solidifying power, anti-West forces rapidly solidifying power Congo and there may be little time left in which take action to avoid another Cuba.[7]

Up to this point the United States was the only major power which was supporting the UN operation. Britain and France had abstained on the resolution which authorized it. They sympathized with Belgium's covert support of the Katanga secession, and the Soviet Union was acting unilaterally in opposition to the UN policy. Now, alarmed by their fear of Soviet influence, Eisenhower and his advisers also decided to intervene directly by covert means. Their purpose was to remove Lumumba from power and so remove the danger that the UN would be asked to leave and Soviet aid would be accepted instead. The U.S. Senate investigation of governmental intelligence activities later showed that the policy included a plan to assassinate Lumumba. There is little doubt that President Eisenhower authorized it, though in this or other cases where the CIA was similarly involved, no such directive was ever put in writing.[8]

The assassination plan was not disclosed to any UN officials, but they too were alarmed by the direct Soviet intervention, and eventually welcomed Lumumba's fall from power.[9]

Congolese president Kasavubu was also alarmed by Prime Minister Lumumba's alliance with the Russians and was urged by the American and Belgian embassies to dismiss Lumumba. Kasavubu told Andrew Cordier, who was then acting as the Secretary-General's representative in the Congo, that he planned to do that. Cordier reports that he warned Kasavubu that such action might provoke a violent reaction. He denied a request from Kasavubu to have the UN force close Parliament and arrest some of Lumumba's followers. Cordier reported these developments to Hammarskjold, who left it up to Cordier to respond to events according to his own judgment.[10]

On September 5, 1960 Kasavubu announced that he was dismissing Lumumba from his position as prime minister, replacing him with Joseph Ileo (a Catholic federalist and president of the Senate).

Lumumba responded with a radio broadcast in which he declared Kasavubu to be no longer chief of state and called on the army and the people to rise in Lumumba's support. He was an effective speaker and better able than Kasavubu to rally popular support.

After announcing Lumumba's dismissal, Kasavubu sent Cordier a letter asking him to close all the Congo's airfields, except to UN aircraft. This was to prevent the Russian transport planes from bringing troops loyal to Lumumba from Stanleyville to Leopoldville, and it may have been suggested to Kasavubu by the Americans. After consulting the UN force commander and other officers of the UN force, as well as the U.S. ambassador, Cordier did order closure of the airfields, and he also directed UN troops to close the Leopoldville radio station to prevent incitement to civil war.[11] A United States aircraft carrier had been stationed off the mouth of the Congo River, and it is reported that the U.S. ambassador was authorized to call on its planes, if necessary, to prevent Soviet troop-carrying planes from landing at Leopoldville.[12]

While Cordier's intercession gave Kasavubu an advantage, Lumumba succeeded in getting declarations of support from both houses of Parliament. The Congolese army then became a critical factor. The soldiers had not been paid or given regular rations for two months, and General Kettani, of the UN's Moroccan contingent, suggested to Cordier that they could be kept quiet if they were paid and fed. Cordier asked the Secretary-General for $1 million for this purpose. The money was provided by the United States, and Cordier reports that, because of the prospect of receiving it, "Lundula, Mobutu, and other ANC commanders joined in opposing an earlier order by Lumumba to attack UN troops guarding the airport."[13]

Lumumba's popular and parliamentary support was so strong that the likelihood of his winning his struggle with Kasavubu was not removed until Mobutu, the army's chief of staff, executed a coup d'etat on September 14. Mobutu declared that he was "neutralizing" all of the contending factions, including Lumumba, Kasavubu, Ileo, and Parliament.[14]

The CIA station had been involved in planning to keep the army from suporting Lumumba, and it conspired with Mobutu in planning his coup d'etat.[15] American money was being dispensed to ensure the soldiers' loyalty to Mobutu. Dayal, of India, who took Cordier's place as the Secretary-General's representative in the Congo on September 8th, reported that

> While the teachers, medical assistants, and other Congolese functionaries remained starving and unpaid... Mobutu's men continued to receive their inflated salaries, becoming by far the most affluent soldiers in Africa. ... ONUC's liaison officers . . . used frequently to report on the constant comings and goings of some Western military attaches who visited Mobutu with bulging briefcases . . .[16]

While supplementing the UN effort with its own secret operations, the Eisenhower administration had thus far supported Hammarskjold's Congo policy. But from September on its policy and that of Hammarskjold were at cross purposes.

Hammarskjold found himself in a dangerously vulnerable position, for not only the Soviet Union, but many of the African states as well, considered that Cordier had engaged in an unwarranted intervention in Congolese politics.[17] Dayal, the new chief of UN operations, recognized that the UN had taken sides and decided "to see how I could, after a decent interval and with plausible reason, rescind the orders which had evoked so much controversy."[18] On September 12 he reopened the radio station and the airports. He also placed Lumumba's residence under a UN guard and resisted urging by the American and European ambassadors to allow Lumumba's arrest. The UN protection made it impossible for the would-be assassins to reach Lumumba before his flight from Leopoldville on November 27th.

Hammarskjold embarked on a conciliation effort. At his request, Dayal prepared a report on the situation to serve as the basis for consideration by the General Assembly. It blamed much of the Congo's instability on the army's intrusion into civilian affairs and suggested the need for a fresh start, which would be based on the Congo's only legitimate political institutions, the office of chief of state and the Parliament. This Dayal report was very unpopular in Washington. Dayal states that "the Western powers, led by the United States, were firmly opposed to a return to constitutional rule following the recall of Parliament, for to them it meant only one thing—the return of Lumumba."[19] With U.S. support, Kasavubu went to New York as head of a Congolese delegation, and the United States lobbied hard to have the General Assembly accept the credentials of his delegation instead of those of a rival Lumumbist delegation. Hammarskjold disapproved of this campaign on Kasavubu's behalf, preferring that the Assembly postpone consideration of the issue until the constitutional crisis had been resolved. He hoped to accomplish that with the aid of a conciliation commission composed of representatives of the African and Asian countries which had contributed troops to the UN force.[20] The United States withheld support from Hammarskjold's plan, and pressed its campaign to seat the Kasavubu delegation to a successful vote on November 24th. Of the members of the UN advisory committee (countries contributing forces for the UN in the Congo), only Senegal supported the Kasavubu credentials.[21]

This victory for Kasavubu undermined the effort to promote reconciliation of the rival factions. It led to Lumumba's flight from UN protection in an effort to join his supporters in Stanleyville. On December 1 he was captured by agents whom Mobutu had sent in pursuit of him. Antoine Gizenga, a Lumumba supporter, then announced the establishment of a new Congolese Government based in Stanleyville. At the end of the year the Lumumbist forces were in control of the country's two eastern provinces, and in January 1961 they invaded North Katanga.

Six months after the UN operation began, the Congo was in a state of civil war and the UN operation was in deep trouble. The Soviet Union charged that the UN had intervened illegally in the Congo's domestic affairs and called for an Asian-African commission to supervise the UN operation. Other critics were an important group of African states which met at Casablanca at the beginning of January and called for measures to disarm Mobutu's troops, release Lumumba and other prisoners, and recall Parliament. They decided to withdraw their contingents from the UN Force if these actions were not quickly taken. This meant loss of the contingents from Morocco, Guinea, the United Arab Republic, and Mali, and was a very serious loss of African support.

It was fortunate for the Secretary-General and ONUC (the UN operation in the Congo) that this crisis coincided with the arrival in Washington of a new administration. Kennedy and his advisers were more disposed than their predecessors to conciliate Asian-African opinion and to work with, rather than against, the Secretary-General.

No less than Eisenhower, Kennedy (as well as Adlai Stevenson, his representative at the UN) was determined to keep Soviet influence out of the Congo. But he had a greater appreciation of the strength of the nationalist sentiments of the new African leaders and he agreed with Stevenson that to keep the cold war out of the Congo it was necessary to ensure the success of the UN operation. The UN and African sections of the State Department, and the mission to the United Nations, were the strongholds of the foreign policy liberals within the Kennedy administration. These included Under Secretary of State Chester Bowles, Stevenson, Harlan Cleveland (assistant secretary for International Organization Affairs), and G. Mennen Williams (assistant secretary for African Affairs). They believed that if the UN could not ensure the unity of the Congo, the Congolese moderates would lose power to more radical leaders who would rely on Soviet support. They thought that American support for effective UN action to preserve the unity of the Congo was crucial for American relations with the large group of developing nations in Africa and Asia. They also feared that failure in the Congo might destroy the United Nations, for it would be faced with loss of confidence of the new nations on top of the campaign being waged by the Soviet government to weaken the office of the Secretary-General.

Just before Kennedy's inauguration on January 20th, the effort of the Eisenhower administration to eliminate Lumumba reached its tragic denoument. Unable to reach Lumumba while he was protected by UN guards, the CIA had helped Mobutu's men to block possible escape routes. When Lumumba did make his escape from Leopoldville, Mobutu's men found and captured him on December 1. He was imprisoned until January. Then, aware that U.S. policy might change after Kennedy's inauguration, his captors decided to deliver their prisoner into the custody of the chief of Kasai province, who was Lumumba's enemy. The CIA station chief almost certainly concurred in that plan. On January 17, while the plane carrying Lumumba and some of his associates was en route to Kasai, it was learned that UN troops were at the airport there, and the prisoners were taken to Katanga instead. There Lumumba and two others were killed on the night of their arrival. The Katanga regime did not announce his death until February 13th, and then said that Lumumba had met his death at the hands of "tribesmen" during an attempt to escape. No one credited that explanation; and a UN commission of inquiry concluded that

Lumumba had been murdered, probably in the actual presence of members of the Katanga government.[22]

Kennedy had set up a task force to consider the Congo problem, and on February 2 he approved their recommendations that the UN should be authorized to use force to bring the opposing Congo factions under control and that the United States should support establishment of a broadly based Congo government, with secession banned. In the midst of outrage at the UN over the killing of Lumumba, the Security Council then passed the first resolution which authorized the UN command to use force, "if necessary, in the last resort," to prevent civil war. It called for the reorganization of the Congolese army to end its interference in politics, and for immediate measures to expel from the Congo all foreign military and political advisers not under UN command, and all mercenaries.[23] The passage of this resolution was made possible by the joint backing of the United States and the Afro-Asian members of the Security Council. The USSR abstained. It had announced that it would support "the lawful government" of acting prime minister Gizenga (the rival Stanleyville regime), and that the USSR would no longer maintain any relations with Secretary-General Hammarskjold. It called for his dismissal and for discontinuance of the UN operation. Adlai Stevenson, making his first speech as the new United States representative to the United Nations, promised American support for the UN operation. He called the UN presence in the Congo "the only way to keep the cold war *out*." He endorsed the principle of the territorial integrity of the whole Congo, including Katanga, and he called for "reconciliation of the political elements in the Congo and a full return to constitutional processes," which meant reconvening Parliament.[24] These were considerable concessions to the Afro-Asian viewpoint. The change in American policy induced India to send a badly needed brigade to join the UN force.

The Kennedy administration was not content with simply supporting Hammarskjold's policy. It was determined to prevent Gizenga, whose government in Stanleyville had been receiving aid from the Soviet Union, from being chosen as the Congo's prime minister. U.S. pressure on Hammarskjold and Nehru compelled them to accept the replacement of Dayal of India, the Secretary-General's Congo representative who was the target of criticism on capitol hill as well as from the Belgian and British governments, for his sympathy for Lumumba. When Parliament was reconvened in the summer of 1961, bribery by U.S. agents and the threat of a new coup by Mobutu induced the Lumumbists to accept the choice of the neutral candidate, Cyrille Adoula, as prime minister, with half of the government ministries going to the Lumumbists.[25]

The problem of Tshombe's "gendarmerie" remained. Originally organized by Belgian officers and composed in large part of native Katangese, it had been reinforced by former French officers from Algeria and by imported white mercenaries. Tshombe balked at attempts by the UN officials to oust his foreign advisers and mercenaries. In September 1961, the UN political and military officers in Katanga, broadly interpreting their own authority under the February resolution and without seeking advance approval from Hammarskjold, launched a military operation to arrest the foreigners and end the secession. Their plans miscarried. Tshombe and his interior minister, Godefroid Munongo, escaped and were given refuge by the anti-UN government of Rhodesia. Tshombe's regime possessed the only fighter plane in the Congo, which harrassed the UN force without opposition. Seeking to secure a cease-fire, Hammarskjold himself undertook a dangerous night flight September 17 to meet with Tshombe in Rhodesia, and was killed when his plane crashed in the jungle.

After the death of Hammarskjold, there was a reassessment of U.S. policy. A recommendation by Stevenson and the State Department's African Bureau, concurred in by the Joint Chiefs of Staff, favored sending U.S. fighter planes to support the UN forces, but such direct intervention was ruled out by the President.[26] State Department Europeanists favored abandonment of the UN peacekeeping operation and acceptance of an independent Katanga. It, at least, would be reliably aligned with Europe and the United States. That course was being urged by a vigorous "Katanga lobby" which was financed and managed by Michael Struelens, the Belgian who ran Katanga's information office in New York. Its supporters included Senator Thomas Dodd of Connecticut, William Buckley, and Richard Nixon. It made much of the argument that Katanga was the best bulwark against communism in the Congo and that, in the words of Barry Goldwater, the United States had been "condoning aggression by international machinery and paving the way for a Communist takeover."[27]

Kennedy turned to George Ball, who soon replaced Chester Bowles as Under Secretary of State, to review and coordinate the administration's Congo policy. Despite some vacillation in the succeeding months in the face of difficulties in getting Congress to provide funds to meet UN Congo expenses, as well as dissent from European allies and Tshombe's continued intransigence, it was Ball's ultimate conclusion, concurred in by the President, that there was no real alternative to backing UN operations to reintegrate Katanga into the Congo. Without that, there seemed no way of avoiding Congolese civil war and Soviet intervention.

Hammarskjold's death produced a strengthening of the UN mandate. A Security Council resolution of November 24, 1961 declared "that all secessionist activities against the Republic of the Congo are contrary to [the Congo's] *Loi Fondamentale* and Security Council decisions." It demanded "that such activities which are now taking place in Katanga shall cease forthwith." It authorized the Secretary-General (now U Thant) "to take vigorous action, including the requisite measure of force, if necessary," to apprehend and deport all foreign advisers and mercenaries.

The United States voted for the resolution and sent U.S. transport planes to airlift UN troop reinforcements to Katanga, and on December 13 Under Secretary Ball announced that the United States would oppose any cease-fire until the UN forces attained their "minimum objectives," to ensure their own protection against further attack as well as their communications and freedom of movement. "There cannot be a repetition of the events of September," he said, "when the United Nations was widely regarded as having suffered a defeat at the hands of the Katanga authorities and the situation further deteriorated."[28] As Tshombe proved unable to control his own forces, renewed fighting between the UN troops and the Katanga gendarmerie took place in December 1961. This time the UN force had military aircraft which it had obtained from Ethiopia, India, and Sweden, and this round of fighting ended with the UN in control of Elizabethville.

With the European governments pleading for a ceasefire, there was then a pause for negotiations between Tshombe and the Congolese government. Though he at first agreed to end the secession, he later backed out of it. In the fall of 1962 the situation took on a new urgency. The Katanga gendarmerie had been joined by additional mercenaries.

There were now several hundred of those and approximately 18,000 Katanga gendarmes. Moreover, the Indian brigade was about to be withdrawn from the UN force because of India's defense needs at home following its frontier conflict with China. If the UN must take military action against Katanga's mercenaries, it would have to be before the Indian withdrawal.

Ball and State Department analysts saw that a choice must be made between the alternatives of "using force to bring about integration or disengaging the United States from the Congo entirely and working to get the UN out as well."[29] Since the second option would offer an oportunity to the Soviets, they concluded that it was the lesser risk to support vigorous action by the UN force. Kennedy agreed. There was then a third brief round of fighting, which ended with UN occupation of the gendarmerie's last stronghold. Tshombe then accepted the end of Katanga's secession. The United States, the UN Secretariat, and the UN representatives of the states with troops in the UN force had worked together in planning the operation. While we have focused on the United States' role, one should not overlook the contribution of the other countries—principally Ethiopia, India, Ireland, and Sweden—whose soldiers fought for the UN in Katanga.

While the Congo would continue to be troubled by tribal disunity, the UN operation appeared to have been a success from the point of view of the United States. Soviet intervention had been prevented and the conflict between Leopoldville and Katanga had been settled in a way that promoted the confidence of the independent African governments in the United States and the UN. It had been accomplished without the commitment of any American troops and at relatively moderate expense.[30] In 1963, however, the UN force was greatly reduced, and it was withdrawn in the first half of 1964 despite the outbreak of a new rebellion in the northeastern part of the country. The principle reason for abandonment of the UN operation was the problem of financing.

2. THE ISSUE OF PEACEKEEPING COSTS

Before 1956, aside from the very few Secretariat staff members sent on peacekeeping missions, no expenses of UN peacekeeping had been paid from the Organization's budget. Where member governments sent their personnel on UN missions, those governments expected to pay their expenses. There was no thought of including in the UN budget the very large costs of the UN military effort in Korea. They were paid for by the governments contributing the forces. But UNEF, the United Nations Emergency Force sent to the Middle East in 1956, was a new type of peace-keeping force, in which the contributors of troops were small nations. It set the pattern for the later Congo operation. In 1956 the General Assembly provisionally approved a "basic rule," proposed by Hammarskjold, "that a nation providing a unit would be responsible for all costs for equipment and salaries, while all other costs should be financed outside the normal [UN] budget."[31] When the question of financing was taken up by the General Assembly in 1957, it was evident that voluntary contributions would not be enough to cover UNEF's costs. The United States and the United Kingdom argued that UNEF expenses were the collective responsibility of the organization. They offered to make substantial voluntary contributions, but only if the remaining expenses were to be assessed on the same scale of assessment as applied to the UN's regular budget. The Soviet Union took the opposite position, that the creation of UNEF by the General Assembly was contrary to the Charter, since the establishment of UN armed forces was the exclusive prerogative of the Security Council. The USSR therefore refused to pay any part of the UNEF expenses and argued that they should be paid entirely by the three states which had attacked Egypt. The formula that the General Assembly adopted was that UNEF's expenses should be assessed on the regular scale, but voluntary contributions over a member's assessed share would be applied to reduce the contributions required from the states with the lowest assessments.

When the matter of financing the Congo operation was taken up, the United States offered to waive reimbursement of its costs for airlifting UN troops and supplies, but argued for the principle that the costs of this operation also should be charged against all members according to the regular scale of assessments. Other means of financing that were proposed included the conclusion of special agreements, in accordance with Article 43 of the Charter, between the Security Council and the countries providing troops, or financing entirely out of voluntary contributions. The former method would require at least acquiescence of all the permanent Security Council members in the terms of the agreements. The United States view had majority support in the General Assembly, but not by any large margin. On December 20, 1960, the General Assembly adopted a resolution which "recognized" that

> the expenses involved in the United Nations operations in the Congo... constitute "expenses of the Organization" within the meaning of Article 17, paragraph 2, of the Charter... and that the assessment thereof against Member States creates binding legal obligations on such States to pay their assessed shares.

Article 17, paragraph 2 states that "the expenses of the Organization shall be borne by the Members as apportioned by the General Assembly." It was obviously to be read with Article 19 in mind, *viz:*

> A Member of the United Nations which is in arrears in the payment of its financial contributions to the Organization shall have no vote in the General Assembly if the amount of its arrears equals or exceeds the amount of the contributions due from it for the preceding two full years.

Despite the adoption of the resolution of December 20th, a number of important states continued to disagree. France, whose sympathies were with Belgium and Katanga, abstained on the original authorization for the UN force and refused to pay any share of the costs. The USSR, which at first voted for the UN intervention since the African states favored it, had turned against it when the Soviet government decided to intervene directly in support of Lumumba, and it was maintaining its position that only the Security Council could decide how to pay for UN armed forces. India, which favored special funding arrangements, also considered that article 17 did not apply. So did Mexico, which suggested that the bulk of the costs should be paid by the permanent members of the Security Council and by states with large investments in the Congo.[32] A factor which had helped win support for the resolution favored by the United States was the provision which reduced assessments for the states least able to pay.

Despite the General Assembly's decision, unpaid assessments for peacekeeping expenses mounted rapidly. By the end of 1961 they had reached $92 million, $59 million on account of the Congo force and $33 million on account of UNEF. The Congo costs were running at the rate of $120 million per year. A bond issue was proposed as a temporary expedient. Most of the loan would have to come from the United States, the one large power which had been a strong supporter of ONUC.

The commitment of the United States to treat the new kind of peacekeeping costs as "expenses of the Organization" of an assessable kind had been taken before the new administration took office in Washington in January 1961. The decisive factor was that the Charter seemed to provide an enforceable sanction. That consideration also lured the Kennedy administration. It faced an uphill battle in Congress over approval of the U.S. purchase of UN bonds. Members of Congress were wont to complain that the United States paid more than a fair share of the UN's costs, and from 1952 on Congress had insisted that the U.S. share of the regular UN budget be kept below one third of the total. It was much easier to rely on the argument that all members, even the Soviet Union, would eventually be compelled to pay their share of peacekeeping costs, and that the United States would get back the money loaned, than it was to base the case for UN financing squarely on the ground that the Congo intervention was serving the interests of the United States, if not those of the Soviet Union or France, by averting the possible need for a much more costly direct American entanglement in African conflicts. In their enthusiasm for the enforcement strategy, American officials underestimated the political risks in the event that France and the Soviet Union should continue their refusal to pay for the operations they considered improper.

To move ahead with the strategy it had chosen, the administration secured General Assembly approval of three resolutions in December 1961. One of them appropriated $80 million for the UN's Congo operations from November 1961 through June 1962 and decided to apportion that amount "as expenses of the Organization" according to the assessment scale for the regular budget, while reducing the assessments for the member states at the bottom of the scale; and it appealed to the permanent members of the Security Council, and to Belgium, to make sizable additional contributions. A second resolution, which said that the General Assembly needed "authoritative legal guidance," requested an advisory opinion of the International Court of Justice on the question whether the expenditures previously authorized by the General Assembly relating to the UNEF and Congo operations constituted "expenses of the Organization within the meaning of Article 17, paragraph 2." The third resolution authorized the Secretary-General to issue United Nations bonds in the amount of $200 million, to make up the deficit temporarily resulting from unpaid assessments. Two per cent interest on the bonds and funding for repayment of the principal over a twenty-five year period were to be included in the regular annual UN budget.[33]

In hearings before Congressional committees on legislation to authorize United States purchase of half of the bonds, administration spokesmen predicted that the court would find the peacekeeping expenses to be "expenses of the Organization;" that the General Assembly would then vote to "accept" the court's opinion; and that afterwards the loss of the Soviet vote would be automatic, requiring no further vote, when their arrears reached the two-year limit. Secretary of State Rusk thought it "very unlikely" that the Russians would choose to withdraw from the Organization. Only Congressman Wayne Hays of Ohio warned that the USSR was not going to accept the World Court's opinion and that in the final count there would not be the votes to deprive Russia of its right to vote. Under Secretary Ball testified that, whatever the holding of the International Court of Justice, "the United States national interest [was] greatly served by the continued availability of the United Nations to continue these operations," and even if the Court's ruling were adverse, "we could still not . . . fail to find financing to continue these operations."[34] But this point was lost sight of in the general enthusiasm for the legal strategy.

The first steps went as planned. Congress authorized purchase of the bonds. On July 20, 1962, the International Court of Justice gave the expected non-binding advisory opinion (though only by a vote of 9 to 5), that peacekeeping expenditures authorized by the General Assembly did constitute obligations of the Organization for which it might make provision under Article 17. On December 19, 1962, by a vote of 76 to 17, the General Assembly voted "to accept" the Court's opinion. It now only remained to apply the sanction contained in Article 19.

It was not until September 1, 1964 that the arrears of the Soviet Union and some other members had reached such an amount that Article 19, if applied, would deprive them of their voting rights. As late as May 15, 1964, speaking before the International Law Association, the State Department's Legal Adviser said that the language of Article 19 was so clear that the loss of the right to vote of a member more than two years behind would automatically apply without the need of any affirmative action of the General Assembly. While conceding that a constitutional battle was impending and that "high politics" was involved, it was also, he said,

> very much a matter of law. . . . It was argued to a court and pronounced upon by judges.
>
> But whether or not the opinion by its own force establishes the law, the General Assembly . . . removed any question about the status of the Court's pronouncement [when it] declared that it "Accepts the opinion of the International Court of Justice . . ."

He rejected "fainthearted counsel [by] those who say we must save the organization by abandoning the charter."[35] Congress also favored a hard line. In August it passed a concurrent resolution, with near unanimity, which expressed its sentiment that the President ought to instruct the United States delegate to "make every effort to assure invocation of the penalty provisions of Article 19."[36]

But the Soviet Union continued to insist that the General Assembly had exceeded its powers, and the prospect of a crisis over Soviet voting rights was causing second thoughts among UN delegations. Twenty delegations requested postponement of the 19th General Assembly from September 1964 to November to give time to find a negotiated solution. With the membership clearly hoping not to have to apply Article 19, Ambassador Stevenson began a long negotiation with the Soviet ambassador in an effort to find a compromise. If the USSR would make some voluntary payment, agreed to be without prejudice to their legal views, the United States would agree to the establishment of a special finance committee, to include the permanent members of the Security Council, with the understanding that the General Assembly would apportion expenses of peacekeeping operations only on recommendation of two thirds of the committee and only after first considering every other method of financing.[37]

In this confrontation it was finally the United States that retreated. Desire of the membership to avoid precipitating a possible Soviet walkout, mounting vulnerability of the United States because of its deepening involvement in Vietnam, and desire to keep open the possibility of accommodation between the United States and the Soviet Union and to balance the Soviet Union against China, were all causing second thoughts. There was also a dawning realization that the United States might not always agree with the majority in the General Assembly and that some day the Assembly might seek to impose financial obligations on the rich states that the United States would be unwilling to accept. Just before the postponed opening of the General Assembly on December 1, the United States accepted an "understanding" that the Assembly would refrain from voting while negotiations continued, and when, on the last day of the session, Albania finally insisted on its right to a vote on its challenge to the ruling of the president that the Assembly had agreed to proceed without voting, Stevenson announced that the United States would not object to the vote and considered that it would not prejudice or affect the question of the applicability of Article 19.[38] This marked the collapse of the American resolve to apply the sanction. Stevenson died in London on July 14, 1965, and on August 16 Ambassador Goldberg, his successor at the UN, told the special committee on peacekeeping operations that the United States would accept "the consensus of opinion in the Assembly . . . against the application [of Article 19]." He also warned that,

> if any Member State could make an exception to the principle of collective financial responsibility with respect to certain United Nations activities, the United States reserved the same option to make exceptions if, in its view, there were strong and compelling reasons to do so.[39]

In this instance, the American decision-makers had been so impressed with the apparent legal sanction that they had underestimated the political risks of insisting on contributions from all members. Great powers could not be compelled to accept advisory opinions of the International Court or decisions of the General Assembly. To insist on applying the sanction might have destroyed the UN. As Britain's Herbert Nicholas wrote, "the Americans did not really want *at any price* the victory of principle on which they averred their hearts were set."[40] The failure of the effort to make dissident members share in the expense obscured the fact that the UN operation had been a political success from the United States' viewpoint, and it reduced the likelihood that Congress would support future UN peacekeeping operations of this kind.

3. AFRICA AFTER THE UN OPERATION

The Congo. After the successful UN military action against the Katanga gendarmerie was completed in January 1963, the UN force was rapidly reduced in strength. Secretary-General U Thant reported that there no longer appeared to be any major threat to the Congo's territorial integrity or political independence. But he warned that "an immediate military disengagement would undo almost everything that has been achieved," and that for some time the central Congolese government would need help in dealing with the "endemic problems of tribal warfare and maintenance of law and order."[41] Prime Minister Adoula asked for a continued presence of UN troops in the Congo, and U Thant felt that they were needed. But he reported in September 1963 that the force could not be reduced below 5000 without loss of the ability to protect itself and its supply lines.

New disorders did erupt at the end of 1963. Lumumbist leaders who had been purged from the Adoula government met in Brazzaville and formed a committee of national liberation to lead a revolutionary struggle, and at the beginning of 1964 they began a major rebellion in the northeast. This crisis came shortly after the death of President Kennedy. Under President Johnson there was less disposition to rely on the UN, and the sensitivity to African opinion which influenced the Kennedy policies also seemed to disappear. President Johnson turned to unilateral measures. To meet the new threat, increased supplies of American military equipment were sent to the Congo government, along with instructors and counter-insurgency experts; and the CIA assembled a small air force of anti-Castro Cubans flying American T-28 fighters. At the end of June 1964, Adoula resigned and Kasavubu recalled Katanga's Moise Tshombe from exile and made him prime minister of the Congo. The United States was reported to be unenthusiastic about the Tshombe appointment, but it did not intervene to prevent it. The rationale behind it was the fact that he commanded the allegiance of some 15,000 former members of the Katanga gendarmerie who were in hiding and a force of ex-gendarmes and white mercenaries who were in training in Portuguese Angola. Faced with the rebellion in the northeast, Kasavubu wanted to prevent at all costs a renewal of Katanga's secession. The Tshombe appointment, however, completely undercut State Department hopes that the Organization of African Unity might sponsor a new peacekeeping force to aid the Congolese Government.[42]

The result was that the Tshombe Government called in Belgian military advisers and recruited white mercenaries from South Africa and Rhodesia, who spearheaded the drive against the rebels in the eastern provinces. Tshombe's interior minister was Godefroid

Munongo, who had held the same post in Katanga during the secession and who was believed to be the murderer of Lumumba. Michael Struelens, who had run the Katanga lobbying effort in New York, now became Tshombe's personal representative to the United States and was accorded a White House reception by President Johnson.[43] The final act in this reversal of American policy was the joint Belgian-American operation to rescue some 2000 foreign residents who were arrested and held as hostages by the rebels following their capture of Stanleyville. The foreigners, including the American consul and vice-consul and a number of American missionaries, were threatened with death if the United States and Belgium did not abandon their support of the central government. George Ball, who again headed State Department planning with respect to the Congo, recommended the joint Belgian-American operation whereby American transport planes dropped Belgian paratroopers to seize control of Stanleyville just ahead of the arrival of a Congolese army column which was led by the white mercenaries. 2000 foreigners were evacuated, but 300 others were executed in retaliation.[44] There were vehement protests and demonstrations against the American-Belgian intervention in a considerable number of African countries.[45]

In 1965 General Mobutu, again backed by the CIA, once more seized power in Leopoldville, dismissing President Kasavubu and proclaiming himself president.[46] In 1966 he abolished the office of prime minister and established a dictatorial regime. He enjoyed generous support from the United States. (In 1971 his country changed its name to Zaire.)

Angola. The next crisis of decolonization that occurred in neighboring Angola in 1975 bore some resemblance to the Congo crisis. The Portuguese rulers of Angola were even later than the Belgians in conceding the inevitability of African independence and they had fought a long war against three Angolan liberation movements before they finally gave up the struggle. The fact that there were rival liberation movements based on different tribal groups invited foreign intervention. The United States, handicapped by its alliance with Portugal in Europe, had not been involved before 1975. But in their previous struggles against the Portuguese, one liberation group, the MPLA, headed by Dr. Agostinho Neto and supported by educated urban Angolans and the Mbundu tribe living around the capital city, Luanda, had been aided by Soviet arms and Cuban advisers. The FNLA, headed by Holden Roberto, an ally and associate of President Mobutu of Zaire, had its support among the Bakongo tribe in northern Angola, and had operated from a base in Zaire. It had received military support from Mobutu and had also some Chinese weapons. In southern Angola the principal liberation movement was UNITA, headed by Dr. Jonas Savimbi. Its support was in the Ovimbundu tribe, and it had received arms and advice from the Chinese. The Portuguese, deciding to give up the effort to hold Angola, agreed in January 1975 to recognize Angola's independence as of November 11, 1975, under a transitional government, with equal participation of the three liberation movements. Portuguese troops were to be withdrawn by February 29, 1976. However, conflict among the three groups made it impossible to effectuate the transitional government. By the summer of 1975, armed conflict was spreading throughout the country, and on August 21 Portugal brought the situation to the attention of the UN Secretary-General and the Security Council. It did not request a meeting of the Security Council, but it announced that it had had to suspend the January agreement temporarily, and it asked vaguely for United Nations support.[47]

In this situation it would have been possible for the United States to press for a United Nations effort to achieve a negotiated solution in Angola, calling for the exclusion of all foreign intervention, suggesting a cease-fire to be monitored by the UN, and seeking assistance from the Organization of African Unity. But this was not done. Possibly it was the popular impression that the UN's peacekeeping in the Congo had been excessively costly that dampened interest in any such initiative. The African Bureau of the Department of State urged that the United States should follow a "diplomatic option" which entailed negotiation with Tanzania, Zambia and Zaire to reduce the flow of arms to Angola and an attempt to promote a UN or OAU meditation effort. But President Ford and Secretary of State Kissinger decided at the end of July 1975 to implement a CIA action plan for aid to Holden Roberto's FNLA, with the arms shipments channeled through Mobutu's government in Zaire, and encouragement to Mobutu to send Zairian troops into Angola to aid Roberto. More or less simultaneously the Soviet Union increased its arms shipments to Neto's MPLA, and in September, Cuban troops came to Neto's support. South Africa, meanwhile, sent weapons and munitions to the FNLA and UNITA and set up a training base for the FNLA in southern Angola. By December 1975, some 10,000 Cuban troops were fighting in Angola on the side of the MPLA against Zairian troops in the north and against a South African strike force which had entered the country from the south.[48] The covert American intervention in this struggle was too large to be kept secret, and too small to be effective. Newspaper reports aroused fears of "another Vietnam," and the *de facto* alliance with South Africa embarrassed the United States in its relations with the other African countries. Under new regulations resulting from the post-Watergate investigations of intelligence activities, Congressional committees had to be advised, and in December and January the Senate and House voted to cut off any further funding of covert military aid to any of the contending factions in Angola.[49]

The American intervention in Angola never grew to significant proportions. South Africa abandoned its intervention in January 1976. The relatively large Soviet and Cuban effort on the side of the MPLA enabled that faction to establish itself in power, though UNITA continued the struggle with much support in the south. The other African countries were united in condemnation of the South African intervention, but divided in their attitude towards Soviet and Cuban support of the MPLA. When a summit conference of the Organization of African Unity was held in Addis Ababa in January 1976, the members split 22-22 on the question of recognition of the MPLA government in Luanda. Half of them supported the alternative of calling for a government of national unity to include all three factions and for withdrawal of all foreign forces. In June of 1975 an OAU summit meeting had been in agreement that all three Angolan independence movements were equally entitled to share in the government to be established after independence. It appeared to be the South African intervention that now caused half the African States to vote to support the MPLA.[50]

Kissinger tried to persuade Congress that intervention was in the United States' interest, not because Angola was important in itself but rather because the United States should balance any Soviet military initiative outside their immediate orbit, in order to force a negotiated rather than an imposed solution, because "demonstration of a lack of resolve could lead the Soviets to a great miscalculation."[51] Congress chose not to play that game in Angola.

Neutrality, combined with UN efforts to mediate among the independence groups and to exclude all foreign intervention in Angola, was an option that the United States might have been able to follow successfully in Angola were it not for paranoia about the Soviet threat. That course might indeed have led to the same result as actually occurred — the coming to power of a regime that had been aided by the Russians and Cubans. But there was no reason to suppose that that meant permanent Russian control. The government of Agostinho Neto declared that it would not need the support of Cuban troops when independence for Namibia should end the threat of South African incursions into Angola, and it was unlikely that the Angolans would be willing to accept any other foreign rule in the place of Portugal's.[52]

Eithiopia and Somalia. In one other African instance adherence to legal principle concerning international use of force helped the United States to avoid being drawn into a local conflict, despite Russian and Cuban involvement. This was the conflict between Ethiopia and Somalia over the region known as the Ogaden. Ethnically Somali, the region had been included within the borders of Ethiopia by agreement between Ethiopia and the British rulers of Somaliland before it gained independence in 1960 as Somalia. The Somalis never accepted that agreement, and in 1977 Somalia's army crossed the border to join in the battle being waged by Somali guerrillas against Ethiopian rule.

Somalia sought U.S. arms and support, and it could be argued that such aid should be provided on anti-communist grounds, for Ethiopia was being actively aided in the struggle against the Somalis by Soviet arms and military advisers, and by Cuban troops participating in the fighting. Somalia was under a government which had proclaimed the country a socialist state following "principles of scientific socialism," and until the Soviet decision to give aid to Ethiopia, Somalia had been a Soviet ally, and its port of Berbera had been a Soviet naval base. But because of Soviet aid to Ethiopia, Somalia expelled its Soviet advisers. If the United States gave Somalia the military aid it wanted, the United States might gain an important air and naval base strategically close to Arabia and the Persian gulf.

But Somalia did not succeed in attracting international support for its claims on territory beyond its inherited border with Ethiopia. Its ambition to unite all Somalis under one government was threatening to its other neighbors, Kenya and Djibouti. The principle of the inviolability of existing international frontiers was of special importance in Africa, since the borders of all of the African states had been drawn up by the former colonial rulers, and there would be no stability on the continent if they were open to question. The Organization of African Unity had therefore adopted a resolution in 1964 which declared "that all Member States pledge themselves to respect the borders existing on their achievement of national independence."[53]

The Carter administration decided that so long as the Somali government was supporting the conflict in Ethiopia the United States would refuse to supply arms to either side and would support efforts of the other African states to end the conflict.[54] With the aid of Russian arms and Cuban troops, Ethiopia succeeded in repelling the Somali invasion (though not in ending the guerrilla resistance of the Ogaden's Somalis). In March 1978 Somalia withdrew its forces from the Ogaden. The Russian-Cuban intervention aroused American fears that the Ethiopian offensive might not stop at the border. Secretary of State Vance had said that there would be a new consideration of American policy in the matter of supplying arms if there were a crossing of the border by the Ethiopians.[55] At the end of February Colonel Mengistu Haile Mariam, head of the Ethiopian government, sent assurance to the United States that Ethiopia did not intend to cross the Somali frontier. Similar assurance had been received from the Soviet Union.[56]

Cuban and Russian combat support for Ethiopia in its effort to repel the Somali invasion had not been seen by the rest of Africa as contravening the rules respecting the use of force. The question of whether it would be legitimate for Cuba and the Soviet Union to aid the Ethiopian government in its long campaign to crush the Eritreans' struggle for national liberation was less clear.

Eritrea's struggle for independence. Eritrea had been an Italian colony. The principle of self-determination within the established colonial boundaries ought to have been applied to it, but the emperor of Ethiopia urged after World War II that the territory should be annexed to Ethiopia, and the United Nations General Assembly, to which the future of the Italian colonies had been referred by the Big Four, decided that Eritrea should constitute "an autonomous unit federated with Ethiopia under the sovereignty of the Ethiopian

Crown." During a transition period under British administering authority, a UN commission would be present and an Eritrean constitution was to be prepared, based on principles of democratic government and including guarantees of human rights.[57] The federation with Ethiopia took effect in September 1952. From that point on, Eritrea was ignored by the UN. The Ethiopian emperor progressively imposed his control, ending by proclaiming unconditional union of Eritrea with Ethiopia on November 14, 1962. The "Eritrean Liberation Front" launched an armed struggle for independence in 1961. In the late 1960's they began to receive external support from some Arab countries, notably Libya and the Sudan, and more recently Saudi Arabia. The military regime in Ethiopia, having repelled the Somali army in the south, turned in 1978 to a redoubled offensive to crush the Eritrean rebels. Ethiopia used Soviet military equipment, but it was notable that no Cuban forces joined the Eritrean campaign.The struggle for Eritrean liberation unites Eritrean Marxists, Christians and Muslims, and to aid Ethiopia in suppressing such a patently genuine national struggle would be embarrassing in terms of international Marxist legitimacy. The United States and most African states, and the United Nations, remained aloof because of the respect accorded to established borders, which left the Eritreans to fight on pretty much alone.

Namibia. On one matter American policy towards Africa remained centered on the UN even after the end of the UN operation in the Congo. This was the dispute over Namibia. There special legal considerations made it inescapable to recognize the central role of the world organization.

South Africa held and administered the former German colony of South West Africa, which was named Namibia by the UN General Assembly in 1968, as a Mandate from the League of Nations. Upon the dissolution of the League, the United Nations was considered to have taken over the League's supervisory responsibilities, but South Africa refused to account for its administration to the UN. After negotiations failed to resolve the issue, the matter was first referred to the International Court of Justice in 1949, when a General Assembly resolution initiated by India, Denmark, Norway, Syria and Thailand and supported by the United States, asked the court for an advisory opinion on the obligations of South Africa. The court held that the obligations South Africa had assumed under the Mandate agreement remained in effect despite the dissolution of the League of Nations, with the League's supervisory functions now to be exercised by the United Nations.[58] The opinion had little immediate effect. South Africa ignored it and proceeded to apply measures discriminating against black Africans in the territory. But the growing Asian-African bloc pressed the issue with increasing insistence. When prolonged negotiations and two more advisory opinions by the court had no effect on South Africa, Krishna Menon of India proposed in the General Assembly's trusteeship committee in December 1956 that a study should be made of other forms of legal action open to the UN "or to former Members of the League of Nations" which might lead to a judgment of the International Court with more legal force than its advisory opinions. He had in mind Article 7 of the Mandate, by which South Africa had agreed that any dispute between the mandatory and another member of the League of Nations relating to the interpretation or application of the provisions of the Mandate should, if it could not be settled by negotiation, be submitted to the International Court. It seemed to open an avenue of compulsory jurisdiction. The Indian resolution, requesting that the UN committee on South West Africa study the possibilities of new kinds of legal action, was adopted by the General Assembly. A working group composed of Brazil, Finland, and the United States analyzed the question and confirmed the apparent firm basis for invocation of the court's jurisdiction by UN members which had been members of the League. On October 25, 1957 the General Assembly voted to draw the attention of member states "to the legal action provided for in article 7 of the Mandate read with Article 37 of the Statute of the International Court of Justice."[59] In 1959, after further fruitless negotiations with South Africa, the General Assembly again called attention to the legal action open to members which had belonged to the League.[60] In June of 1960 the second conference of independent African States, at Addis Ababa, also urged the initiation of contentious proceedings against South Africa, and in November 1960 Ethiopia and Liberia, former League members, did file such actions, asking the court to declare that South Africa was in breach of the Mandate and was obliged to accept United Nations supervision of its administration of the territory.

The Asian and African states had taken the lead in the effort to require South African compliance with the Mandate, and the United States had been content to follow their lead. It now welcomed adjudication of the issue. Ethiopia and Liberia were represented before the court by an American lawyer, Ernest Gross, who had been a U.S. ambassador to the United Nations. In December 1962, in an 8 to 7 decision, the court dismissed preliminary objections and ruled that it had jurisdiction. The United States confidently expected a decision against South Africa. On July 15, 1966, as the long proceedings neared conclusion, it warned South Africa of the obligation of UN members under Article 94 of the Charter to comply with decisions of the court in cases to which they were parties. It stated that the United States, as well as the "overwhelming majority" of UN members, intended to support the decision.[61] The U.S. government was therefore shocked by the court's 7 to 7 ruling of July 18, 1966 which, by virtue of the casting vote of the court's president in the case of a tie, in effect reversed the court's 1962 decision. The new majority determined that Ethiopia and Liberia lacked any legal right or interest in the performance of the general obligations of the Mandate except for those provisions which conferred specific rights on them or their nationals. As the latter were not in issue, the claims were rejected.[62]

In the General Assembly U.S. Ambassador Goldberg called the decision "most disappointing." When South Africa protested the United States note of July 15 as unwarranted interference and asked, in the light of the decision, that the United States should "instruct its representatives at the United Nations to oppose any renewal of the vendetta against South Africa," the United States replied that the court's decision on the narrow issue of the legal right or interest of Ethiopia and Liberia in no way diminished the authority of the court's advisory opinions on South Africa's obligations under the Mandate and the right of the UN to exercise supervision.[63]

The unexpected ruling of the court spurred the General Assembly to action. It voted 114 to 2 (with the United States joining the majority, while Britain and France abstained) to terminate South Africa's Mandate and assume direct UN responsibility for administration of South West Africa.[64] It appointed a UN council for South West Africa, intended to assume control and prepare the transition to independence, and it later renamed the territory Namibia. At that stage, the United States, Britain and France were unwilling to support any enforcement action to compel South Africa to recognize the UN's authority. It was not until January 1970 that the Security Council was finally induced to take action. It then reaffirmed the General

Assembly's decision terminating the Mandate and declared that all acts taken by South Africa concerning Namibia after the termination of the Mandate were illegal and invalid.[65] It secured from the International Court of Justice another advisory opinion that the General Assembly had the right to end the Mandate for breach of its terms by the mandatory and that the decisions of the Security Council to bring an end to South Africa's illegal acts were proper and binding. The court advised that South Africa was under obligation to end its occupation of Namibia.[66]

The United States was content to accept the court's opinion on the legal consequences for states of the South African occupation. Secretary of State Rogers assured the General Assembly that it would do so. On June 6, 1975 a joint veto by the United States, Britain, and France defeated a Security Council resolution which would have determined that South Africa's illegal occupation constituted a threat to international peace and security and would have imposed an embargo on the supply of weapons or military equipment to South Africa. In November 1977, however, following a series of South African attacks against Namibian liberation forces within Angola, and harsh repressive measures in Namibia, the Carter administration joined in a unanimous Security Council vote for such an arms embargo.[67] The five Western members of the Security Council at that time (United States, Britain, France, Canada, and West Germany) also began negotiations with South Africa and SWAPO, the Namibian liberation movement, on a plan for a transition to independence to be assisted by a United Nations peacekeeping force. The negotiations are still continuing, with no final settlement yet in sight.

CHAPTER IX

IRAN AND AFGHANISTAN

In Iran* the United States has allowed itself to become the focus of pent-up national resentment against almost two hundred years of indignities and onslaughts suffered at the hands of the Western powers. It is instructive to review the process by which this came about. The critical change of American policy came in 1953, when the Eisenhower administration decided to attempt the overthrow of Mohammed Mossadegh. From that point on the United States replaced Britain as the foreign power with dominant influence in Iran. As with Indochina, where a year later we assumed a burden of foreign intervention that France had decided to relinquish, the American involvement was undertaken, not so much because Iran was in itself important to the United States,[1] but with the intention of making Iran a barrier against communism. In consequence we became enmeshed in Iranian politics, for which, as foreigners, we were inherently unqualified.

1. IRAN AS A PAWN IN THE TWO WORLD WARS

Pressure of the European powers on Iran began early in the 19th century, with a series of Russian wars. Besides losing its claims to territory in the Caucasus, Iran was forced to grant to Russia in 1828 a regime of capitulations, exempting Russian subjects from the jurisdiction of Iranian courts. Similar concessions were subsequently extracted by the other Western countries. Iran was similar to China in being an ancient nation with a proud and distinctive national culture and these impositions by foreigners were resented in the same way in both cases. Beginning in the 1870s Iran also became a field of European economic exploitation, with an increasing number of exclusive concessions obtained by foreign financiers. A noteworthy example was the tobacco concession obtained by an English company in 1890, which gave that company an exclusive monopoly over the curing and sale of tobacco in Iran. The Iranian government was to

---

* For consistency, I shall use the name of Iran throughout, although until 1935 it was officially known as Persia.

receive £15,000 per year and a share of profits. The use of tobacco was an established Iranian custom, and this foreign intrusion aroused intense national opposition. To compel cancellation of the concession religious leaders forbade the use of tobacco, and the government was forced to concede their demand when the entire nation went "cold turkey" in response to the religious summons. In other respects, foreign control of the nation's economy intensified. Most important was the oil concession granted to British financiers in 1901. Oil was discovered in 1908, and became of great value when the British navy began to convert to oil. The British government then bought a controlling interest in the oil company.

Being a border country, Iran was saved from complete colonial subjugation by the European balance of power. In 1907 England and Russia agreed, without consulting Iran, on spheres of influence in the region. Russia conceded that Afghanistan was to be a British sphere of influence, as was southeastern Iran, bordering India and Afghanistan. Northern Iran, including Teheran, was declared to be a Russian sphere of influence, with a neutral zone of equal economic opportunity in between, including the shore of the Persian Gulf. This agreement, which made possible the Anglo-French-Russian Entente, rested on a real balance of military might between England and Russia. On England's side of the balance were not only her navy but also her powerful Indian army.

In Iran, xenophobia was intensified by foreign occupation throughout both World Wars. Iran proclaimed its neutrality in 1914, but it was made a battleground as soon as Turkey entered the war on Germany's side. British forces landed at Basra to fight the Turks, and occupied the Iranian oilfields. Russian armies occupied Northern Iran, which was also invaded by the Turks, and in March 1915 England and France secretly agreed that, upon victory over the Central Powers, Russia should receive Constantinople and control of the Black Sea Straits. In turn, Russia agreed that the neutral zone of Iran, including the oilfields and the Persian Gulf coast, should be added to the British sphere of influence.[2] In 1917 the Bolsheviks published this and other secret agreements of the allies to show the predatory designs of the imperialists. The Bolsheviks themselves concluded a Treaty of Friendship with the Iranian government on February 26, 1921 in which Russia renounced what it called the "criminal" policy of the Tsarist government "which infringed upon the independence of the countries of Asia and which made the living nations of the East a prey to the cupidity and the tyranny of European robbers." Ending consular jurisdiction, it made Russians in Iran subject to Iranian laws and courts, and it renounced all former economic concessions and debts to Russia, as well as the agreement with Britain concerning spheres of influence. Included, however, was a new proviso (Art. 6) which gave Russia a right to conduct defensive military operations in Iran if any foreign power should conduct armed intervention in Iran or use its territory as a base for an armed attack on Russia.[3] The Bolshevik Revolution thus produced a temporary reduction of foreign pressure on Iran. Britain had prevailed on Iran's government to conclude a new Anglo-Iranian treaty of August 9, 1919, which provided that Britain would supply any civilian and military advisers found to be needed by the Iranian government, and provide military equipment at Iran's expense. A substantial British loan to Iran was to be secured by the revenues of Iranian customs. The British had rejected an Iranian claim to abolish consular jurisdiction. This treaty, which was considered in Iran to make the country a British protectorate, aroused strong nationalist opposition. Its ratification by the Majlis, Iran's parliament, became increasingly doubtful, and after the conclusion of the Russian treaty, the treaty with Britain became a dead letter.[4] In 1927, the new Iranian monarch, Reza Shah, denounced all treaties with other states which related to the regime of capitulations and opened negotiations to replace them with new treaties based on the principle of equality. Iran also attempted to cancel the 1901 oil concession which, since 1909, was held by the Anglo-Iranian Oil Company. The British government protested that this was a violation of the company's contract rights and took the dispute to the Council of the League of Nations. Resulting negotiations produced a revised concession agreement by which the company still retained the lion's share of the oil profits.

Xenophobia in Iran was stimulated by the renewed experience of foreign occupation in World War II. Iran again declared its neutrality, but it was not respected. A plan to occupy Iran was formulated by the British in July, 1941. They had three major concerns — desire to open up a route for sending munitions and supplies to the Soviet government, a need to ensure continued British access to Iranian oil, and concern about the activities of the numerous German advisers in Teheran.[5] On August 13, 1941 the British and Russian governments agreed to intervene jointly unless Iran agreed to expel the Germans. Iran vainly appealed for United States support against the impending invasion. The chief of the State Department's Division of Near Eastern Affairs reported on a conversation with the Iranian Minister,

> The minister then launched into a recital of the tragic history of Iran during the past century or more, when she had been subject to constant threats and menaces of both Russia and Britain, rivals for a position of supremacy in the ancient kingdom. This struggle had led to the practical extinction of Iran as a sovereign power in 1907 and the total disappearance of Iran was only avoided by the defeat of Czarist Russia in 1917 and the new orientation in the foreign policy of the Soviet Union assumed in the Soviet-Persian Treaty of 1921.[6]

Iran's appeals for American intercession were met with the statement that Britain's cause and the United States' were the same and that Iran must appreciate the overriding importance of the struggle against Naziism. British and Russian forces entered Iran on August 25. The British were opposed by the Iranian army, but overcame its resistance in a three-day campaign, with losses of twenty-two killed and forty-two wounded. In his history of the war, Churchill summed it up as "this brief and fruitful exercise of overwhelming force against a weak and ancient state. Britain and Russia were fighting for their lives. *Inter arma silent leges.* We may be glad that in our victory the independence of Persia has been preserved."[7] The Soviet government invoked Article 6 of the Friendship Treaty of 1921 ("the right belonging to the Soviet Union of temporarily sending its troops into Iranian territory in the interests of self-defense") as legal justification of the Russian intervention.[8] The British and the Russians remained in joint occupation of Iran throughout the war, the Russians in the north and the British in the south, and there was also present an American Persian Gulf Command comprising 30,000 troops engaged in the movement of lend-lease supplies. Teheran was turned over to Iranian control after Reza Shah abdicated in favor of his son, Muhammed Reza Pahlevi, and a new government, satisfactory to the occupiers, was installed. On January 29, 1942 it signed a treaty of alliance with Britain and the Soviet Union, giving them full powers to control all routes and means of communication, and agreeing to cooperate with them to maintain internal security and to enable them to obtain supplies and recruit labor to maintain and improve the means of communication. Otherwise, Britain and the Soviet Union undertook to respect the territorial integrity, sovereignty and political independence of Iran, and to withdraw from Iranian territory not later than six months after the end of hostilities. On that date also the alliance would terminate.[9] At their meeting in Teheran, in December 1943, Roosevelt, Churchill and Stalin affirmed their desire for the maintenance of the independence and integrity of Iran. In September 1945 the British and Soviet foreign ministers fixed the date for withdrawal of their forces as not later than March 2, 1946. British and American forces were withdrawn as agreed, but the Russians overstayed the time limit, supported Azerbaijanian separatists, and demanded that Iran agree to a concession for exploitation of oil resources in northern Iran by a joint Soviet-Iranian company. They refused to allow the Iranian government to send troops to Azerbaijan to put down the rebellion against its authority. On January 19, 1946, Iran decided independently to ask the UN Security Council to consider the situation created by Soviet interference, and to recommend terms of settlement. Although the United States had not urged Iran to make this appeal, and the British had favored conceding an autonomous Azerbaijan which would be under Russian influence, balanced by an autonomous Khuzistan (the oil province in the south) where the British could be expected to exercise strong influence,[10] the United States now earned Iran's gratitude by coming to Iran's support.[11] When Soviet troops were not withdrawn on time, the United States protested, reminding the Russians of the treaty commitment to withdraw and stating that it considered the continued presence in Iran of Soviet troops a violation of the tripartite Declaration of Teheran and of the principles of the United Nations.[12] On March 8th it again requested information on Soviet intentions.[13] In a public speech on February 28 Secretary of State Byrnes spoke of the United States' responsibility to enforce the Charter commitment against the use of force, adding

> We will not and we cannot stand aloof if force or threat of force is used contrary to the purposes and principles of the Charter. We have no right to hold our troops in the territories of other sovereign states without their approval and consent freely given.[14]

On the breakdown of bilateral negotiations with Moscow, Iran was encouraged by the United States and Britain to make renewed appeal to the Security Council. The United States announced its intention to insist that the Iranian complaint be placed at the head of the agenda. Just before the scheduled meeting on March 26, the USSR announced that it had started withdrawal of its troops from northern Iran. There were further delays, but the last Russian troops were reported to have left in May. The Iranian government compromised by agreeing to establish a joint Iranian-Soviet company to exploit oil in the northern provinces, subject to approval by the Majlis. In December Iranian government troops were sent into Azerbaijan, and the separatist regime collapsed. By this time the United States had begun a program of military assistance designed to organize and equip the Iranian army "to maintain internal security."[15] The Iranian government attributed its success to American help and the American ambassador in Teheran reported that Iranians generally shared that opinion.[16] With Azerbaijan once more under central government control, the Majlis in 1947 rejected the Soviet-Iranian oil contract. At the same time it called for renegotiation of the Anglo-Iranian concession so as to regain Iran's "national rights."

2. THE STRUGGLE BETWEEN BRITAIN AND IRAN, 1949-1953

Despite Iran's formal status as an ally, the wartime occupation by British, Russian and American forces had created widespread xenophobia. After the rejection of the Russian oil concession, the next target of Iranian nationalism became the control by the British over the valuable southern oil resource. Negotiations were begun between the Iranian minister of finance and the oil company. A supplemental oil agreement was signed in July 1949, but a year later the Oil Commission of the Majlis, headed by Mohammed Mossadegh, a fervent nationalist, recommended its rejection. After the assassination of a prime minister who had favored a negotiated solution, Mossadegh was swept into office as prime minister, and his measure to nationalize the company's oil properties became law on May 1, 1951.

Iran acknowledged an obligation to pay compensation to the company for the nationalized properties. Truman and Acheson attempted mediation. It was their view that the British would be wise to accept nationalization and to seek a compromise on compensation and on a role for the company in marketing the oil, if not in production and refining. As Acheson wrote in his memoirs,

> Our view was that their own folly had brought them to their present fix, which Aramco had avoided by (in Burke's phrase) graciously granting what it no longer had the power to withhold. Having lost their chance to

negotiate the desirable way, they now had to use the Iranian vocabulary; the longer they delayed, the more difficult the Iranians would be. Our interest lay in the threat that this controversy held for everyone's interest in the Near East: it upset relations with the oil-producing states and opened rare opportunities for Communist propaganda; Britain might drive Iran to a Communist *coup d'etat,* or Iran might drive Britain out of the country. Either would be a major disaster. We were deeply concerned.[17]

The British Labour government, however, refused to accept nationalization. Extending diplomatic protection to the company it controlled, it charged breach of contract and embarked on a struggle to reverse the Iranian action. It counted first on economic pressure, hoping that Iranians could not run the refineries or sell the oil without British cooperation. Secondly, it filed suit against Iran in the International Court. Britain also seemed to contemplate military intervention, as it was sending naval forces into the Persian Gulf. Mossadegh's nationalist party warned "that the first shot fired would 'signal the start of World War III.' "[18]

As we have noted previously, Acheson preferred to consider military options from a practical rather than a legal viewpoint, but in this instance he was strongly opposed to forcible aciton. He feared that British intervention in southern Iran would provoke Soviet intervention in Azerbaijan. He later recalled,

On the basis of a National Security Council decision, I warned British Ambassador Franks on May 17 that a substantial difference was developing between our views on the permissible use of force in Iran and those to which some elements in London appeared to be adhering. Only on invitation of the Iranian Government, or Soviet military intervention, or a Communist *coup d'etat* in Teheran, or to evacuate British nationals in danger of attack could we support the use of military force.[19]

Averell Harriman was dispatched to Teheran to try to start negotiations. "To the great credit of the Labour Government," according to Acheson, "it stood against jingo pressures," and rejected the military option.[20]

The economic boycott was not working. Although the Iranian oil industry was almost completely shut down for three years (because none of the major foreign companies were willing to buy Iranian oil for fear of establishing a precedent favoring nationalization), neither side was willing to retreat. At the end of September 1951, Mossadegh decided to expel the British oil technicians who remained in Iran and the British responded by blocking the conversion of Iranian deposits in England, and by sending more warships. They also complained to the United Nations Security Council that Iran had failed to comply with provisional measures ordered by the International Court of Justice to prevent aggravation of the dispute while the court was considering Iran's objection to its jurisdiction. After inconclusive debate in the Security Council, the matter was adjourned, pending a ruling by the court. In July of 1952, the hope of strengthening Britain's position with a favorable judicial determination was disappointed. The court decided that it lacked jurisdiction, because Iran was bound by its acceptance of compulsory jurisdiction only as to treaty disputes, and the concession issued in 1933 was a contract with private investors rather than a treaty.[21]

In October 1951, the Conservative Party was returned to power in England. Anthony Eden was the new foreign minister. He and his associates were determined not to give in to Mossadegh. They counted on his eventual displacement by another government that would be more willing to compromise, and Acheson feared that they were considering a "push" to hasten Mossadegh's downfall.[22]

3. THE AMERICAN INTERVENTION

Acheson's fear was well-founded. In November 1952, the British Foreign Office suggested to the American CIA, through Kermit Roosevelt, a grandson of Theodore Roosevelt and an experienced CIA operative who had worked in Iran, a cooperative venture to secure the ouster of Mossadegh as Iran's prime minister. Representatives of British Intelligence in Iran would work with the CIA, but the British proposed that Roosevelt should be "field commander" for the operation.[23] According to Roosevelt, the CIA decided to defer consideration of the British proposal until after the inauguration of President-Elect Eisenhower, because Allen Dulles, then Deputy Director and slated to become Director of the CIA, did not think Truman and Acheson would approve of the plan.

The new administration did decide upon intervention. Under an assumed name, and avoiding acquaintances in Iran, Roosevelt entered the country, where he was assisted by several other agents of the CIA and British intelligence. An intermediary arranged a secret rendezvous with the shah, and Roosevelt's authority to speak for Eisenhower and Churchill was verified by code words inserted in an Eisenhower speech and in a BBC broadcast. He met with the shah several times on plans for the coup. The shah agreed to sign orders dismissing Mossadegh and appointing army general Zahedi as his new prime minister. In case things went wrong, the shah arranged to be away from Teheran, at a retreat on the Caspian Sea from which he could fly abroad, when the order was delivered.

Also working with Roosevelt were two unidentified Iranian "allies," who proved to be highly effective organizers. Summoning up a team of supporters, they could, as Roosevelt told the shah, "distribute pamphlets, organize mobs, keep track of the opposition— you name it," and they were counted upon to bring crowds into the streets at the proper time to demonstrate in the shah's favor. Iranian army officers considered reliably loyal to the shah were asked to be ready to provide support. At the last moment there was an almost-fatal set-back. The plot was betrayed, by someone unknown, to the pro-Mossadegh chief of staff, General Riahi, who ringed Mossadegh's house with troops. Colonel Nassiri, commander of the shah's palace guard (and later to be the head of SAVAK, the shah's secret police) was therefore unable to arrest Riahi, as had been planned. He was able to deliver the dismissal decree to Mossadegh's house, but he barely escaped arrest by the troops supporting Mossadegh. Roosevelt hastily hid General Zahedi to prevent his arrest. The radio announced that the shah, incited by foreign elements, had tried to dismiss the Prime Minister, but that the plot had failed. Mossadegh was himself assuming full power. Soldiers and demonstrators were in the streets supporting him. Nothing daunted, Roosevelt organized a counter-attack. On August 19th his Iranian allies brought *their* crowds into the streets, and with them, soldiers and police who were on the shah's side. They brandished copies of the shah's portrait and his decrees replacing Mossadegh. They succeeded in gaining control of the Teheran radio station, where they broadcast the shah's instructions that Zahedi was the new prime minister. Mossadegh's house was stormed by the crowd with the aid of soldiers loyal to the shah, and Mossadegh was arrested. An army colonel loyal to the shah, who commanded a force of armored vehicles, responded to a call to bring his force to the capital. It arrived in time to consolidate the victory. The shah, who had fled abroad when the coup appeared to have failed, returned in triumph.

Roosevelt stopped in London on his way home and gave a full report on the operation to British intelligence. He was warmly congratulated by Winston Churchill. The limited British role in the coup was kept a much better secret than the role of the United States. But, as we noted when the Suez episode was discussed, Eden's knowledge of Eisenhower's willingness to topple unfriendly governments by forcible means helps to explain his bewilderment at the lack of American support for Britain's resort to force against Nasser in 1956. Eden considered Nasser to be a menace fully as dangerous as Mossadegh had been.

While American participation in the overthrow of Mossadegh was a vital catalyst, it is important to note that it could not have been accomplished without the support of Iranians loyal to the shah. In his recent book, Roosevelt says that he stressed that point when he reported on his successful operation at the White House before President Eisenhower and his senior advisers:

> We were successful in this venture because our assessment of the situation in Iran *was* correct. We believed—and we were proven right—that if the people and the armed forces were shown that they must choose . . . between their monarch and a revolutionary figure backed by the Soviet Union, they could, and would, make only one choice. With some help from us . . . the populace made a choice. . . . The people and the army came, overwhelmingly, to the support of the Shah. . . .

He says that he also warned against trying to repeat a similar venture under different conditions:

> But Foster Dulles did not want to hear what I was saying. He was . . . leaning back in his chair with a catlike grin on his face. Within weeks I was offered command of a Guatemalan undertaking already in preparation. A quick check suggested that my requirements [clear support of people and army] were not likely to be met. I declined the offer. Later, I resigned from the CIA—before the Bay of Pigs disaster underlined the validity of my warning.[24]

The American intervention of 1953 inaugurated a decisive change in American relations with Iran. Until then the United States role had been neutral and mediatory. The national resentment focused against Great Britain for its interventions in southern Iran and for its control of the nation's oil wealth thus did not extend to the United States. But from the moment of Mossadegh's overthrow, the United States was held responsible for the shah's misdeeds. Mossadegh became a national hero and a symbol of independent Iran. American complicity in the coup was not kept secret. Partisans of the CIA frequently boasted about it. The shah's aid to Israel by supplying its oil imports was an offense to Islamic sensibilities. The oil settlement with the British, concluded by the shah's government following Mossadegh's downfall, brought in the five major American oil companies as part of a new international consortium to market Iranian oil. Over the next twenty-five years Iranian resources were squandered on enormous quantities of American weapons and on the shah's American-trained army. The CIA helped him to set up his intelligence agency, SAVAK,[25] whose cruel and repressive measures outside the law were therefore blamed on the United States. SAVAK became a kind of Frankenstein's monster which operated illegally, even in the United States, against critics of the shah's regime. Its misdeeds were tolerated by the United States because Iran was thought to be indispensable as a base for American intelligence surveillance of the USSR, and as a military guardian of American interests in the Middle East. SAVAK forbade American intelligence to make independent contacts with the shah's opponents, and it became the only source of American intelligence on Iranian politics. The American presence in Iran became extremely visible. It included a large military advisory mission, and Washington's focus on the Soviet threat so blinded it to local political reality that in 1962 it demanded full diplomatic immunity for all of the American military advisors. Roy Parviz Mottahedeh, professor of Islamic history, has compared this highly unpopular demand, which the Majlis finally approved in 1964 as the price of American economic aid, to the regimes of capitulations from which Iran, like China and Turkey, had only freed itself after a great struggle.[26] Mottahedeh notes that the Ayatollah Khomeini was exiled in 1964 because he had led a campaign of opposition to this demand for diplomatic immunity for the American military advisers, which he proclaimed to be an insult to Iran and to Islamic law.

In retrospect, it seems clear that it was not wise policy for the United States to intervene so blatantly in Iran or to identify the shah's regime so closely with the United States. We are now reaping the fruits of the earlier interventionist policy, and would now happily settle for an independent and neutral Iran if we only could. But, hypnotized by a Soviet menace which our imagination had magnified out of proportion, Americans had no appreciation of the depth of Iranian opposition to "America's shah." The revolution of 1978-79 was in part a revolt against American influence.

4. THE IRANIAN REVOLUTION

Beginning at the end of 1977, the country was swept by rioting of ever-increasing intensity. Despite the use of troops, which fired on the crowds, the shah's regime was unable to restore order. On January 16, 1979, the shah left the country, entrusting leadership to a provisional government headed by Shahpur Bakhtiar. Bakhtiar, however, lacked the support of the Ayatollah Khomeini, who had inspired and led the revolution in absentia. Khomeini returned to Iran in triumph on February 1. Soon afterwards, the commanders of the army, many of their soldiers having defected to the side of the revolution, withdrew their troops from attempts to control demonstrators. On February 11, Bakhtiar resigned and was replaced by a new provisional government approved by Khomeini, who was now in full control.

The Carter administration had inherited the very close relationship of the United States with the shah and his generals. As the crisis deepened, the shah was himself uncertain of the best course to follow, and seemed to want the United States to make a decision for him between an attempt to undercut the opposition by transferring authority to a new civilian government, which would include democratic opposition leaders, and the "iron fist" alternative of giving power to the military leaders and calling on the army to crush the opposition by stern repressive measures. Secretary of State Vance favored the first alternative, while National Security Adviser Brzezinski was urging the second. The President himself was unwilling to make a decision for the shah, or, after the shah's departure, to sponsor a military coup.[27] Brzezinski has described these divided opinions:

> To the others, it was not for America to decide what transpired within Iran. . . . They felt that the United States . . . should not assume the responsibility for plunging another country into a bloody and cruel confrontation. I was not unsympathetic to this argument, for it was a compelling one, and hence my clear preference was for the Shah to make the decision that I favored. . . . [But] the Shah chose not to or, perhaps more correctly, was simply too weak a person to make the decision himself . . . Thus I gradually came to believe that we had no choice but, for overriding strategic and geopolitical factors, to make the decision for him.

> The President . . . felt otherwise and would not cross the elusive line between strong support . . . and the actual decision to embark on a bloody and admittedly uncertain course of action. Carter felt that we gave the Shah all the backing and encouragement that he needed, but that it was historically and morally wrong for the United States to go any further.[28]

According to Secretary of State Vance, the result of the internal policy divisions within the administration was that the United States "dissipated" its potential influence. The President tried to follow the middle course. General Robert E. Huyser, who had served in Iran as adviser to the Iranian army, was sent to Teheran on January 3, 1979 to open a direct line of communication to the military leaders. He was to assure them of continuing U.S. support, to ask them to remain in the country after the shah's departure, and to help them formulate a "contingency plan" for a military coup in case of failure of the new government of Shahpur Bakhtiar. Thus the coup option was not completely ruled out. Nevertheless, through Huyser, the generals were urged to support the Bakhtiar government. Ambassador Sullivan thought that to be a mistake. He considered the Iranian armed forces to be the instrument essential to preserve an independent Iran, and thought American policy should therefore aim "to preclude the armed forces from being chewed up in the revolution." He favored sending an emmisary to Khomeini in Paris to promote an understanding whereby some senior officers would leave Iran, installing new commanders acceptable to the revolutionary leaders. He was convinced that Bakhtiar had no popular support.[29] Vance supported Sullivan's proposal and indirect contact was made with Khomeini, but the special U.S. emmisary was not sent. When the military leaders did attempt to use their troops in support of the Bakhtiar government in fighting against the revolutionaries, the result was mutiny and the disintegration of the army which Sullivan had foreseen, with many weapons falling into the hands of the revolutionary factions. The U.S. Military Assistance Advisory Group was with difficulty extricated from the fighting.

Throughout these events, the Carter administration had maintained in public a non-interventionary posture. The President and Secretary of State replied to all questions that the future of Iran must be decided by the Iranian people and that, while the administration hoped that the shah would be able to restore order, and later that the Bakhtiar government would succeed in reconciling the internal conflicts of

Iran, the set policy of the United States was not to interfere in Iran's internal affairs.

It was some nine months later, on Nov. 4, 1979, that U.S. relations with revolutionary Iran entered a new crisis. Vance remarks, in retrospect, that "every faction seeking to dominate the revolution harbored paranoid fears of residual 'pro-shah' forces in the country and suspected that the United States would try, as it had in 1953, to restore the shah to his throne."[30] This may partially account for the attack on the American embassy by militant students after the shah was admitted to the United States, and their holding the embassy's staff as hostages against their demand for extradition of the shah. Apparent support of the students, for whatever reasons, by the Ayatollah Khomeini and the revolutionary government aggravated the injury and caused a surge of national indignation in the United States. By siding with the occupiers of the embassy, the Iranian authorities were challenging the most universally accepted rule of international law— the immunity of diplomats and the inviolability of embassy premises.

In these circumstances a military response, proportional to the offense, could reasonably be defended as an exercise of the right of self-defense, and this was among the options considered. Naval forces in the Indian Ocean were augmented. It was soon realized, however, that the military options were very limited. The embassy was in the heart of Teheran, far from the city's airport, and some 800 miles from the closest possible approach of American aircraft carriers. Any military operation other than a hit-and-run raid would require larger ground forces than the United States could possibly assemble in the Persian Gulf, to say nothing of the probability that it would cause a counter-intervention by the Russians in northern Iran, for which they had shown a proclivity in the past.

While planning went forward for a possible rescue attempt if it should appear that the hostages were about to be harmed, the administration turned its attention to diplomatic, legal, and economic measures. To respond to the immediate pressure for some response, the President directed strict enforcement of immigration laws against Iranian students in the United States (some of whom had become involved in disorders in American cities), and he ordered the discontinuance of imports of Iranian oil. When Iran, demanding the return of the shah and his property to Iran, attempted to apply financial pressure by declaring its intention to withdraw its funds from American banks, President Carter responded on November 14 with an order blocking all Iranian government deposits in American banks and their branches in foreign countries. Since Iran had clearly violated American legal rights, it was also a natural response to pursue legal channels of redress. This satisfied in some part the international expectation that the United States must react, and it provided a welcome excuse, both domestically and internationally, for deferring consideration of the unattractive military option. On November 29 the United States applied to the International Court of Justice for a judgment that the Iranian government had violated its legal obligations and should immediately procure the release of the Americans being detained and pay reparation for the injury. It seemed assured that the court would act, because of the unusual circumstance that its jurisdiction was compulsory in this dispute. Iran and the United States were both at this time parties to the Vienna Conventions on Diplomatic and Consular Relations, of 1961 and 1963 (which Iran had plainly violated), and parties also to the Optional Protocol attached to each convention which extended the compulsory jurisdiction of the International Court to any disputes arising out of the interpretation or application of the conventions. On December 15th, at the United States' request, the court ordered provisional relief, directing Iran to restore the embassy to the United States and to free the hostages.[31]

While Iran did not obey the court's order, its failure to do so added another count to the grievance of the United States, which it pursued also in the forum of the UN Security Council. On November 25, 1979 Secretary-General Waldheim placed the dispute on the Security Council's agenda, exercising his power under Article 99 of the Charter to bring to the Council's attention any matter which in his opinion threatened the maintenance of international peace and security. Iran had previously asked for a meeting on November 13, complaining that the United States was threatening war, but the United States had then opposed a hearing for Iran until the hostages were freed. Now, however, it welcomed the Secretary-General's initiative as a way of moving beyond an apparent impasse. Iran declined an invitation to be represented, but the Council, by a unanimous resolution of December 4, 1979, called on Iran to release the Americans. It also urged both Iran and the United States "to exercise the utmost restraint" and asked the Secretary-General to lend his good offices to implement the resolution.

After the December 15 judgment of the International Court, the United States again took the matter to the Security Council, asking it to condemn Iran for failure to comply with the previous Security Council resolution and the order of the International Court. It also asked that the Council decide to apply sanctions at a future meeting if the hostages had not been released by then. A watered-down resolution "deplored" the continued detention of the hostages and decided that the Council should meet on January 2 to adopt further measures. In the meantime the Secretary-General was asked to intensify his mediation effort.[32] The next meeting, deferred until January 13th, saw a Soviet veto of an American draft resolution calling for the imposition of economic sanctions against Iran. The vote for the resolution was 13 to 2 (USSR and East Germany).

The United States had achieved almost unanimous legal and verbal support from the International Court, the United Nations, and governments around the world, but this had not moved Iran to release the hostages. Economic pressure in the form of the cut-off of oil imports and the blocking of Iranian assets in American banks had also produced no result.

Conciliation was tried as well. Iran had asked for four concessions by the United States:

(a) Return of the shah to Iran for trial;
(b) Return of the shah's wealth in the United States;
(c) An admission by the United States that it had committed "crimes" in Iran;
(d) A promise by the United States "never again to interfere in Iran's affairs."

As to the demand for the return of the shah, he had moved from the United States to Panama in December. After that Iran was encouraged to seek his extradition from Panama through legal channels. As to the other demands, the U.S. position was made clear in a statement approved by the President on January 12, and sent to the Iranians through Secretary-General Waldheim:

> 1. The safe and immediate departure from Iran of all U.S. employees of the Embassy in Tehran and other Americans held hostage is essential to a resolution of other issues.
>
> 2. The United States understands and sympathizes with the grievances felt by many Iranian citizens concerning the practices of the former regime.... The United States is prepared to cooperate in seeking through the auspices

of the UN to establish . . . a forum or commission to hear Iran's grievances and to produce a report on them. The U.S. Government will cooperate with such a group in accordance with its laws, international law, and the Charter of the UN.

3. The U.S. Government will facilitate any legal action brought by the Government of Iran in courts of the United States to account for assets within the custody or control of the former Shah that may be judged to belong to the national treasury of Iran by advising the courts, and other interested parties, that the U.S. Government recognizes the right of the Government of Iran to bring such claims before the courts and to request the courts' assistance in obtaining information about such assets from financial institutions and other parties.

* * * *

6. The U.S. Administration is prepared to make a statement at an appropriate moment that it understands the grievances felt by the people of Iran, and that it respects the integrity of Iran, and the right of the people of Iran to choose their own form of government. The U.S. Government recognizes the Government of the Islamic Republic of Iran as the legal government of Iran. The United States reaffirms that the people of Iran have the right to determine their own form of government.[33]

But conciliation was also ineffective. A UN commission went to Iran in February to conduct the inquiry into Iran's grievances, but it had to suspend its work on March 10 because the Iranian government failed to carry out a prior understanding that the commission would be allowed to meet with the hostages and that there should be progress towards their release. Political power in Iran seemed to be so utterly fragmented, between the embassy militants, the Ayatollah Khomeini, and the Revolutionary Council (which itself comprised discordant religious and political factions), that Iran's president and foreign minister were unable to decide on anything except inaction.

As the crisis continued without any real progress towards release of the hostages, the administration sought new ways of applying pressure. On April 7th President Carter announced that the United States would break diplomatic relations and embargo United States exports to Iran, and would initiate legislation allowing the hostages' families to file claims against the blocked Iranian assets. Europe and Japan were pressed to join in an economic blockade of Iran, and the United States also threatened more explicitly to impose a naval blockade if the hostages were not freed soon. On April 25th there was the announcement of an attempt to free the hostages by a surprise airborne rescue mission, which suffered an accident within Iran and was therefore aborted before any fighting took place. The hostages were then dispersed among a number of places of custody to make rescue more difficult than ever.

After the rescue failure, there was a return to the effort to negotiate a solution. The strongest card possessed by the United States, and the key to a settlement, proved to be, not the threat of military action, but the blocked Iranian assets within American control. $5 billion of the Iranian assets were deposits in foreign branches of the major American banks. Those banks had also made extensive loans to Iran and were involved in litigation with Iran in the United States and several other countries, in which the banks had attached the Iranian deposits as security for payment of the debts. Soon after the aborted rescue attempt, on May 2, 1980, lawyers for Citibank were approached by a lawyer for Iran asking negotiations concerning the frozen deposits and the bank claims. On May 13 the United States government gave its approval to the negotiation with Iran by the bank's lawyers. It was specified that they did not represent the United States, but only Citibank, but the Iranians understood that the United States government would have to approve the settlement and that it would not approve unless the hostages were released. Negotiations began on a proposal offered by the bank for using the frozen European deposits to pay off all bank debt claims and for another part of the frozen assets to go to a settlement fund for other nonliquidated claims. These would be processed through an adjudication procedure. Negotiations on this basis started in June 1980. The basic features of Citibank's original proposal were quite close to the settlement which was ultimately agreed to. At a later stage the other banks were brought into the negotiations.[34]

Iran delayed agreement with the United States through the November election and the last days of the Carter administration, in an obvious effort to extract the maximum concessions, and then agreed to terms on the day before the Carter presidency expired.[35]

Part of the settlement was the agreement reached between Iran and the banks, whereby the banks' claims against Iran, up to $5.285 billion (subject to arbitration of disputed amounts) were to be paid in full, with interest (these funds coming from the Iranian deposits in the banks' foreign branches). Other Iranian assets were returned to Iran, via the Algerian Central Bank, except for $1 billion retained in that bank as security for the payment of other claims. Claims of American citizens and corporations against Iran (if not settled by agreement between the parties concerned, as had been the bank claims) were referred to an international arbitral tribunal empowered to make final and binding settlements. It was directed to decide all cases on the basis of law, "applying such choice of law rules and principles of commercial and international law as the Tribunal determines to be applicable." With this agreement for settlement of claims, the United States agreed to preclude the prosecution in American courts of claims growing out of the detention of the American hostages or other injury to United States nationals or their property "as a result of popular movements in the course of the Islamic revolution in Iran." The United States also agreed to end all trade sanctions which were directed against Iran in the period after the embassy seizure. The released Iranian funds were held in escrow by the Algerian bank until all 52 American hostages had safely left Iran.

Another part of the agreement specified that the United States would withdraw all claims pending against Iran before the International Court of Justice. It agreed also to freeze all identifiable property and assets in the United States controlled by the estate of the former shah or close relatives of the shah who had been named as defendants in U.S. litigation initiated by Iran to recover such property. The freeze would remain in effect until the termination of the litigation. The United States undertook to aid in the identification of such assets by ordering all persons within U.S. jurisdiction to report all information known to them with respect to such assets.

The agreement also contained the following pledge of nonintervention:

> The United States pledges that it is and from now on will be the policy of the United States not to intervene, directly or indirectly, politically or militarily, in Iran's internal affairs.

In a real sense this ending to the hostage crisis was a victory of legal procedures. It was true that the United States withdrew from further proceedings before the International Court of Justice, abandoning its claim for monetary reparation. It "settled out of court." But the important principles of law had been affirmed by the world court in its judgment of May 24, 1980. The United States, in pledging not to intervene in Iran's internal affairs was only acknowledging a legal obligation which it had previously conceded. And the parties agreed to accept judicial settlement of respective claims — the claims of

American nationals against Iran which were referred to compulsory international arbitration, and the claims of Iran to the shah's assets which were left to be determined by American courts. It was only to be regretted that the parties had not been able to agree much earlier to leave these questions of legal right to judicial determination.

5. SOVIET INTERVENTION IN AFGHANISTAN

At the end of December 1979, the Soviet Union, supporting a bloody *coup d'etat* against the government then in power in Afghanistan, moved its troops into that country to combat a growing Muslim rebellion there. The Soviet military intervention came on the heels of the violent anti-American explosion in Iran, and the American reaction to it must be appreciated in relationship to the Iranian crisis.

There was general international condemnation of the Soviet armed intervention. Fifty-two countries appealed jointly to the Security Council. A resolution sponsored by six third-world countries, which called for immediate withdrawal of foreign troops from Afghanistan was blocked by the expected Soviet veto, whereupon the Security Council majority called for consideration of the matter by an emergency special session of the General Assembly. In the General Assembly a resolution which said the intervention was a contravention of the fundamental principles of sovereignty and national independence, and which called for withdrawal of "foreign troops," was adopted on January 14, 1980 by 104 votes to 18, with 18 abstentions. A meeting of foreign ministers of 35 Islamic countries also agreed on a resolution denouncing the Soviet use of force against Afghanistan. It was also soon apparent that the Soviet invaders would face long-term resistance from the Afghans.

The reaction of the Carter administration went far beyond that of other governments. The coincidence of the Soviet move into Afghanistan with other events of the preceding year increased the sense of alarm. The collapse of the shah's government in Iran, which had seemed to provide a strong shield in the region, the presence of Russian and Cuban military personnel in Ethiopia and South Yemen, the attack on the embassy in Teheran and detention of its staff, and the seizure of the Great Mosque of Mecca by Muslim dissidents who held out for two weeks against a Saudi military seige, together with this new Soviet move, caused the administration to think increasingly about military options to insure American access to the oil of the Persian Gulf. In one passage of his State of the Union Message (January 21, 1980) the President said:

> In recent years, as our own fuel imports have soared, the Persian Gulf has become vital to the United States [and to] our friends and allies.... The denial of these oil supplies—to us or to others—would threaten our security and provoke an economic crisis greater than that of the Great Depression 50 years ago, with a fundamental change in the way we live.

And in his Address before Congress he issued the warning that was soon labeled "the Carter Doctrine:"

> An attempt by any outside force to gain control of the Persian Gulf region will be regarded as an assault on the vital interests of the United States of America, and such an assault will be repelled by any means necessary, including military force.[36]

Within the administration, National Security Adviser Brzezinski had particularly sounded the alarm, warning of a possible Soviet push to the Indian Ocean, and advised Carter that he must show toughness and "be like President Truman." It was he who proposed the wording of the President's warning, modeling it on the Truman Doctrine. He advised the formation of a new regional security framework to include the United States, Egypt, Saudi Arabia, Pakistan, and Turkey, and also a move towards a new U.S.-Chinese defense relationship.[37]

The Soviet move into Afghanistan generated new thought about possible American counter-intervention in case of a threatened unfriendly change of government in one of the neighboring countries. The United States now opened negotiations with Kenya, Somalia, and Oman for access to base facilities in those countries, and there was stepped-up planning to create a "rapid deployment force" that would enable the United States to send a 100,000 man army on short notice to any trouble spot in the region. New thought was also being given to the means available to the United States to meet a possible direct Soviet military challenge in the Gulf area. The only possible countermeasure seemed to be the use of nuclear weapons. That this was the trend of thinking was indicated by Defense Secretary Harold Brown, who said in a talk to the Council on Foreign Relations that the United States held open the option of using nuclear weapons to defend Western access to the oil of the Persian Gulf.[38]

In his State of the Union Address the President also declared that "the Soviet Union must pay a concrete price for their aggression" and that "while this invasion continues we cannot continue business as usual." He therefore announced a far-reaching series of punitive measures:

1. An embargo on the shipment to the USSR of high technology or strategic equipment;

2. Denial of future permits for Soviet fishing operations in the 200-mile U.S. fishery zone;

3. Cutting off American grain deliveries to the Soviet Union;

4. A decision to boycott the Moscow Olympic Games;

5. Interruption of the U.S.-Soviet cultural exchange program;

6. A request that the U.S. Senate defer consideration of the SALT II arms limitation treaty;

7. A request that Congress reaffirm the 1959 executive agreement which declared the independence and integrity of Pakistan to be vital to the national interest of the United States, and that it renew military aid to Pakistan (which had been cut off earlier because of Pakistan's apparent program to develop a nuclear weapon).

The major question about President Carter's response to the Russian intervention in Afghanistan is whether it was an overreaction. None of the decisions he took were likely to help the Afghan people. It was certainly appropriate to join in the worldwide condemnation of the Soviet intervention. President Carter referred to Afghanistan as a non-aligned country, and the Soviet action was thought to be particularly significant as "the first example since World War II of Soviet military occupation of a non-Communist-bloc country."[39] Yet Soviet weapons, advisers, and some troops had been in Afghanistan since 1978, aiding the Marxist government which took power in April of that year, in its struggle against a growing Muslim revolt. The overriding reality was that there was no international balance of military power in that region, and that the situation of Afghanistan was therefore very much like that of Eastern Europe. It was quite different from the situation of nations far enough from the Soviet border to be able to choose with complete independence between Soviet or Western assistance. In the colonial era there had indeed been a balance of power in the region between the British and Russian empires, which composed their interests in 1907 by assigning northern Iran to the Russian sphere of influence and southern Iran and Afghanistan to the British sphere. But that balance had disappeared when Britain relinquished its Indian empire in 1947. To the south of Afghanistan there was no longer a single united India, but the successor states of India and Pakistan, whose attention was focused on their own internecine struggle. John Foster Dulles had promoted the alliance of Turkey, Iran and Pakistan, backed by the United States and Britain, as an instrument of containment of the Soviet Union, but that alignment had collapsed with the Iranian Revolution. India, having defeated Pakistan decisively in December, 1971, in the war over Bangladesh, was now the only potentially strong power in the region.

The threatened struggle between the superpowers for control of the Persian Gulf region would be significantly different from their earlier confrontations. The first such struggle, over Europe, ended favorably for the West when the United States and the Western European countries closed ranks and firmly indicated their determination to hold the line in Germany and Berlin. The second, between the United States and China, was essentially the result of an American delusion—the assumption that Communist China and Communist Russia were but parts of a single communist monolith. That illusory struggle ended with the Nixon visit to China and American withdrawal from Vietnam. America had discovered that Communist China was still an independent power with a vital interest in a plural world, and therefore one we could live with. In Europe, the United States was able effectively to counter Soviet power not just because it enjoyed an advantage in nuclear weaponry at that time or because it had an American army in Germany. The decisive factor was the common civilization and common commitment to democratic institutions that were shared by the United States and the European countries. The peoples of the North Atlantic Alliance were indeed one in their determination to defend this way of life, and the Soviet Union would have faced enormous continuing resistance to any attempt to subject Europe to its control. But between the United States and the peoples of the Persian Gulf region there are no common civilization, no shared institutions, and few common values. The crisis between the United States and Iran demonstrates the wide gulf that separates our two societies. This was inhospitable terrain on which to build a strong common defense.

Leaving aside the legal objections to use of force other than military assistance to a government facing a foreign attack from outside its borders, there must be great doubt about the practicality of relying on American military action to ensure access to the Persian Gulf oil fields.

It would entail very great risks. Less powerful countries, such as Japan and the Western European nations, which lack the capability, and so the temptation, to intervene militarily in the oil-producing countries, rely instead on buying the oil on the best terms they can obtain in the market place. Given the need of the producing countries to sell their oil for profit, and the high costs of war, the market place strategy may be the least expensive.

While American support for an initiative by other concerned nations, particularly those in the region, might have found a face-saving formula which would permit the Soviet Union to demilitarize Afghanistan, there seemed no prospect that American demands or punitive actions not backed by any realistic military power in the area would force the Soviets to withdraw. The abandonment of the SALT II treaty was as likely to damage American security as that of the Soviet Union. In all, President Carter's response to the Afghan situation, like his earlier attempts to intercede in favor of dissidents within the Soviet Union,[40] did little to help those injured by the Soviet actions, but it played into the hand of those American crusaders who saw no security short of "victory" over "world communism."

CHAPTER X

QUESTIONS OF NEUTRALITY

We have noted that, despite assumptions made in 1945 that collective security under the aegis of the UN had made neutrality obsolete, the not infrequent outbreaks of military conflict, whether within one state or between states, still make it necessary for outside governments to consider whether to maintain a neutral position or to give active support to one of the belligerent parties. It is clear that neutrality does not preclude efforts to bring the conflict to an end, whether pursued individually or through international organizations. The choice between neutrality and taking sides is linked with the role the nation making the decision wants the UN to perform with respect to the conflict. Where one party is clearly perceived to be an aggressor, neutrality may be seen as inappropriate and, along with giving aid to the victim of aggression, the UN may be asked for help in bringing the aggression to an end. In other cases, where there is no clear answer to the question which party is to blame, neutrality may be the best adjunct to efforts to restore peace.

Questions of this kind have been raised by the recurrent conflicts between Israel, the Palestinians, and the Arab states. For the reasons which were stated in the Introduction, those decisions, except with regard to the attack on Egypt in 1956, which involved Britain and France as well as Israel, are not considered in this book.

Other regional conflicts in which American policy-makers faced a choice whether to remain neutral or to take sides, included the conflicts between India and Pakistan and the one between Britain and Argentina over the Falkland Islands.

1. RELATIONS WITH INDIA AND PAKISTAN

Ever since the partition of British India, the primary problem of foreign policy for India and Pakistan alike has been their relations with each other. In the conflict between them over Kashmir in 1947-1948, the United States supported mediation by the Security Council. That brought a cease-fire on January 1, 1949, but no peace settlement. Kashmir continued to be a bone of contention. There were also other serious causes of friction between the two countries. There was constant danger of renewed war between them.

From independence on, India had followed a policy of nonalignment. While it was an active member of the United Nations, it refused to be drawn into the power struggles between East and West. Pakistan, however, was willing to associate itself with Dulles' attempt to create an anti-communist defensive alignment in the Middle East, to include Turkey, Pakistan, and Iran, and it also joined the Southeast Asia Treaty Organization. The crucial first link between Pakistan and the United States was the Mutual Defense Assistance Agreement of May 19, 1954.[1] The United States agreed to provide Pakistan with military equipment for its own defense and "to permit it to participate in the defense of the area." Pakistan agreed not to use the equipment for aggressive purposes. There were provisions for an American military mission to accompany the U.S. arms. Pakistan agreed to make the full contribution permitted by its manpower and resources to "maintenance of its own defensive strength and the defensive strength of the free world," and to cooperate with U.S. measures "to control trade with nations which threaten the maintenance of world peace."

While the United States intended by this agreement to enlist Pakistan in efforts to contain communism, Pakistan saw the American military equipment as a means of strengthening itself against India. India's Prime Minister Nehru had objected that American military aid to Pakistan would increase military tension in the area. President Eisenhower reassured him that the aid was not directed against India and that the United States would take "appropriate action" if American aid to any country was misused for aggression. He offered to consider sympathetically an Indian request for similar aid. Nehru rejected the suggestion and reiterated India's opposition to the military aid as "a form of intervention in Asian affairs."[2]

As Secretary of State Dulles continued with his pact-building efforts focused on the assumed communist menace, the American commitment to Pakistan ripened into alliance with the Agreement of Cooperation between the United States and Pakistan of March 5, 1959. It provided:

> In case of aggression against Pakistan, the Government of the United States of America, in accordance with the Constitution . . . , will take such appropriate action, including the use of armed forces, as may be mutually agreed upon and as is envisaged in the Joint Resolution to Promote Peace

and Stability in the Middle East,* in order to assist the Government of Pakistan at its request.³

Between 1954 and 1962 Pakistan received over $850 million dollars worth of American military equipment.

The history of American involvement in the India-Pakistan conflict did not end with the Eisenhower administration. In 1962 the alignment between the United States and Pakistan cooled and the United States drew closer to India when conflicts over the Chinese-Indian border brought a limited Chinese military attack against India. The attack inflicted a severe defeat on Indian troops and caused fear of further attacks. Pakistan sided diplomatically with China. In that emergency India turned to the United States and Britain for help. They promptly sent India military equipment valued at seventy million dollars. Negotiations on a long-term program of U.S. military aid to India were begun, but were dropped in 1964 because of unwillingness of the State and Defense Departments to jeopardize the relationship with Pakistan, and in particular the large American air base which had been constructed in the Eisenhower years at Peshawar, and which was used for U2 flights and other means of monitoring scientific developments in the Soviet Union. Unable to obtain the military equipment it needed from the United States, India negotiated to buy arms from the Soviet Union.

In 1965 there was renewed fighting in Kashmir, and a counter-offensive by India against Pakistan in the Punjab. The UN Security Council worked to restore the cease-fire, without attempting to assess blame. The United States and Great Britain both terminated weapons shipments to either party and supported the UN efforts to restore peace, but neither formally declared neutrality. The American tanks and planes which had been supplied to Pakistan were used against India, despite the previous American assurances to India that they would not be.⁴

In 1971 there was again war in the subcontinent. It began as a Pakistani civil war and grew into war between India and Pakistan when India intervened to support the demand of the Bengalis (the people of East Pakistan) for a separate nation of Bangladesh. This time

---

* This was the Congressional Resolution which authorized the president to use military force in aid of nations in the Middle East which asked for assistance "against armed aggression *from any country controlled by international communism.*" (Italics added)

President Nixon clearly sided with Pakistan, though stopping short of military intervention. The "tilt" in favor of Pakistan, which was decided upon by Nixon and Kissinger against the wishes of the State Department, occasioned public controversy when the minutes of National Security Council committee meetings were leaked to columnist Jack Anderson.

East Pakistan (Bengal) was separated by the breadth of the subcontinent from West Pakistan, and was the more populous section of the country. The Bengalis felt that the national government based in West Pakistan was not responsive to their needs, and in December 1970 a national election resulted in a resounding victory for the Awami League which was demanding autonomy for East Pakistan. The existing government, in West Pakistan, refused to make concessions despite the election result, and in March of 1971 President Yahya Khan decided to establish military rule over East Pakistan, suppressing the Awami League and arresting the Bengali national leader, Sheikh Mujibur Rahman. The result was civil war — a war for the independence of Bangladesh, characterized by atrocities perpetrated against the Bengalis by West Pakistan's army, by determined resistance by Bengali guerrillas against the government troops, and by the flight of ten million Bengali refugees into India. When the war continued through the summer and fall, with the very large numbers of refugees creating severe problems for India, the government of Indira Gandhi became more and more insistent that Pakistan must grant independence to Bangladesh. India gave increasing support to the guerrillas. At the end of November Indian troops made forays into East Pakistan, claimed to be defensive, and on December 3 full scale war broke out between India and Pakistan, initiated by Pakistani attacks on Indian airports close to West Pakistan. On December 16th the Pakistani forces in the East surrendered to the Indians and the war ended with the independence of Bangladesh.

The policy followed in this instance by President Nixon and Henry Kissinger, his National Security Adviser, was not determined by anti-communist ideology, but by a concept of power balancing. Rejecting a neutral attitude, they threatened to side with Pakistan in order to promote rapprochement between the United States and Communist China. Relationships between the United States and India and Pakistan were relegated to a subordinate position.

Nixon and Kissinger had both become convinced early in the administration that sharpening conflict between China and Russia, which was particularly evident in 1969, opened an opportunity for understanding between the United States and China, and that the relationship which would result would make both communist powers more conciliatory in their dealings with the United States. Pakistan had established a close relationship with China to gain support against India, and starting in August of 1969 Nixon had asked Yahya Kahn to convey to Peking Nixon's interest in improving U.S.-Chinese relations. Other signals and contacts were also exploited, but from that point on "the Pakistan channel" proved the most reliable contact with the Chinese leaders.

China responded with indications of interest and what Kissinger described as an "intricate minuet" developed.[5] Kissinger and Nixon assumed that China and the United States had a common interest in global equilibrium. China offered to consider "whatever ideas and suggestions the U.S. Government might put forward in accordance with the five principles of peaceful coexistence."[6] Neither insisted on immediate settlement of the long-standing points of conflict between them. Contacts were interrupted for five months following the American military intrusion into Cambodia, but in October 1970 a message from Chou En-lai to Nixon was transmitted through Pakistan in which Chou said "a special envoy of President Nixon's will be most welcome in Peking," to discuss, he said, "the subject of vacation of Chinese territories called Taiwan." Nixon responded that the United States was prepared for talks "which would not be limited only to the Taiwan question but would encompass other steps designed to improve relations and reduce tensions."[7] On April 27th the Pakistani ambassador in Washington delivered a message suggesting that Kissinger should be the envoy to come to China. As a result of further messages interchanged through Pakistan, the Kissinger visit was scheduled for July 1971. Pakistan was his point of departure and he travelled in a Pakistani plane.

In opening contact with Communist China, Kissinger has written, the United States did not intend to take sides in the Sino-Soviet dispute. Its concern with global equilibrium, however, meant that the United States had an interest in preventing a Soviet attack on China. The two communist countries would be judged by their actions and not by their ideology. Kissinger considered his and Nixon's objective to be "to purge our foreign policy of all sentimentality."[8] Whether they were successful is open to question. In working to bring its Chinese and American allies together, Pakistan was not a disinterested party, and the debt of gratitude which the White House owed to the Pakistani leaders for collaborating in their China diplomacy gave Pakistan a sentimental advantage with respect to American policy in the Indo-Pakistani conflict.

The contacts with China were handled by the White House entirely outside of State Department channels and Secretary of State Rogers was not even told of Kissinger's China trip until it was over.

When the civil war in East Pakistan began, the Department of State took the neutral action of suspending delivery of military supplies to Pakistan, and did so without first seeking White House clearance. President Nixon was disturbed by the embargo, but the action was allowed to stand because it was supported by strong public sympathy for the Bengalis.

As Pakistan's war against the Bengalis continued and the flow of refugees into India increased, the Indian Government concluded a friendship treaty with the Soviet Union, on August 9, 1971, under which the signatories agreed to consult upon appropriate action in case either party was attacked or threatened with attack. The purpose was evidently to protect India from intervention by China or the United States if there were war between India and Pakistan.

When war did come, with India's intervention in East Pakistan to force an end to the civil war there and establish the independence of Bangladesh, President Nixon was determined to "tilt" to the side of the West Pakistani government, overruling State Department sentiment in favor of neutrality. The United States called for an immediate meeting of the UN Security Council to denounce India's intervention. In a CBS interview George Bush, U.S. delegate to the UN, called it "clear aggression." American economic aid to India was slashed. In the Security Council a U.S. draft resolution calling for withdrawal of Indian and Pakistani forces to their own sides of the border was vetoed by the Soviet Union. The United States then supported referral of the question to the General Assembly, which adopted a resolution calling for cease-fire and withdrawal. China had supported Pakistan in denouncing the Indian invasion, and the USSR had supported India's position that any withdrawal of troops had to include the withdrawal of Pakistan's occupation troops from Bangladesh. Britain and France abstained from voting on any of the resolutions, taking the position that the resolutions would not contribute to a settlement and that the UN role should be confined to mediation.

In National Security Council sub-committee meetings Kissinger insisted that the United States should publicly side with Pakistan, even though it was "an exercise in futility as the Soviets can be expected to veto." He emphasized the President's desire *not* to be evenhanded. He asked whether the United States could challenge India's sea blockade of East Pakistan, but was told by the State Department that there was no legal case for a protest, as "belligerent nations have a right to blockade when a state of war exists."[9] Kissinger argued that the 1959 agreement between the United States and Pakistan made Pakistan an ally whom the United States must aid against India. The State Department disagreed, citing the reference in the treaty to the Eisenhower Doctrine which authorized American military intervention only in the case of "aggression from any country controlled by international communism." The treaty had never been considered by the United States as directed against India.

In the final stage of the conflict, before the Pakistani surrender in East Pakistan on Dec. 16th, Nixon and Kissinger professed to see a danger that India would not be satisfied with the independence of Bangladesh (a practical accomplished fact) but intended to continue the war against West Pakistan and bring about its disintegration as well, wiping out West Pakistan's army and seizing all of Kashmir. They envisaged China's going to the aid of Pakistan and a Soviet assault on China. India's declared aim had been only to end the Pakistani denial of independence to Bangladesh which India recognized as a state on Dec. 6. Before the Security Council on December 12th the Indian foreign minister said that India sought no territorial gains either in West Pakistan or in Bangladesh. But Kissinger states that on December 10 he gave a warning to the Soviet embassy that the United States would consider itself obligated to go to the assistance of Pakistan if India launched an offensive against West Pakistan. To back up the warning, an aircraft carrier task force was sent into the Bay of Bengal. Kissinger told Huang Hua, China's representative at the UN, that the United States was acting to protect West Pakistan.[10] Nixon decided, according to Kissinger, "that if the Soviet Union threatened China we would not stand idly by . . . We would have had no choice but to assist China in some manner against the probable opposition of much of the government, the media, and the Congress."[11] He claimed that it was these threats that produced Prime Minister Gandhi's statement, read by the representative of India in the Security Council on Dec. 16, that, since the Pakistani armed forces in Bangladesh had surrendered, India had ordered its forces to cease fire on the Western front. It reiterated that India had no territorial ambitions.

There is very little to indicate that the specter of an Indian offensive to crush West Pakistan, of Chinese intervention and of an attack by Russia on China was anything more than a figment of Nixon's and Kissinger's imagination. A major purpose of the American gestures in support of Pakistan seems to have been to impress China as to the value of the United States as an ally. Kissinger acknowledged to Haldeman on Dec. 11th, "We are running a tremendous bluff in a situation in which we are holding no cards."[12] The affair raises basic questions as to the relative merits of alliances with regional powers (which are intended to build a defense against the Soviet Union, but which draw us into regional conflicts), as opposed to the policy of neutrality and UN mediation, which was preferred by Britain and France and in this instance by the State Department. If reconciliation with the United States was recommended to China by its own interests, was it necessary to pay the price of alienating India? India had theretofore clung tenaciously to its policy of non-alignment, but it now looked increasingly to the Soviet Union for support.

During the Carter administration American military and economic assistance to Pakistan was terminated because of Pakistan's refusal to allow inspection of its nuclear development program, but in reaction to the Soviet invasion of Afghanistan in December 1979, a $400 million program of economic and military aid was again offered, despite Pakistan's apparent intent to develop nuclear weapons. President Zia rejected that offer as inadequate. It would have included essentially defensive weapons that would not represent a threat to India. In May of 1980 India reached agreement with the Soviet Union on an increased program of purchases of Soviet arms on low-interest terms. In June, 1981 the Reagan administration went far beyond the Carter offer and agreed to provide Pakistan with economic support, development assistance, and loans to cover military sales, to a total amount of $3 billion over a six-year period. It specifically committed itself to sell

Pakistan F-16 fighter-bombers, high performance aircraft certain to be seen as a threat by India.[13]

2. ARGENTINA'S SEIZURE OF THE FALKLANDS (MALVINAS)

In the India-Pakistan situation it was never obvious that one party was the aggressor and the other the victim. Furthermore, the ability of outside nations to bring peace to the subcontinent was strictly limited. The international community could do little more than press the parties to cease or refrain from hostilities. A quite different choice between neutrality and commitment to uphold the no-force principle of the Charter was posed by the Argentine seizure of the Falkland Islands in April 1982.

Argentina had been in possession of the islands from the 1820s to 1833, claiming ownership as the successor to Spain. In 1833 the British government took possession of the islands by force, asserting an old and dubious claim of sovereignty and ousting the Argentine authorities.[14] The islands then remained in British possession from 1833 to 1982, although the Argentines always insisted that they were the rightful owners. The present inhabitants of the islands, numbering approximately 1900, are descendants of settlers from the British Isles, engaged in sheep raising.

From 1965 onwards the dispute concerning sovereignty over the islands was a subject of consideration by the UN General Assembly, which regularly urged the two parties to negotiate a settlement. The Assembly characterized the Falklands situation as a "colonial situation." Initially, that seemed to call for implementation of the Assembly's 1960 Declaration on the Granting of Independence to Colonial Countries and Peoples, and the British declared their willingness to apply the principle of self-determination. The difficulty was that the islands' inhabitants were firmly opposed to acceptance of any form of Argentine sovereignty. They wanted to remain a British colony or an independent country within the Commonwealth. The position of Argentina was that the applicable principle was not self-determination, but the principle of the territorial integrity of Argentina, which had been violated by the British in 1833. The matter was complicated by the potential value of the oil resources and fisheries in the surrounding waters and continental shelf.

The question as to whether a particular colony should be accorded the right of self-determination, or whether it should be merged in another nation in the name of territorial integrity was not new. It was a debate that traced back at least to the General Assembly's 1960 Declaration on the Granting of Independence to Colonial Countries and Peoples.[15] After declaring that the subjection of peoples to alien subjugation was "contrary to the Charter of the United Nations," it further declared that "all peoples have the right to self-determination" (para. 2), and that "any attempt aimed at the partial or total disruption of the national unity and the territorial integrity of a country is incompatible with the purposes and principles of the Charter" (para. 6). The question which of these principles to apply had been debated in a series of instances, including West Irian, Belize, and Gibraltar. This last case was undoubtedly a factor in the considerations of the British decision-makers. Spain had long insisted that continued British control of Gibraltar violated Spain's right of territorial integrity. Britain had met the call for decolonization by insisting on the right of self-determination for the "Gibraltarians," whose ancestors came from diverse parts of the Mediterranean region. It held a referendum in 1967 in which the population voted to retain their link with Britain, with democratic local institutions, in preference to the other alternative of passing under Spanish sovereignty. With negotiations between Britain and Spain concerning Gibraltar at a critical stage, it would damage the British case to concede that the territorial integrity of Argentina was offended by British control of the Falklands.

On April 2, 1982 Argentine forces invaded the islands, quickly overcoming the small garrison of British marines. To this resort to force by Argentina, Prime Minister Thatcher reacted very much as President Truman reacted to the North Korean attack in 1950. Secretary of State Haig reports that she spoke of the lesson of Munich and told him, "Do not urge Britain to reward aggression, to give Argentina something taken by force that it could not attain by peaceful means and that would send a signal round the world with devastating consequences."[16]

The UN Security Council agreed with Britain that Argentina had no right to seize the islands. It adopted a British draft resolution which referred to Argentina's action as an "invasion" and found the existence of a breach of the peace. It "demanded" an immediate cessation of hostilities and an immediate withdrawal of all Argentine forces from the islands. It took no position on the merits of the dispute over sovereignty, but called on Argentina and the United Kingdom to seek a diplomatic solution to their differences (Security Council Resolution 502, April 3, 1982). The vote was 10 in favor to 1 against (Panama). There were 4 abstentions (China, Poland, Spain, and the Soviet Union). It was noteworthy that neither China nor the Soviet Union chose to exercise the veto.

When President Reagan learned that an Argentine invasion was about to occur, he telephoned President Galtieri with a plea to cancel the plan. He reportedly told the Argentine president that if Argentina used force to take the islands it would wreck the friendship between Argentina and the United States because the American people and Congress would regard it as an act of aggression.[17] His plea was in vain.

Previous conduct of the Reagan administration had probably encouraged the Argentine military junta to expect United States acquiescence, if not support. Where the Carter administration had denounced the Argentine military regime for its violations of human rights and had cut off U.S. military assitance, military aid had been resumed under the Reagan administration, which embraced the theory of Jeane Kirkpatrick, Reagan's ambassador to the UN, that the United States should cooperate with such merely "authoritarian" regimes in opposition to communist "totalitarians." The administration had drawn the Argentines into its own semi-secret plans to train and equip Nicaraguan exiles and infiltrate them into Nicaragua for the purpose of guerrilla warfare against Nicaragua's leftist government.[18]

The Argentine gamble on resort to force had also been encouraged by the gradual erosion of the no-force rule. Distracted by its rivalry with the Soviet Union, the United States had pursued a wavering course with respect to forcible actions by non-communist states. Cases in point were India's seizure of Portuguese Goa in 1961 and Indonesia's resort to force to acquire West Irian in 1962 and East Timor in 1975. In the case of Goa, the United States had roundly denounced India for its forcible action and pressed for a Security Council resolution "deploring" it. The draft resolution was defeated by a Soviet veto, and third world support for India prevented taking the case to the General Assembly. (It should be noted that the case of Goa was quite unlike that of the Falklands, for Goa was a colonial enclave on the Indian mainland, with a population ethnically Indian, and Portugal, ruling without any mandate from the local population, had little excuse for retaining it after Britain had conceded India's independence and France had given up its small colonial enclaves at Chandernagore and Pondicherry.) In the case of West Irian (the Western part of New Guinea) Indonesia's President Sukarno embarked on the use of force to make good his claim that the territory was part of Indonesia. The Netherlands, which had been insisting on the Papuans' right of self-determination, escaped the problem by agreeing to transfer the territory to UN administration, and the UN allowed Indonesia to take control without any plebiscite to determine the wishes of the population. When Indonesia subsequently invaded the former Portuguese colony of East Timor in 1975, to overthrow the government established there by the leftist FRETILIN (Revolutionary Front for the Independence of East Timor), the UN General Assembly did issue repeated calls for Indonesian withdrawal and affirmations of the right of the Timorese to self-determination and independence. The United States repeatedly voted with Indonesia in opposition to those resolutions. Its appreciation of Indonesia as an anti-Communist ally and as a provider of oil supplies evidently prevailed over dedication to UN principles.

In the Falklands conflict there were divided counsels within the Reagan administration. Secretary of State Haig states that he saw the matter as a test of the credibility of the American-British alliance and of American support for the rule of law.[19] Opposing him within the administration was Ambassador to the UN Jeane Kirkpatrick, who thought it more important not to alienate Argentina. While Haig's view was reflected in the U.S. vote for the Security Council resolution demanding the withdrawal of Argentine forces, Ambassador Kirkpatrick was the guest of honor at a dinner at the Argentine embassy on the evening after the invasion, and on April 11, on "Face the Nation," she even suggested that the Argentine claim to own the islands might justify the use of force.

During the first four weeks following the Argentine invasion the United States did little to back up the UN demand for Argentine withdrawal. Acting as a mediator, Secretary Haig shuttled back and forth between London and Buenos Aires trying to find a compromise that would save face for both sides.

There was much that the United States might have done. It was not necessary to take a position on the question of sovereignty. There the United States could offer friendly mediation, suggesting measures such as a UN trusteeship or special guarantees for local self-government by the islanders, and perhaps separating out the questions concerning the surrounding waters and continental shelf and the ownership of South Georgia and other outlying dependencies. The critical point, however, was enforcment of the rule against seizure of territory by force, and the first requirement was to make it clear that the United States intended to take the necessary action to make Security Council Resolution 502 effective. Such action would certainly include the application of maximum economic and financial pressure — action such as President Eisenhower had taken against Britain to compel withdrawal of the force landed in Egypt in 1956. Beyond that, an American aircraft carrier might even have been ordered to the South Atlantic as a precautionary measure, as Eisenhower had sent one to the Congo in the crisis there and as Nixon had done, in more questionable circumstances, in the India-Pakistan conflict. It is likely that clear indication of the United States' intention to make Resolution 502 effective, combined with the actions taken by the European Economic Community, would have compelled Argentina to retreat from its use of force.

After the delay of four weeks, when the U.S. mediation effort collapsed because of Argentina's refusal to retreat, President Reagan and Secretary Haig issued declarations that "armed aggression of that kind must not be allowed to succeed" and that "the United States cannot and will not condone the use of unlawful force to resolve disputes." It was also announced at this time that the United States would suspend military exports to Argentina and withhold Export-Import Bank credits and loan guarantees and would "respond positively to requests for material support for British forces." American weapons were sold to the British as needed. These measures, while helpful to Britain, came too late to influence the Argentines. The battle for the islands began with the sinking of an Argentine cruiser on May 2, and continued until the Argentine forces were overcome on June 14th.

The United States thus left Britain to act alone in defense of the important UN principle, incurring heavy expense and risk to its navy, which was exposed to damaging attacks by Argentine shore-based aircraft. That we would take no action in such circumstances would have been inconceivable twenty years earlier. The episode showed how far the United States had departed from its original commitment to the principles of the UN Charter.

The Falklands conflict also demonstrated how, in the face of weakened confidence in the likelihood of enforcement of those principles, more and more nations were taking positions with a view to protecting their own separate interests, or were thinking of how the present case might affect their own unsatisfied claims, rather than heeding an interest in world order. Thus China evidently was comparing the Argentine effort to recover "their Malvinas" with its own desire to recover Taiwan, Spain was influenced by its desire to recover Gibraltar, Guatemala by its desire to annex Belize, and Venezuela by its old claim to part of Guyana, to mention only a few of the irredentist claims which might threaten world peace. U.S. conduct was influenced by the administration's plans to ally itself with anti-communist Argentina to combat revolutions in Central America, and the Soviet Union was inclined to side with Argentina by its dependence on imports of Argentine wheat, as well as by its desire to wean allies away from the United States.

Argentina appealed to the OAS for support against the British campaign to retake the islands. After the British military beachhead was established on East Falkland, the OAS adopted a resolution on May 29 which condemned "the unjustified and disproportionate armed attack ... by the United Kingdom." It endorsed efforts of the UN Secretary-General to achieve a peaceful settlement, and called on the United States to respect "inter-American continental solidarity" and to end the "coercive measures" it had applied against Argentina. The United States abstained, along with Chile, Colombia, and Trinidad. Its representative stated that the sanctions against Argentina would be lifted "when United Nations Resolution 502 is implemented." Argentina also sought support from the coordinating bureau of the group of 94 "non-aligned" nations, which met in Havana at the beginning of June. The bureau adopted an ambiguous resolution which voiced support for Argentina's claim of sovereignty and deplored the British military offensive, but also expressed support for the Security Council's resolutions. It rejected Argentina's appeal to label the British action "aggression."

CHAPTER XI

SUMMING UP

National decision-makers react to the image of a situation as it appears to them. Part of that image is a perception of legality, including relevant treaties, customary rules, and the vested rights of their own nation and other parties. Where decision-makers perceive foreign action as encroachment upon their nation's clear legal rights, there is an increased likelihood that they will take an unyielding stand, including readiness to use force to defend those rights.

Perceptions of law also affect calculations of probable support or counter-action from other nations. For that reason decision-makers normally try to give the appearance of legality to actions they take publicly with respect to other nations. That is seen as an aid to persuading them to accept the actions decided upon. In the case of the United States, it also helps in obtaining support from Congress and from the American people, for we like to consider ourselves a law-abiding people.

Considerations of legality compete, however, with other factors influencing decision-making. Sometimes interests at stake are thought to be important enough to justify acting illegally if necessary. A powerful nation can choose to act in defiance of the rules if it considers that to be in its national interest. Yet clear decision that national interest requires overt action contrary to an acknowledged rule of law is rare. More frequently, choices are made between possible national positions as to what international law requires. In such cases, if an arguable legal theory is available to support a line of action that certain policy-makers favor for other reasons, the chance of such action being decided upon is improved, even though the decision-makers know that the theory in question may be rejected by other nations. If decision-makers decide upon action for which *no* plausible legal justification can be offered, they generally try to keep their action secret.

After action has been taken publicly, it is accepted routine for governments to defend what they have done with arguments that law is on their side. Because of the fact that they can ordinarily avoid submitting to third-party determination as to the legality of their actions, it is possible for them to insist indefinitely that their interpretation of international law is correct, however much other nations may disagree. National decision-makers can therefore take advantage of strained interpretations of legal principle which would be likely to be rejected if the issue came before an international tribunal.

The introduction into international law of rules against the use of force. There are rare occasions when the development of new rules of international law or new international legal institutions has been in itself an important policy question. The most striking instance of an American law-building effort of that kind was the American leadership in creating the League of Nations and the United Nations, together with the new rules limiting the use of force which were incorporated in 1945 in the UN Charter.

Rules limiting the use of force were a radical change in international law, and were difficult to enforce, especially after the victorious superpowers became bitter rivals. Both of them have violated the rules on occasion, invoking evasive excuses or taking illegal action of a covert kind, and the precedent set by departures from the rules by the superpowers may have encouraged less powerful states to follow their example. With a few notable exceptions, actions that the UN majority has found it possible or practical to take to deal with outbreaks of conflict have been confined to resolutions condemning acts of force that were clearly in violation of the Charter, or calling for cease-fires in order to end hostilities as quickly as possible.

There is striking evidence, nevertheless, that there is still wide international agreement in principle as to what uses of force are lawful and what ones are not. Invasion across the established border of one state by another is proscribed. It is legitimate to use force in defense against a foreign attack, as an exercise of the inherent right of self-defense. Unless and until the United Nations acts to restore peace, other nations may legitimately aid the nation attacked. If the United Nations undertakes action to restore peace, member nations have a duty to assist the UN effort and to refrain from giving assistance to any state against which the United Nations is taking such action. The right of a people to revolt against an oppressive government is not affected by the international rules. Foreign states have a duty not to intervene forcibly in civil strife in another state, and not to finance or assist terrorist or armed efforts to overthrow another state's government. An exception to this principle, which has been insisted upon by the anti-colonial majority in the UN membership, is a right to give military support to a people who are struggling to free themselves from foreign colonial rule, or from domination by an alien racist minority. Also, not infrequently, the claim is heard that foreign intervention may be excusable if it has been requested by the legitimate government of the country in question.

Decisions of Truman and Acheson. Except for sending military advisers and equipment to help the Greek government combat communist rebels, the first resort to force by the United States after 1945 was the decision to send U.S. combat forces to Korea in June 1950 to help repel the North Korean attack on the Republic of Korea. That use of force was in aid of a UN police action to repel aggression that violated the UN Charter.

Reference of this matter by the United States to the UN, instead of responding with unilateral counter-action, was unopposed by any of the officials who took part in the decision. There were other reasons besides defense of the UN Charter in favor of a forcible U.S. response—especially the need to show small allies that they could rely on U.S. protection and to show the communists that the United States would not permit piecemeal aggression—but besides showing that the rules of the Charter were to be taken seriously, backing of the great majority of the UN membership for a strong response seemed assured, and the UN connection would bring both legitimation and significant foreign participation to the military effort led by the United States.

Part of President Truman's response, however, was the naval action to "neutralize" Formosa, which was taken by the United States alone, without any request for UN authorization. It was this action which finally entangled the United States in the Chinese civil conflict. One factor which promoted this linking of Formosa with the U.S. response to aggression in Korea was the assumption by the President and his advisers that the aggressor was not the North Korean regime, nor even their Soviet allies, but an entity spoken of as "international communism," of which the Chinese Communist government was assumed to be a part. Formosa was thus treated as another front in a single worldwide conflict.

That action concerning Formosa might not have been taken were it not for the existence of a legal theory which could be invoked to support it. This was the theory of continuing Japanese sovereignty

SUMMING UP

over the island. It was not a very good justification, and the United States showed its lack of confidence in it by its failure to put the matter before the Security Council. However plausible it might have been as an excuse for taking Formosa back from Chinese administration at an earlier stage, it had been greatly weakened by President Truman's previous declaration that the United States considered the island to be Chinese territory.

Until the reversal of policy occasioned by the crisis in Korea, Acheson had struggled hard to avoid entanglement in the Chinese civil conflict, and it is a little hard to understand why, in his previous resistance to Republican pressure to intervene militarily to keep Formosa out of the hands of the Chinese communists, he had never made the argument that, the island having been conceded to be part of China when it was delivered to Chinese control, for the United States to intervene between the Chinese Nationalists and the Chinese Communists would be a use of force in international relations which would violate the UN Charter. The explanation may be that his not doing so reflected his belief that the UN rules were largely irrelevant where the struggle between the Communist bloc and the "free world" was concerned.

The UN police action in Korea was at first highly successful, both repelling the invasion and demonstrating American determination to enforce the rule against international use of force. The later unwise decision to advance across the 38th parallel into North Korea, which brought on a limited war with China, was influenced by the openness to conflicting interpretations of the Security Council resolution which authorized action "to repel the armed attack and to restore peace and security in the area." Even the United States conceded that the legality of applying force north of the 38th parallel depended on finding justification for it in that resolution. But it was possible to argue for either a strict interpretation of the resolution (repel the attack means return to the 38th parallel) or a broad interpretation (restore peace and security in the area means compel the submission of North Korea to UN control in order to remove the likelihood of renewed aggression). If the United States chose to interpret the resolution broadly, it could defend that position so long as it could muster enough votes to prevent a contrary UN interpretation. That was the course chosen. It was a wholly American decision, only accepted after the fact by an acquiescent General Assembly.

As Acheson later bitterly observed, the defeat of MacArthur's forces by the unexpected Chinese counter-offensive "was an incalculable defeat to U.S. foreign policy and destroyed the Truman administration."[1] Once the 38th parallel was crossed, the administration had found it difficult politically to stop short of the northern border, although many of Truman's advisers would have liked to do so. To stop at the 38th parallel *could* have been defended politically on the basis of legal principle—the argument made by India and Communist China, and the position taken initially by the British, that there was no authority in law for the use of force to alter the status quo north of the 38th parallel or to give effect to the General Assembly's previous political recommendations.

Decisions of Eisenhower and Dulles. The foreign outlook of Eisenhower and Dulles was dominated by their image of world communism as a force transcending nationalism and bringing nations under the power of the USSR. While Eisenhower followed a cautious policy wherever he saw a danger of war that might escalate beyond acceptable dimensions, that image led him to concur with the view of Dulles that the United States should not shrink from the use of force to prevent the extension of communist influence wherever it seemed that it might do the job at acceptable cost. That attitude was an essential rejection of the central principle of the UN Charter.

Already in the Truman administration, the concern about communism had affected the attitude of the United States towards struggles for national independence. Because Ho Chi Minh was a communist, his struggle for Vietnamese independence did not attract the American sympathy and support that was given to the Indonesian struggle for independence. But while the Truman administration embarked at the beginning of 1950 on a program of American aid for the purchase of arms for France's Indochinese war, it never intended American forces to be used in Indochina except as defense against a hypothetical Chinese armed intervention. And, despite Acheson's lack of enthusiasm for the UN, the Truman administration is not known to have embarked on any secret operations for forcible overthrow of foreign governments.

Eisenhower and Dulles contemplated overt use of force against communist governments on several occasions. The first of these was when it was proposed that the United States should intervene to help France defeat the communist insurrection in Indochina. What dissuaded the administration from doing so was not the Charter's prohibition of the use of force, but the absence of Congressional support for intervention, the refusal of the British to participate, and the negative military prospects as seen by General Ridgeway and by Eisenhower, himself. Had intervention been thought expedient, Dulles would have insisted that the help provided by Communist China to the Viet Minh constituted "armed attack," justifying invocation of the right of collective self-defense.

While this administration participated reluctantly in the Geneva Conference on Indochina, it refused participation in the plan, supported by Britain, Russia, and Communist China, for a guarantee by the five big powers of a settlement to be based on an internationally supervised cease-fire, withdrawal of foreign troops, independence of the three Indochinese states under a guarantee of their neutrality, and internationally supervised elections for Vietnam. It supported South Vietnam in its repudiation of the election plan and set out to make permanent the temporary partition of Vietnam that the Geneva agreements had intended.

The Eisenhower administration also intervened in the Chinese civil war, participating secretly in the use of force by the Chinese Nationalists against the mainland, and threatening the use of force, including the use of nuclear weapons, to protect the Chinese Nationalists against attacks on their coastal island positions.

Dulles insisted that what the United States was doing was legal, relying on the fact that it could not be compelled to submit to any third-party judgment on the question of legality. One device that he used was his characterization of Communist insurrections as "aggression by international communism." That argument was applied both to the insurrection against France in Indochina and to the Chinese civil war.

Another device which he exploited was insistence on the right of the United States to recognize, or not to recognize, any government it chose, regardless of the requirement of factual control. Only by a fiction could the government on Formosa be considered the government of China, but the United States continued to treat it as such. It gave a cloak of legality to its intervention in Chinese affairs by formalizing it in a mutual defense treaty with the exile regime. As a commitment to intervention, the treaty was fundamentally inconsistent with the UN Charter. Yet the treaty stated the parties' intention to "refrain in their international relations from the threat or use of force in any manner inconsistent with the purposes of the United Nations." Having, by its own intervention, made a separate Chinese regime on Taiwan possible, the United States now insisted that its protection of that regime from the government of the rest of China was an exercise of the right of collective self-defense. It would be hard to find a more extreme example of the manipulation of international law by national decision-makers.

The traditional American policy with respect to recognition of new states and governments, in which the element of *de facto* control of territory and population was the decisive criterion, had been a policy supportive of effective application of international law. It did not denote approval of any recognized government, or relinquishment of claims against it. Indeed, one of the purposes of such a recognition policy, as Canning had said in 1825, was to hold new governments responsible for their actions under international law. Britain had in the main stuck to that policy. The new American practice, denying any obligation in the matter, ensured that no generally accepted rules of recognition could be pointed to. It was a practice subversive of effective international law, as well as one which threatened to make the UN unrepresentative of the world's actual governments.[2]

A major new initiative by the Eisenhower administration was the planning to make secret illegal operations into a much more active tool of American policy than it had been previously. Eisenhower authorized the secret operation to overthrow Mossadegh in Iran, which resulted finally in the shah's authoritarian rule, as well as the ill-concealed assault against the Arbenz government of Guatemala that deprived that nation of an opportunity for much-needed social reform, and the plan for an expedition against the government of Cuba that was passed on to the next administration. To prevent the spread of communism had become such an overriding goal that even action that would normally be considered criminal was now open to consideration. Among the new options were plots to assassinate certain foreign leaders. The CIA expanded to fill the new role assigned to it, and the types of secret operations initiated under Eisenhower were further pursued under later administrations.

Except for measures to counter what he saw as the aggressive plans of "international communism," Eisenhower remained convinced of the importance of adhering to the rule against the use of force. Taking personal control in the final stage of the Suez Crisis, after Dulles had been hospitalized, he took very strong measures, in support of the UN Charter, to compel the withdrawal of British, French, and Israeli troops from Egypt. In the months before the British and French intervention, however, his injunctions against the use of force had been slightly ambiguous, and Dulles' seeming participation in planning to make Egypt accept an imposed solution, combined with recollection of past American willingness to use force against Iran and Guatemala, probably contributed to British misjudgment of the expected American reaction to their military intervention.

The failure of intervention in Vietnam. Presidents Kennedy and Johnson held essentially the same perception of the menace of international communism as did Eisenhower. They continued the struggle to prevent unification of Vietnam under communist control which led, under Johnson, to the second costly limited war fought by the United States. This one did not have UN support, and it showed the very limited effectiveness of foreign military intervention as a way of influencing the internal political development of another country. The likelihood of counter-intervention by China kept the United States from sending its troops into North Vietnam. And there was a real internal political struggle in South Vietnam such as had not been present in South Korea. The United States was unable to prevent the North Vietnamese from intervening and, as foreigners, the Americans could not compete with the North Vietnamese for influence in the South Vietnamese political struggle.

In its inception the American intervention in Vietnam had been seen as an aspect of the containment of Communist China. Yet the war took on a life of its own because it was thought that to admit defeat would damage American prestige, and so the war continued well beyond the point when President Nixon had decided that Communist China, remaining an independent nation with interests different from those of the Soviet Union, represented no threat and could have cooperative relations with the United States. Taken together, the end of the American intervention in Vietnam, American recognition of the Chinese government (and termination of the mutual defense treaty with Taiwan which that recognition required), and Chinese participation in the United Nations, have effectively ended the cold war in the Far East.

Differing degrees of risk. In some of the instances we have considered, the decision-makers were more conscious than in other situations that they were in a direct confrontation with Soviet power that might escalate into all-out war. Such confrontations have become ever more dangerous as nuclear weapons have accumulated on both sides. Those are the cases where the "chicken" game is played. In the Berlin case, Khrushchev sought to take by threats a position where the Western powers had well-founded legal rights. The determination of the United States, Britain and France to stand firm, even at the risk of war, was increased and was give credibility by the fact that legality was on their side. On the other hand, American decision-makers gave no serious thought to contesting the Soviet decision to close off their zone of German occupation. To contest the Berlin wall, the West would have had to take the offensive in a way that was not only dangerous, but of dubious legal validity. They could argue that the wall contravened agreements to treat Berlin as a single area with free internal communication, but their arguments here would be no better than the Soviet arguments that the West had already violated the same agreements by separate measures put in effect in their zones. In effect these agreements had long since become dead letters, important only as part of the process by which the four wartime allies had acquired occupation rights in their sectors and zones.

Forcible Soviet interventions in the internal affairs of the Eastern European nations have flagrantly violated the independence and territorial integrity of those countries and have been properly condemned by the UN General Assembly, but they have not been the subject of "chicken" games because the United States has recognized that it could not help those nations by military means without risking a third world war. The best hope of those nations is their own determination to resist foreign domination. The United States has rejected Soviet claims of a right to intervene in Eastern Europe, but has tacitly accepted Soviet military preeminence there.

Latin America would seem to be the other side of this coin. It is close to the United States, far from the Soviet Union, and an area of historic U.S. concern. It was therefore a reckless move on Khrushchev's part to challenge the United States with his plan to install missiles in Cuba. President Kennedy's response was not based on any perception of American legal rights being violated by the Soviet action, comparable to the perception that motivated the Western powers in Berlin. Instead, what made credible the United States' determination to get the missiles out no matter what the cost were the strategic and psychological considerations which were peculiarly present at that geographical location. For the Soviet Union there was no comparable interest to justify its risking war.

While there was no publicly stated threat, the brief confrontation which occurred in 1973 when the Soviet Union informed the United States that it was considering sending a Soviet force to Egypt to compel Israel to observe a UN cease-fire resolution, and the United States, opposing any Soviet intervention, responded with an alert of its forces, was made dangerous by the fact that the two superpowers had approximately equal commitments to the opposing parties in the Middle East conflict, and both considered their interests to be important.

The Soviet intervention in Afghanistan in December 1979 was apparently undertaken to quell a growing Muslim revolt and establish a reliable pro-Soviet regime, thus limiting the spread of Muslim fundamentalism beyond Iran to another country immediately bordering Soviet Central Asia. It was clearly illegal and the UN General Assembly declared it to be a violation of fundamental principles and called for withdrawal of foreign troops. So close to the Soviet border, military intervention by the United States to help the Afghans was too dangerous to contemplate. However, coming on top of the collapse of Iran as a military power in the region, it so alarmed the Carter administration that it began to plan intensively to build a U.S. military capability to go to the aid of friendly countries in the region of the Persian Gulf, or to intervene militarily in case of internal conflict in those countries. There was a serious danger that intervention by either superpower in a local conflict in that region might bring counter-intervention and another playing of the game of "chicken."

Decisions concerning Latin America. It is in Latin America that the United States has most persistently violated the non-interventionist norm. Yet while American interventions in that region are comparable to those of the Soviet Union in Eastern Europe, they have been less massive and determined, and they have been the subject of continuing domestic controversy. This was an issue on which American opinion was deeply ambivalent. On the one hand was the tradition that viewed Latin America as a special U.S. sphere of influence, the tradition of the

Monroe Doctrine. On the other was the American belief in the general principle of the right of all peoples to self-determination, the corollary of which was the principle of non-intervention.

A division of the world which would assign spheres of influence to the respective great powers was a method of accommodating their rivalries that long antedated the UN. Stalin and Churchill had been attracted to the idea, but Roosevelt and Truman had rejected it. If the United States was determined to try to retain control of Central America and willing to repudiate its treaty commitments, it could offer a deal to the Soviet Union whereby the latter would acknowledge a U.S. right to have governments it considered friendly to it in Central America and the Caribbean, in exchange for acknowledgement by the United States of a Soviet right of intervention in Eastern Europe. Revived talk of the Monroe Doctrine by American officials brought that suspicion to the minds of some Latin Americans. But Americans were not so willing to give up the UN principles as to forego the right which those principles gave them to criticize Soviet intervention in Poland and Afghanistan.

The failure of the Carter administration to get OAS support for its proposal of an inter-American peacekeeping force for Nicaragua in 1979 shows that if the United States is determined to prevent revolution in Central America, it will have to act alone. The Latin American governments continue to be strongly attached to the non-intervention principle.

The European powers had come to accept their inability to control their former dependencies in Africa and Asia. Without resort to force, they retained considerable influence through trade, economic aid, and diplomatic relations. Sooner or later the United States must make the same adjustment. It should recognize that its true interest is in the independence of Latin American governments rather than in their ideological purity. If the United States would recommit itself unequivocally to the principle of non-intervention, it might be able to persuade the OAS to adopt the principle that the establishment of any Soviet or non-American base or troops in the American hemisphere would be an impermissible threat to peace and security of the continent. There was precedent for that in the resolution of the OAS which declared Soviet missiles in Cuba to be a threat of that nature and supported action to secure their removal.

Decisions concerning Africa. Because it was a region remote from both superpowers, and one where the United States was historically uninvolved, it was in Africa that the United States had the best chance to avoid direct political or military involvement and to make maximum use of the United Nations. For those reasons the Eisenhower administration welcomed the UN intervention in the Congo, and vigorous support by President Kennedy enabled the UN to end the Katanga secession and foreign intervention. However, the failure of the campaign to make discontented UN members pay for peacekeeping operations to which they were opposed caused loss of enthusiasm for UN peacekeeping as a way to deal with African conflicts, and willingness to consider direct U.S. intervention instead.

In the one case of Namibia, where Black Africa was solidly ranged against South Africa's attempt to perpetuate its control, United States policy continued to be centered on the UN. Since the territory was a former League of Nations Mandate, South Africa had never enjoyed full sovereignty. The attempt to invoke the influence of the International Court in this matter confronted the same problem of inability to coerce South Africa as was present in the case of the USSR, France, and peacekeeping expenses, but in this instance the support of the UN majority for the legal principles laid down by the court in its advisory opinions was much firmer, and the legal pressures on South Africa were a significant element in the continuing political struggle to end South African rule.

When to be neutral and when to take sides. In the conflicts between India and Pakistan the United States had no good reason not to preserve good relations with both sides. Neutrality would not have been inconsistent with support of UN efforts to preserve or restore peace. It was the focus on the presumed Soviet menace which caused the United States to ally itself with Pakistan, although Pakistan was far less concerned with any danger of Soviet aggression than it was interested in profiting from American military aid to prepare itself for conflicts with India.

The Falkland Islands conflict, by contrast, presented a direct challenge to the rule against the use of force in international relations. The flagrant illegality of the Argentine seizure of the islands left no face-saving way out for the United Kingdom short of a forcible response. The British had long been willing to negotiate a transfer of sovereignty if a formula could be found that was acceptable to the islands' inhabitants, but they could not accept seizure of the islands by force. Because it was so clearly a violation of the UN Charter, Britain was able to secure the necessary support for a Security Council resolution finding a breach of the peace and demanding Argentine withdrawal. It provided legitimation for British invocation of the right of self-defense.

This was the type of situation in which it was supposed after World War II that the United States would never again be neutral, yet the United States now experimented with neutrality before it finally tilted towards Great Britain. If the United States had from the start supported the British in their insistence upon Argentine withdrawal and a return to peaceful means of resolving the questions at issue, it might have been able to prevent the conflict from becoming a full-scale war.

The chimera of "world communism." The record of American decision-making since we committed ourselves to the UN (and OAS) principles is a mixed one. Successive decision-makers have held differing views in the matter. Nor is the United States alone in having departed from those principles. We have noted that the Soviet Union has repeatedly intervened in the countries contiguous to the USSR (Eastern Europe and Afghanistan), and that those countries have been deprived of their right of self-determination as a result. Notable instances where the United States has supported or deferred to the UN principles included President Truman's decision to enforce the UN Charter by sending U.S. forces to participate in the UN police action in Korea; President Eisenhower's insistence that the United States' allies withdraw their military forces from Egypt in 1956; President Kennedy's decision (following failure of the illegal U.S. operation in aid of the Cuban exile brigade) *not* to reinforce the Cubans with U.S. forces; the support by Eisenhower and Kennedy for the UN operation in the Congo; President Carter's decision *not* to intervene in Nicaragua against the Sandinist revolution; and President Reagan's support for Britain in the Falkland Islands conflict.

Where the United States has departed from its commitment to the UN principles, it was a consequence of an obsessive fear of communism, which led the decision-makers to reject all restraints on their choice of means to fight it.

This has been a peculiarly American obsession. Europeans, who have long been accustomed to Socialist parties and governments, have never had the same fear. The Communist parties of France, Italy, Spain, and Portugal are seen to be national parties. They are feared by the middle class for their radicalism, but they are not regarded as agents of the Kremlin. It is only in those Eastern European countries which were so unlucky as to be behind the lines of the Russian armies at the end of World War II that Communist governments were put in power and kept in power by Russians. Events in Hungary, Czechoslovakia, and Poland have shown that socialism in those countries would deviate substantially from the Soviet model and their politics would approach a Western multi-party model were it not for the repressive Soviet presence. With no possibility of Soviet military occupation of the United States, those who fear that communism might be planted in this country show a strange lack of confidence in the American system.

The first indication that "international communism" in the sense in which Dulles perceived it ("that farflung clandestine political organization operated by the leaders of the Communist Party of the Soviet Union") in reality does not exist outside of Soviet-controlled Eastern Europe, came in 1948, with Yugoslavia's break with the Soviet Union. The fact that nationalism had prevailed over ideology was demonstrated again in the 1960's by the public conflict between the USSR and Communist China. President Nixon's opening to China resulted, and Communist China's independence from Soviet control is now an acknowledged cornerstone of the world power balance. Countries that at one time relied on Soviet military support have later rejected it, and turned to the United States for support, as was the case with Egypt and Somalia. The alliance of Cuba and Vietnam with the Soviet Union is based less on common political principles than on convergent interests. Fidel Castro turned to the Soviet Union because he needed a protector against the United States and a source of economic support. His anti-imperialism is a Cuban, not a Russian, phenomenon, and it is misleading to label him a "proxy" or a puppet of the Russians.

The assumption that communism was the major cause of world conflict was also incorrect. Some of the most dangerous conflicts have had nothing to do with communism. Cases in point have been the conflicts between Israel, the Palestinian Arabs, and the surrounding states, and conflicts between India and Pakistan, Iran and Iraq, Iran and the United States, and Argentina and Great Britain. The most serious conflict of all, the nuclear confrontation between the United States and the USSR, has less to do with doctrinal differences than with the simple fear on each side of the terrible weapons with which both are equipped. The conflicts in Central America, and between the United States and Cuba, bear some resemblance to the conflicts in Eastern Europe. They are in essence revolts against the dominance of those nations by the United States and the local oligarchies which have depended on US protection, and the attraction to Marxism has been less a cause than a consequence of those conflicts. So also, contemporary conflicts between the northern nations and the newer, poorer nations are not produced by communism, but by resentment of inequality and economic and political dependence.

By its own departures from the UN and OAS principles, the United States has weakend the force of the rules and made it easier for others to violate them. Thus U.S. interventions in Guatemala, Cuba, and the Dominican Republic made U.S. objections to Soviet interventions in Hungary and Czechoslovakia seem hypocritical. Britain and France expected American abstention on the issue of their intervention against Egypt at Suez as the equivalent of their abstention when the issue of Guatemala was brought to the Security Council. The Argentine dictatorship expected the United States to tolerate its assault on the Falkland Islands because the United States had shown itself willing to use force as a tool of its national policies and had demonstrated tolerant acceptance of resort to force by Israel and some other nations.

The departure from our commitment to the UN principles was defended as a return to *realpolitik*. Its practitioners considered the UN and its Charter to be utopian and impractical, and their own anti-communism to be more realistic. Yet in fact the non-ideological UN model of world politics has turned out to be more realistic than the cold warriors' vision of world politics as a struggle between "the free world" and "international communism."

The UN principles and American foreign policy. The question whether the United States should refrain from using force except as permitted by the UN principles does not involve a choice between altruism and "the national interest." Indeed it can be said that all debates about foreign policy are debates about what is in the national interest. The question at issue is whether or not American interests are best served by keeping our use of forcible means within the guidelines set by the UN principles.

It should first be said that the preservation of peace and prevention of international aggression, the right of national self-determination and the right of a people to revolt against oppressive government, and the impermissibility of foreign interference in the internal affairs of other nations, which are the Charter's principles, are basic American principles as well. It is ironic that the United States and the Soviet Union, both of which began as champions of the rights of man, are today the greatest supporters of counter-revolution. Where the Soviet Union suppresses popular revolts of the peoples of Eastern Europe, the United States tries to prevent the peoples of Latin America from exercising the right of revolution as a remedy for misrule. It can certainly be argued that we have an interest in being respected by other nations, not merely for military power, but for our national commitment to universally respected principles. Actions such as our interventions in Guatemala, El Salvador, and Nicaragua, the campaign by the Nixon administration to undermine the legitimate constitutional government of Chile and replace it with a military dictatorship, and undercover plots to assassinate foreign leaders, have violated our own principles as well as those of international law, and they did great damage to the good name of the United States and to the respect of other peoples for our government.

From Iran to Latin America, preoccupation with "the communist threat" has led us to ally ourselves with repressive dictatorships, often creating hostility to the United States among the peoples of the countries concerned. In the case of Iran it produced the most virulent anti-Americanism. Where discontent boiled over and finally brought revolutionary governments to power, the hostility of our government to such regimes tended to force them to seek Soviet protection. If we had been willing to accept those radical upheavals as possibly necessary stages of development of those nations, there is no reason to suppose those new governments would not have chosen independence in foreign policy and friendly relations and trade with the United States. There is, furthermore, no indication that communist governments, or socialist regimes not calling themselves communist, hesitate to trade with capitalist countries or to enlist the services of capitalist corporations when it is good business to do so.

Our attempts to attain political objectives by the use of force have been notably unsuccessful. The long and costly war with China in Korea would not have occurred if we had been content with merely repelling the invasion of South Korea. Avoidance of intervention in the internal affairs of Vietnam would have saved us from that unnecessary war. There was no need for us to incur the enmity of China by intervening in its civil war. The attempts of Eisenhower and Kennedy to overthrow Castro helped to bring on the dangerous Cuban missile crisis. The situation in Guatemala today is much worse because we did not permit the Arbenz revolution to take its course in 1954. Current U.S. operations against the government of Nicaragua, and to prevent revolution in El Salvador, show little prospect of success. They have tended to radicalize the revolution in both countries.

What changes in our policies would a recommitment to the UN principles entail?

It would require a decision to stop interfering in the internal affairs of other nations.

It would require that we not engage in counter-revolution.

It would require willingness to accept Marxist governments in some Latin American countries.

It would require renunciation of secret operations to overthrow other governments.

It would permit us to continue to supply friendly governments with arms to defend themselves, but it would not seek to maintain them in power where they were incapable of defending themselves against internal opposition.

Rather than planning on costly use of force to gain or protect access to oil supplies, it would rely on the continuing need of the producing countries to sell their products, and on our ability to buy them on the world market.

While it would be non-interventionist with respect to the internal affairs of other nations, it would not be a return to isolation. It would maintain the commitment to joint defense of our allies against any external attack. Because of the clear illegality of external attack on governments friendly to us, that is much less likely than is domestic civil conflict within a nation.

Insofar as we rely on use of force unmindful of the UN principles, we are running risks of war that are not justified by any American interests—risks of divisive, unsuccessful wars of the Vietnam type, and, even worse, risks of nuclear war. There is too great a likelihood of miscalculation somewhere down the line. It is rational for us to assume that the Soviet leaders have the same interest we have in avoiding thermonuclear war. There is no rational motive for them to attack us unless they fear that we intend to attack them. Limiting our own propensity to resort to force offers us the best insurance against becoming involved in an escalating spiral of actions that might lead to nuclear war. Recommitting ourselves to observance of the UN principles, pledging non-intervention, but declaring our intention to protect our allies against external attack, we would stand a better chance of inducing the Soviet Union to abide by those rules also. That course, if pressed also upon our respective allies, would help the United States and the Soviet Union to avoid the dangerous game of "chicken."

NOTES

INTRODUCTION

1. I have long been interested in this subject. For a study of U.S. decisions relating to the revision of treaties, see Hoyt, "Law and Politics in the Revision of Treaties Affecting the Panama Canal," *Virginia Journal of International Law*, 6 (1966): 45-76, and, in more detail, Hoyt, *National Policy and International Law: Case Studies from American Canal Policy* (University of Denver Monograph Series in World Affairs, Vol. 4, no. 1 (1966). Cf. several short studies on the role of law in international crises which were sponsored by the American Society of International Law: Thomas Ehrlich, *Cyprus 1958-1967* (Oxford University Press, 1974); Robert Bowie, *Suez 1956* (Oxford University Press, 1974); Abram Chayes, *The Cuban Missile Crisis* (Oxford University Press, 1974); Georges Abi-Saab, *The United Nations Operation in the Congo 1960-1964* (Oxford University Press, 1978); and Roger Fisher, *Points of Choice* (Oxford University Press, 1978). Pioneering work in this field was done by Percy Corbett in *Law and Society in the Relations of States* (New York: Harcourt, Brace & Co., 1951) and *Law and Diplomacy* (Princeton University Press, 1959).

CHAPTER 1: WORLD ORGANIZATION AS A POLICY OBJECTIVE

1. The principal target of American imperialism in those times was Latin America, as to which Theodore Roosevelt asserted the U.S. intention to exercise "an international police power." This first imperial experiment appeared to end in 1933, with the departure of the last marines from Nicaragua, the conclusion of new treaties with Panama and Cuba which relinquished the former treaty right of the United States to send its troops to those countries to maintain order, and the conclusion in December 1933 of the Montevideo Convention on Rights and Duties of States. By its eighth article the United States agreed with its Latin American neighbors that "No State has the right to intervene in the internal or external affairs of another." A second era of North American intervention, this time in the cause of anti-communism, opened with the action taken against the Arbenz government in Guatemala in 1954.

2. U.S. Department of State, *Papers Relating to the Foreign Relations of the United States* (hereafter cited as "For. Rel. U.S."), *The Lansing Papers 1914-1920*, 2:495.

3. Ibid., 477, 497. The phrase was taken from Article 4 of the U.S. Constitution, in which the United States guaranteed a republican form of government to every state.

4. One of the most thoughtful and erudite critics of the collective security concept was the international lawyer, John Bassett Moore. He wrote in 1933: "Neutrality always has had . . . the highly moral and expedient object of preventing the spread of war; and it furthermore prohibits the doing in time of peace of acts designed to contribute to the starting of wars abroad. [Formerly] neutrality was chiefly offensive to war-mongers and profiteers. Today, however, . . . it is even more detested by the devotees of peace through force. But even they should be willing to reflect on the fact that its abolition would make every war potentially a world war . . ." (Moore, "An Appeal to Reason," *Collected Papers of John Bassett Moore* [New Haven, Conn.: Yale University Press, 1944] 6:440). Moore noted that it was not at all easy to determine objectively, in most cases of conflict, which party initiated it. Ibid., 337. In an earlier contribution to a collection of essays on the League of Nations Covenant, he drew attention to the fact that "the causes that operate to produce international wars likewise produce civil wars," and that the latter were as frequent and as destructive as the former ("Some Essentials of a League for Peace" [1919], reprinted in *Collected Papers*, 5:67-70).

5. Winston Churchill, *Triumph and Tragedy*, vol. 6 of *The Second World War* (Boston: Houghton Mifflin Co., 1953), 227-35.

6. J. William Fulbright, "In Thrall to Fear," *The New Yorker*, Jan. 8, 1972, 41.

7. Dean Acheson, *Power and Diplomacy* (Cambridge, Mass.: Harvard University Press, 1958), 41-2.

8. "The very existence of the Greek state is today threatened by the terrorist activities of several thousand armed men, led by Communists, who defy the Government's authority at a number of points, particularly along the northern boundaries. A commission appointed by the United Nations Security Council is at present investigating disturbed conditions along the frontiers. . . . The Greek army is small and poorly equipped. It needs supplies and equipment. . . ." (*New York Times*, March 13, 1947).

9. Acheson, *Present at the Creation* (New York: W.W. Norton & Co., 1969), 223.

10. Arthur H. Vandenberg, Jr., ed. *The Private Papers of Senator Vandenberg* (Boston: Houghton Mifflin Co., 1952), 344-6.

11. In the summer of 1949 Yugoslavia received a loan from the Export-Import Bank, and an export license for a steel finishing mill. Yugoslavia later received other American loans and military equipment.

The apparent success and very moderate cost of the American intervention in Greece invites comparison with the disastrous results of the later American intervention in Vietnam. There were significant differences. As the United Nations Commission of Investigation found, the rebellion drew on support from the three countries to the north. Some of the soldiers in the guerrilla army were from ethnic minorities interested in the creation of a Macedonian state in a projected Balkan federation. The Greek government, monarchist, rightist, and repressive as it was, was a far more independent and national regime than any of the governments in Saigon. And there were much closer historical, cultural and political links between the Greek people and those of the United States than between Americans and Vietnamese. If the United States had not intervened, the E.A.M. might have come to power, as Britain felt unable to continue to support the government. It is fruitless to speculate as to what "Greek socialism" might have been like, or whether it would have been better or worse than the Greek governments since 1949. It seems unlikely, however, that a leftist Greek regime would follow the Russian pattern. Cultural and historical differences are too great for that.

CHAPTER 2: WORLD ORDER TODAY

1. General Assembly Res. 2625 (XXV), October 24, 1970. The Legal Adviser of the Department of State relied on this Declaration, along with the Charter itself, as establishing the illegality of the Soviet intervention in Afghanistan. Memorandum of Legal Adviser Roberts B. Owen to Acting Secretary of State Warren Christoper, December 29, 1979, quoted in Marian L. Nash, "Contemporary Practice of the United States Relating to International Law," *American Journal of International Law* 74 (1980):418-9. Rejecting a Soviet claim that their action was justified by a 1978 treaty with Afghanistan, the Legal Adviser's memorandum stated:

"No treaty between the USSR and Afghanistan can overcome these Charter obligations of the USSR. Article 103 of the Charter provides: 'In the event of conflict between the obligations of the Members of the United Nations under the present Charter and their obligations under any other international agreement, their obligations under the present Charter shall prevail.'

"Nor is it clear that the treaty between the USSR and Afghanistan, concluded in 1978 between the revolutionary Taraki Government and the USSR, is valid. If it actually does lend itself to support of Soviet intervention of the type in question in Afghanistan, it would be void under contemporary principles of international law, since it would conflict with what the Vienna Convention on the Law of Treaties describes as a 'peremptory norm of general international law' (Article 53) namely, that contained in Article 2, paragraph 4 of the Charter. While agreement on precisely what are the peremptory norms of international law is not broad, there is universal agreement that the exemplary illustration of a peremptory norm is Article 2, paragraph 4."

2. Previously, on December 11, 1946, the General Assembly had unanimously affirmed the principle recognized in the Charter of the Nuremberg Military Tribunal that the planning or making of aggressive war was an international criminal offense. UN General Assembly, *Official Records*, 1st Session, 1144.

3. General Assembly Res. 3314(XXIX), Dec. 14, 1974.

4. It thus restated the cardinal Pan-American principle of non-intervention which the United States, after habitual violations of the principle between 1903 and 1933, had finally accepted in 1933 and which was enshrined in the Convention on the Rights and Duties of States, signed at Montevideo in

December 1933. It became the foundation of Roosevelt's "Good Neighbor Policy."

5. Nehru claimed Indian heritage for the "Panch Shila" or "Five Principles of Coexistence," but the principles were no more than those stated in the UN Charter. They had been proclaimed also in Mao Tse-tung's 1949 statement of the basis on which diplomatic relations should be established between Communist China and other countries. Mao Tse-tung, *Selected Works* (New York: International Publishers) 5:408.

6. The conflict between the Arab states and Israel, which has produced a whole series of wars, is *sui generis*, a prolongation and extension, in effect, of the original civil war in Palestine which erupted when Britain relinquished its Mandate over that territory.

7. When Chinese Vice Premier Deng Xiaoping visited President Carter in Washington in February 1979, he gave the United States advance notice of China's intention to undertake a limited military action against Viet Nam as punishment for Viet Nam's invasion of Cambodia. The Carter administration was anxious not to damage the new cordiality between the United States and China, but decided it could not approve action that was "tantamount to overt military aggression." Zbigniew Brzezinski, *Power and Principle* (New York: Farrar, Straus, Giroux, 1983), 409-12. Deng was advised in restrained terms that the international consequences were likely to be adverse. In subsequent Security Council debate, the U.S. representative called for observance of the Charter rules against the use of force and against interference in other States, and took refuge in a call for withdrawal of *all* foreign troops, lumping together the Chinese who had attacked Viet Nam and the Vietnamese who had invaded Cambodia.

8. The Korean conflict was an unusual and exceptional case. The Communist side apparently expected that it would be treated as a civil conflict and that outside nations would refrain from intervention. The UN majority, however, focused on the transgression of an internationally established boundary between separate *de facto* entities and saw an act of international aggression, to which it responded with a UN-approved enforcement action.

9. The United Nations itself was not authorized to intervene in matters of domestic jurisdiction, without prejudice to the application of enforcement measures under Chapter VII (Art. 2, para. 7).

10. Declaration on the Inadmissibility of Intervention, General Assembly Res. 2131 (XX), Dec. 21, 1965. The sole abstention of the United Kingdom was based on its view that the declaration was more political than legal, and too vague and imprecise.

11. General Assembly Res. 2625 (XXV), Oct. 24, 1970.

12. General Assembly Res. 1514 (XV), Dec. 14, 1960. See also the Declaration on Elimination of All Forms of Racial Discrimination, which was adopted unanimously in 1963. General Assembly Res. 1904 (XVIII), Nov. 20, 1963.

13. Zdenek Cervenka, *The Organization of African Unity and its Charter* (New York: Frederick A. Praeger, 1969), 37-8.

14. Louis Henkin reaches a different conclusion. Following a discussion of the political difficulties in the way of applying rules against intervention, he writes: "For the present, then, it may be better to leave the authority of Article 2 (4) clear and undisputed to cover at least cases of direct, overt aggression that are generally capable of objective and persuasive proof. The battle of interventions . . . will have to be fought with little help from law" (Henkin, *How Nations Behave*, 2d ed. [New York: Columbia University Press, 1979], 160).

15. Patrick M. Norton, "Between the Ideology and the Reality: the Shadow of the Law of Neutrality," *Harvard International Law Journal* 17 (Spring, 1976): 249-311.

16. United States, *Department of State Bulletin* 56 (1967):949-50.

CHAPTER 3: DECISIONS THAT RISK NUCLEAR WAR

1. Office of Technology Assessment, *The Effects of Nuclear War* (Washington, D.C.: GPO, 1979). That study, which had the cooperation of the executive branch, stresses the very high degree to which the extent of damage from any nuclear conflict is impossible to predict. Damage might vary enormously depending upon the time of day when a nuclear strike occurs, the season of the year, winds and weather, and the megatonnage of the weapons used. *See also*, R.P. Turco and others, "Nuclear Winter: Global Consequences of Multiple Nuclear Explosions," *Science* 222 (Dec. 23, 1983):1283-92; Paul R. Ehrlich and others, "Long-term Biological Consequences of Nuclear War," ibid., 1293-1300; and Carl Sagan, "Nuclear War and Climatic Catastrophe," *Foreign Affairs* 62 (Winter 1983/84): 257-92.

2. McGeorge Bundy, "To Cap the Volcano," *Foreign Affairs* 48 (October 1969): 9-10.

3. Ibid., 12.

4. Herman Kahn, *On Escalation* (New York: Frederick A. Praeger, 1965), 10-5, 291-2; Karl Deutsch, *The Analysis of International Relations*, 2d ed. (Prentice-Hall, 1978), 143-61.

5. *For. Rel. U.S.* (1948) 2:1188, 1192. Regret that the United States had ever let itself get into such an exposed and militarily indefensible position was felt by General Bedell Smith, U.S. ambassador in Moscow. Ibid., 1194.

6. When the Soviet military command first claimed a right to inspect U.S. military trains in the early spring, General Clay did dispatch "a test train with a few armed guards" towards Berlin to probe Soviet intentions. The Russians shunted the train onto a siding. It was then withdrawn. Clay's proposal to send an armed convoy, with engineering equipment and after notice of intention to the Russians, was made after the Soviet military administration had stopped all rail traffic on the pretext of "technical difficulties." *For. Rel. U.S.* (1948) 2:911-2, 917-8, 957-8; cf. Acheson, *Present at the Creation*, 262.

7. Article 37, para. 1 provides: "Should the parties to a dispute of the nature referred to in Article 33 fail to settle it by the means indicated in that Article, they shall refer it to the Security Council."

8. Philip C. Jessup, "The Berlin Blockade and the Use of the United Nations," *Foreign Affairs* 50 (1971): 163-73; Jessup, "Park Avenue Diplomacy—Ending the Berlin Blockade," *Political Science Quarterly* 87 (1972): 377-400.

9. Russia gained a technological advantage in 1957, achieving, with "Sputnik," the first successful launching and re-entry into the earth's atmosphere of a potentially military payload, but the United states quickly caught up and then outdistanced the Soviet Union in the number of missiles in its arsenal.

10. *Dept. State Bull.* 40 (1959): 81-9.

11. U.S. reply to the Soviet note, Dec. 31, 1958, *Dept. State Bull.* 40 (1959): 79; U.S. Memorandum, "Legal Aspects of the Berlin Situation," ibid., 5; U.S. note to the USSR July 17, 1961, *Dept. State Bull.* 45 (1961): 223; Report to the Nation by President Kennedy, July 25, 1961, ibid., 267.

12. Richard Stebbins, *The United States in World Affairs, 1959* (New York: Harper, 1960), 182.

13. Dwight D. Eisenhower, *Waging Peace* (New York: Doubleday, 1965), 334.

14. *New York Times Magazine*, Mar. 8, 1959.

15. Eisenhower, *Waging Peace*, 331.

16. Ibid., 340.

17. Ibid., 341.

18. *New York Times*, March 12, 1959. In this statement the President seemed to agree with the view expressed in the Soviet note of November 27, 1958 that "only madmen can go to the length of unleashing another world war over the preservation of privileges of occupiers in West Berlin." The trouble was that Khrushchev seemed to think that he had shifted this burden to the United States, which would be the initiator of any overt military action.

19. *Dept. State Bull.* 41 (1959): 152-3.

20. The decision for a program of illegal U-2 overflights of the Soviet Union was a highly risky venture. Eisenhower has described the way the decision was made and how the program grew. The justification for the program was the new Soviet capacity for surprise attack against the United States. Eisenhower was asked to authorize the program in November 1954 by John Foster Dulles, CIA Director Allen Dulles, and Defense Secretary Charles Wilson. Total cost: $35 million. Secrecy limited the number of advisers in on the discussion. "A good deal of design and development work had already been done." "Go ahead and get the equipment, I said, but before initiating operations come in to let me have one last look at the plans." Then came the decision to use the U-2s to intrude over Soviet territory. CIA and military advisers argued that the risks were small: 1) The unique configuration of the plane was such that it was unlikely to be mistaken for a bomber. 2) Soviet radar might not be able to track it and Soviet fighter planes could not reach its altitude. 3) Its construction was so fragile that "in the event of mishap the plane would virtually disintegrate." So the flights were begun in 1956. It was learned that the Soviets knew of the flights, had unsuccessfully tried fighter interception, and were working to

develop defensive rockets. In the light of this knowledge, with each new series of flights there was a meeting to decide whether it was wise to continue. Eisenhower expressed concern that "if ever one of the planes fell in Soviet territory a wave of excitement mounting almost to panic would sweep the world. . . . The others disagreed. Secretary Dulles, for instance, would say laughingly, 'if the Soviets ever capture one of these planes, I'm sure they will never admit it. To do so would make it necessary for them to admit also that for years we had been carrying on flights . . .' " The flights had produced important intelligence, especially of a negative character, showing proof that the feared "missile gap" in favor of the Soviet Union had not materialized. Finally, bureaucratic inertia militated against bringing the flights to an end. "With the record of many successful flights behind us," Eisenhower recalled, "the intelligence people became more and more confident that the outcome of each venture was almost a certainty." Eisenhower again approved a spring program of flights for 1960. The U-2 was shot down on May 1. Eisenhower, *Waging Peace*, 544-7.

21. Ibid., 557.

22. Arthur M. Schlesinger, Jr., *A Thousand Days* (Boston: Houghton Mifflin, 1965), 390.

23. In his address of October 22, 1962, Kennedy included a warning that "any hostile move anywhere in the world against the safety and freedom of peoples to whom we are committed—including in particular the brave people of West Berlin—will be met by whatever action is needed" (*Dept. State Bull.* 47 [1962]: 718).

24. U.S. Department of State, *Treaties and Other International Acts Series* (hereafter cited as "TIAS"), no. 7551.

25. Ibid., p. 92; *New York Times*, Dec. 18 and Dec. 21, 1971.

26. Abram Chayes, *The Cuban Missile Crisis* (New York and London: Oxford University Press, 1974).

27. Schlesinger, *A Thousand Days*, 830. In his address to the nation Kennedy warned that the United States would "regard any nuclear missile launched from Cuba against any nation in the Western Hemisphere as an attack by the Soviet Union on the United States, requiring a full retaliatory response upon the Soviet Union." With respect to a possible Soviet countermove against West Berlin, he was less specific. See note 23, above.

28. Robert F. Kennedy, *Thirteen Days* (New York: W.W. Norton & Co., 1969), 108-9.

29. Henry Kissinger, *Years of Upheaval* (Boston: Little Brown & Co., 1982), 575-99.

30. David Shipler, "Scorn for U.S. in Israel," *New York Times*, March 1, 1984.

CHAPTER 4: LIMITED WAR IN KOREA

1. On this early period of the military occupation, see Soon Sung Cho, *Korea in World Politics 1940-1950* (Berkeley, Calif.: University of California Press, 1967), 65-100.

2. *For. Rel. U.S.* (1945) 6:1144-8.

3. On the proceedings in the "Little Assembly," see Philip Jessup, *The Birth of Nations* (New York: Columbia University Press, 1974), 31-42.

4. All UN members except the Soviet bloc saw what had occurred as external attack rather than civil rebellion. "The Soviet view that Korea at that stage was one legal entity was untenable" (Rosalyn Higgins, *United Nations Peacekeeping 1946-1967* [London and New York: Oxford University Press, 1970], 2: 176).

5. Philip Jessup recalled the President's mood after his hurried return to Washington on June 25: "As we were gathered in the outer room before dinner and the President had heard the latest news . . . he sat on the window seat and I heard him repeating, half to himself, 'We can't let the UN down! We can't let the UN down!' " (Jessup, *The Birth of Nations*, 10).

6. *Congressional Record*, 81st Cong., 2d sess., 96: 9320 (June 28, 1950); Acheson, *Present at the Creation*, 414-5.

7. *Dept. State Bull.* 23 (1950): 173-7.

8. *For. Rel. U.S.* (1950) 7: 148, 176-7, 229.

9. Before the question of command of the UN forces was decided, Secretary-General Trygve Lie had circulated to the U.S., British, and French delegations a draft resolution which would have established a "Committee on Coordination of Assistance for Korea." It would be composed initially of Australia, India, New Zealand, Norway, the United Kingdom, and the United States, with a representative of the Republic of Korea, and the Secretary-General as Rapporteur. It was intended to keep the United Nations "in the picture" and to furnish liaison between the Security Council and the command. Lie states that the United Kingdom, France, and Norway liked the idea, but that the United States turned it down. Lie, *In the Cause of Peace* (New York: Macmillan, 1954), 333-4.

10. *Dept. State Bull.* 23 (1950); 43, 46; Harry Truman, *Memoirs* (New York: Doubleday, 1956) 2: 341.

11. *For. Rel. U.S.* (1950) 7: 272.

12. Ibid., 386. Korean President Syngman Rhee had also begun to argue vehemently for seizing the opportunity to unify Korea.

13. Ibid., 453-4.

14. Ibid., 528-9.

15. Ibid., 646, 653.

16. Ibid., 712, 716.

17. Ibid., 668-70.

18. U.S. Senate, *Reviews of the World Situation: 1949-1950,* Hearings Held in Executive Session Before the Committee on Foreign Relations, 81st Cong., Historical Series (1974), 350-1; *For. Rel. U.S.* (1950) 7: 747-8.

19. *For. Rel. U.S.* (1950) 7: 781, 793n, 826n, 860n.

20. Article 12 of the UN Charter provides: "1. While the Security Council is exercising in respect of any dispute or situation the functions assigned to it in the present Charter, the General Assembly shall not make any

recommendation with regard to that dispute or situation unless the Security Council so requests."
21. *For. Rel. U.S.* (1950) 7: 763-4.
22. Ibid., 790-4, 809-10.
23. Richard Neustadt, *Presidential Power* (New York: John Wiley & Sons, 1960) 139.
24. *For. Rel. U.S.* (1950) 7: 870, 896-7.
25. Ibid., 948-60.
26. Acheson, *Present at the Creation*, 468.
27. *For. Rel. U.S.* (1950) 7: 1242-8, 1276-82.
28. *Dept. State Bull.* 22 (1950): 79. This statement was timed to coincide with British recognition of the Chinese communist government.
29. *For. Rel. U.S.* (1946) 8: 175.
30. *For Rel. U.S.* (1948) 7: 604.
31. Ibid., 662.
32. *For Rel. U.S.* (1949) 9: 343.
33. Ibid., 271, 348-50.
34. Ibid., 826-34, 295, 466.
35. *Dept. State Bull.* 22 (1950): 80.
36. *For. Rel. U.S.* (1949) 9: 21-3.
37. Ibid., 8: 350, 357-60.
38. Fugh was a Chinese who was almost an adopted son to Leighton Stuart. For a brief biographical sketch of this remarkable man, see Stuart, *Fifty Years in China* (New York: Random House, 1954), 121-5, 291-4.
39. *For. Rel. U.S.* (1949) 8: 741-69, 791. For an earlier attempt by Mao and Chou to secure recognition by the United States, *see* Barbara Tuchman, "If Mao had come to Washington," *Foreign Affairs* 51 (1972): 44-64.
40. U.S. Department of State, *United States Relations with China*, Dept. State Pub. 3573 (August 1949).
41. *For Rel. U.S.* (1949) 8: 544-5; 9: 93, 117-8.
42. *For. Rel. U.S.* (1949) 9: 151-4.
43. Michael Hunt, "Mao and Accommodation with the U.S.," in Dorothy Borg and Waldo Heinrichs, *Uncertain Years: Chinese-American Relations 1947-1950* (New York: Columbia University Press, 1980), 204.
44. *For. Rel. U.S.* (1950) 6: 270-2, 286-9; Warren Cohen, "Acheson and China," in Borg and Heinrichs, *Uncertain Years*, 40-1.
45. *For. Rel. U.S.* (1950) 6: 321-2, 327-9.
46. *Congressional Record*, 81st Cong., 1st sess. (1949) 95: 472.
47. Ibid., 1554-8.
48. Rusk had been Deputy Under Secretary of State and took a reduction of pay to fill the FE position. "On record for his outspoken anti-Communist views [and] having had no part in the previous formulation of China policy, Rusk was free of any taint of mistrust or suspicion.... [He] was expected to command—and indeed did—far more confidence among members of the congressional China bloc than any of his predecessors in the Far Eastern

Division" (Foster Rhea Dulles, *American Policy Toward Communist China 1949-1969* [New York: Thomas Y. Crowell Co., 1972], 82).

49. *For. Rel. U.S.* (1950) 1: 314-6. A strong argument for U.S. intervention to save Formosa was also sent to Washington by MacArthur on June 14. He described the island as an essential link in the island defense line which included the Aleutians, Japan, and the Philippines, and argued that the promise to return it to China "was given in consonance with a political situation entirely different from that which now exists."

50. *For. Rel. U.S.* (1950) 6: 347-9.

51. *For. Rel. U.S.* (1950) 7: 158, 180.

52. UN Security Council, *Official Records*, 490th Meeting (Aug. 25, 1950).

53. Security Council, *Official Records*, 474th Meeting (June 27, 1950).

54. Royal Institute of International Affairs (London), *Documents on International Affairs* (1949-50): 633-4. On August 24th Chou addressed a formal complaint of U.S. aggression to the Security Council, with a request for action to secure withdrawal of the American fleet. Security Council, *Official Records*, 490th Meeting (Aug. 25, 1950), 9. It was not until the end of November that the question came up for debate. That was after the Chinese communist forces had attacked the UN forces in Korea, and only the Soviet Union favored a resolution to condemn the United States (India did not participate in the voting).

55. *For. Rel. U.S.* (1950) 7: 330, 349.

56. Ibid., 430.

57. Ibid., 1406.

58. *The Works of Thomas Jefferson*, ed. Paul L. Ford (New York, London: G.P. Putnam's sons, 1904-5) 7: 283.

59. John Bassett Moore, *Digest of International Law* (Washington, 1906) 1: 78. Italics added.

60. Herbert A. Smith, *Great Britain and the Law of Nations* (London, 1932) 1: 166-70.

61. *For. Rel. U.S.* (1913), 100.

62. Questions of claims remained unsettled. On the British side the claims were for financial obligations of the Tsarist government. There were Soviet counterclaims growing out of British participation in the Allied military intervention of 1918-19. The distinction between *de facto* and *de jure* recognition is made particularly by the British. While *de facto* recognition was not accompanied by formal diplomatic relations, it indicated acceptance of the new regime as the government of a state, possessing the rights and obligations assigned to governments by international law. In the course of the Spanish Civil War, the British government recognized the Franco regime "as a government which at present exercises *de facto* control over the larger portion of Spain." But this was little more than a recognition of insurgency or belligerency. Britain was observing the role of a neutral between the Franco government and the government in Madrid which was still recognized as the *de jure* government of Spain.

63. *For. Rel. U.S.* (1920) 3: 463-8.

64. J.B. Moore, "Candor and Common Sense," *Collected Papers*, 6: 360, 363-4.
65. Ibid., 471.
66. Henry Stimson and McGeorge Bundy, *On Active Service in War and Peace* (New York: Harper, 1948), 101.
67. Stimson's diary recorded Hoover's statement that "he would fight for Continental United States as far as anybody, but he would not fight for Asia" (ibid., 243-4).
68. Green Hackworth, *Digest of International Law* (Washington: GPO, 1940), 1:344.
69. *Public Papers of the Secretaries-General of the United Nations*, vol. 1, *Trygve Lie 1946-1953*, ed. Andrew Cordier and Wilder Foote (New York: Columbia University Press, 1969), 261-6.
70. Trygve Lie, *In the Cause of Peace* (New York: Macmillan, 1954), 261.
71. *For. Rel. U.S.* (1950) 2: 256-7.
72. Ibid., 280-5, 289-90.

CHAPTER 5: THE POLICIES OF EISENHOWER AND DULLES

1. Robert Dallek, *Franklin D. Roosevelt and American Foreign Policy, 1932-1945* (New York: Oxford University Press, 1979), 39, 78-81.
2. Jessup, *The Birth of Nations*, 43-92.
3. *For. Rel. U.S.* (1943) 3: 37, 39; ibid. (1944) 5: 1206; ibid. (1945) 1: 124, 6: 293.
4. *For. Rel. U.S.* (1945) 6: 307.
5. "Causes, Origins, and Lessons of the Vietnam War," Hearings Before the Senate Committee on Foreign Relations, 92d Cong., 2d sess. (1972), 319.
6. *For. Rel. U.S.* (1945) 6: 313.
7. Bernard B. Fall ed., *Ho Chi Minh on Revolution, Selected Writings* (New York: Frederick A. Praeger, 1967), 143-5.
8. *For. Rel. U.S.* (1946) 8: 27.
9. *Pentagon Papers*, Senator Gravel ed. (Boston: Beacon Press, 1971), 1: 18.
10. *For. Rel. U.S.* (1946) 8: 36.
11. It did not recognize the Government of the Democratic Republic of Vietnam until January 1950.
12. *For. Rel. U.S.* (1947) 6: 67-8.
13. *For. Rel. U.S.* (1948) 6: 43-9.
14. *For. Rel. U.S.* (1950) 6: 43.
15. *For. Rel. U.S.* (1952-1954) vol. 13, *Indochina*, 1137ff., 1236-7, 1252.
16. Ibid., 1241-3, 1252-3.
17. Ridgeway based his argument on reports of a team of experts he sent to Indochina. His analysis of the prospects of intervention was accurate and prophetic. *Soldier: The Memoirs of Matthew B. Ridgeway* (New York: Harper, 1956), 275-80. The Army estimated that 7 to 12 U.S. divisions might be required *(Pentagon Papers*, Gravel ed., 1: 471-2).
18. *For. Rel. U.S.* (1952-1954) 13: 1251.

19. *Dept. State Bull.* 30 (1954): 539-42.
20. *For. Rel. U.S.* (1952-1954) 13: 1211-2.
21. Ibid., 1174ff.
22. Ibid., 1224-5.
23. Ibid., 1230, 1239-40.
24. Anthony Eden, *Full Circle* (Boston: Houghton Mifflin, 1960), 103.
25. Ibid., 105.
26. *For. Rel. U.S.* (1952-1954) 13: 1423.
27. Ibid., 953, 1262.
28. Ibid., 963.
29. Ibid., 1441, cf. 1410-11, 1431-49.
30. Ibid., 1410-11, 1473-5, 1467-70. Secretary Dulles expressed anger at what he considered betrayal by Foreign Secretary Eden. The dislike and distrust between the two, which was later evident in the Suez negotiations of 1956, dated from this period.
31. *For. Rel. U.S.* (1952-1954) 16: 1352, 1390, 1430.
32. Eden, *Full Circle*, 134, 139, 142-3.
33. Robert F. Randle, *Geneva 1954: The Settlement of the Indochinese War* (Princeton: Princeton University Press, 1969), 109-10.
34. Eden, 71, 126-8.
35. China had warned that outside intervention in support of the French would mean "another Korea" (Randle, 154).
36. *For. Rel. U.S.* (1952-1954) 16: 1504-42.
37. Ibid., 1500.
38. Ibid., 1464-5, 1477-8, 1497; Council on Foreign Relations, *Documents on American Foreign Relations* (1954), 315-6.
39. Eisenhower, *Waging Peace*, 337-8, 372.
40. *Pentagon Papers*, Gravel ed., 573-83.
41. *For. Rel. U.S.* (1952-1954) 3: 656.
42. *Dept. State Bull.* 30 (1954): 540-1.
43. *For. Rel. U.S. (1952-1954) 3: 758.*
44. *For. Rel. U.S.* (1950) 6: 543-4.
45. Peter Lyon, *Eisenhower* (Boston: Little Brown & Co., 1974), 622-3.
46. Townsend Hoopes, *The Devil and John Foster Dulles* (Boston: Little, Brown & Co., 1973), 263-6.
47. TIAS 3178.
48. Lyon, *Eisenhower*, 640.
49. Report of the Security Council covering the period from 16 July 1954 to 15 July 1955 (A/2935), General Assembly, *Official Records*, 10th Sess., Supplement no. 2: 19.
50. Security Council, *Official Records*, 689th Meeting (Jan. 31, 1955), 10-11.
51. *Dept. State Bull.* 66 (1972): 437-8.
52. *Dept. State Bull.* 79 (February 1979): 24-5.
53. U.S. Senate, Select Committee to Study Governmental Operations with respect to Intelligence Activities, *Final Report*, 94th Cong., 2d sess., 1976, S. Rept. 94-755, Book 4: 29-33, 36-8. George Kennan, a sponsor of such a

capability in 1948, testified in 1975: "It did not work out at all the way I had conceived it or others of my associates in the Department of State. We had thought that this would be a facility which could be used when and if an occasion arose when it might be needed. There might be years when we wouldn't have to do anything like this. But if the occasion arose we wanted somebody in the Government who would have the funds, the experience, the expertise to do these things" (ibid., 31). It was perhaps naive to assume that such a facility could be created without a program of ongoing activities to employ the personnel. "With budgeting," as the Senate Report notes, "came the need for ongoing activities to justify future allocations" (ibid., 32).

54. Eisenhower, *Waging Peace*, 163.

55. That operation is detailed in Chapter 9.

56. It was concern to prevent communist gains, rather than concern to protect the United Fruit Company, that caused Eisenhower to embark on the operations against Arbenz. UFC had, it is true, labored to convince the U.S. Government and the public that the Guatemalan Government which expropriated their property had communist connections.

57. *Dept. State Bull.* 30 (1954): 419.

58. A description of the operation, based on previously unpublished sources, is given in Blanche W. Cook, *The Declassified Eisenhower* (Garden City, N.Y.: Doubleday, 1981), 263-91; *see also* Lyon, *Eisenhower*, 588-92, 609-15.

59. Security Council, *Official Records*, 675th Meeting (June 20, 1954).

60. Brian Urquhart, *Hammarskjold* (New York: Knopf, 1972), 92.

61. Dulles conceded privately that this U.S. blockade was illegal. Lyon, *Eisenhower*, 609.

62. Cook, *Declassified Eisenhower*, 268, 281-2.

63. In 1965 the CIA again participated in a revolt against Sukarno, which this time produced the bloody overthrow of his regime. Thomas Powers, *The Man Who Kept the Secrets: Richard Helms and the CIA* (New York: Knopf, 1979), 88-92.

64. Eden's memoirs were published before the first revelations of American complicity in the Iranian coup d'etat, and said nothing about foreign influence on that event, but Eden was well aware of the action the United States had taken. The Guatemalan intervention was already common knowledge, and of it Eden wrote: "We could not help contrasting the American attitude [in the Suez Crisis] with our own attitude at the time of the Guatemalan campaign. In that country the United States had encouraged the overthrow of a Communist-influenced government, which it considered a menace to the peace of Central America. We had understood her action there and done what we could not to hamper her in the Security Council. The United States was now behaving in a precisely contrary manner towards us. When this point was put to the United States officials, they had no answer" (Eden, *Full Circle*, 634). Another member of the British Cabinet under Eden later reported that, before Suez, British and American officials had also discussed together the possibilities of organizing a coup in Egypt "on the lines

of the one which had overthrown Mossadeq in Iran" (Anthony Nutting, *Nasser* [New York: E.P. Dutton, 1972], 136).

65. Eisenhower, *Waging Peace*, 665, 666.

66. Dulles, who brought Eisenhower's message, told the British and French foreign secretaries, in Eden's paraphrase, "Force was the last method to be tried, but the United States did not exclude the use of force if all other methods failed" (Eden, *Full Circle*, 486-7).

67. Hoopes, *Devil and John Foster Dulles*, 350-1.

68. It stated that it would be willing to join with the other signatories of the Convention of 1888 in sponsoring a conference of all the states using the canal in order to reconsider the Convention.

69. Eisenhower, *Waging Peace*, 46.

70. U.S. Dept. of State, *The Suez Canal Problem* (Washington: GPO, 1956), 174-5. Hoopes notes that this could have been a turning point in the crisis: "The American President was ready and willing to put his weight behind a proposal that Nasser would almost surely have accepted, that was supported by . . . India, Russia, Indonesia and Ceylon. If vigorously led by the United States, this combination could almost certainly have isolated Britain and France at the conference and brought about a negotiation with Nasser which London and Paris could have threatened to disrupt by military action only at great peril to their reputations and security . . . [Eisenhower] too readily receded from his instinctively sound feeling for the middle ground where serious negotiation was possible" (Hoopes, 354-5).

71. Eisenhower, *Waging Peace*, 46.

72. Ibid., 184-9; *Dept. State Bull.* 36 (1957): 387-91.

73. He expressed these thoughts forcefully and repeatedly in personal letters to Eden and Churchill. Eisenhower, *Waging Peace*, 664-71, 678-81.

74. Ibid., 665, 667, 669-70.

CHAPTER 6: MILITARY INTERVENTION IN VIETNAM

1. Professor Henkin has aptly pointed out that the arguments depended on debatable alternate characterizations of the facts:

A. Civil war in an independent state of South Vietnam, with the United States and a separate state of North Vietnam both intervening on opposite sides;

B. Civil war in a single state of Vietnam, with the Vietcong and the Hanoi government on one side and the Saigon regime on the other, and with outside intervention by the United States; or

C. An armed attack by North Vietnam, and its Vietcong agents in the South, against an independent South Vietnam, with the United States participating in South Vietnam's defense. Henkin, *How Nations Behave*, 306-8.

The official justification of American intervention was based on the third characterization. Department of State, "Aggression from the North," Dept. State Pub. No. 7839, printed as House Doc. 136, 89th Cong., 1st sess., March 11, 1965; "The Legality of United States Participation in the Defense of Vietnam"

(Memorandum by the State Department's Legal Adviser, Leonard C. Meeker), *Dept. State Bull.* 54 (1966): 474-89.

2. UN General Assembly, *Official Records*, 21st Sess., 1420th Meeting (Sept. 28, 1966).

3. Arthur M. Schlesinger, Jr., *Robert Kennedy and His Times* (Boston: Houghton Mifflin, 1978), 765-6; cf. 703-4. DeGaulle offered to join in an effort to establish a unified Vietnam, to be free from all foreign influence. According to Schlesinger, Kennedy was attracted to the idea, but perhaps felt he could not pursue a political settlement before the 1964 election. Ibid., 719-23.

4. Charles de Gaulle, *Memoirs of Hope* (New York: Simon & Schuster, 1971), 256.

5. In August 1964, American planes struck North Vietnam in retaliation for an alleged attack on American destroyers in the Tonkin Gulf. In February 1965 a continuing program of American air attacks was begun. In March 1965 the United States first sent American ground combat units to South Vietnam.

6. Schlesinger, *Robert Kennedy*, 701.

7. Boston: Little, Brown & Co., 1972.

8. *New York Times,* July 31, 1979.

9. Besides the overt U.S. intervention in Vietnam, secret paramilitary operations by the CIA reached their peak during the Vietnamese war. President Johnson authorized a secret war by a native army led and supported by the CIA in Laos (violating the neutralization of that country which had been agreed to in the 1962 Geneva Agreement on Laos). He also used the CIA to organize and support South Vietnamese raids into North Vietnam from the sea. These raids, of which Congress was not informed, were supported by the U.S. Navy and were one of the material causes of the North Vietnamese attack on American destroyers which Johnson, without telling Congress of the secret hostile actions of U.S. naval forces, used as the basis for his appeal to Congress to authorize overt military action, ostensibly defensive, in Vietnam. During the Nixon administration, bombing raids on neutral Cambodia, which were concealed from Congress and the public by intentionally false military reports, long preceded the American invasion of that country in May 1970, and the CIA's secret war in Laos was greatly augmented. The habit of illegality which developed from these and other secret actions had subversive consequences within the United States. In clear violation of American laws, officials of the executive branch were falsifying reports and lying to Congress. This made it difficult for Congress to perform its function as participant in decisions on war and peace and as a check against presidential usurpation. More broadly, the principle of free discussion and debate on public policy was subverted. The press was impeded from performing its proper role. And from the use of secret and illegal methods against foreigners it was a short and easy step to the use of the same methods and police powers against domestic political opponents. Since the breaking of the Watergate case, there have come to light numerous instances of executive misuse of the CIA and the FBI to violate the civil rights of Americans. False slanderous attacks on individual reputations, illegal wiretaps, and "black bag jobs" against domestic critics or dissidents became

commonplace under Nixon. American Socialists, civil rights activists, and anti-war groups were the principal victims. The Watergate affair produced fortunate corrective action, but the issues raised by official resort to illegal methods are still alive.

CHAPTER 7: COMBATTING REVOLUTIONS IN LATIN AMERICA

1. Philip Bonsal, U.S. ambassador to Cuba, believed that these raids, which violated the American anti-filibustering law, were the illegal acts of private persons. He thought that up to March of 1960 the United States had been strictly adhering to its non-intervention commitments under hemisphere treaties and the UN Charter. Of the raid on Havana on October 21, 1959, in which anti-Castro leaflets were dropped and several Havana residents were killed by anti-aircraft shell fragments, Bonsal wrote: "I do not know how Diaz-Lanz [a Cuban exile] acquired the plane in question [a B-25 bomber converted to cargo-carrier]. . . . I cannot suppose that at this stage of the game any American government agency would have involved itself in a project of this kind. The flight was a most regrettable one and one which . . . was bad from the point of view of a United States government trying sincerely to find a reasonable basis of relations with the Cuban government. It could benefit only those endeavoring to sow hatred and distrust of the United States in Cuba, that is, Castro and the people who were increasingly dominant in his councils. Untroubled by any considerations of truth or good faith, the Cuban authorities distorted the facts of the matter and accused the United States of a responsibility going far beyond negligence" (Philip W. Bonsal, *Cuba, Castro, and the United States* [Pittsburgh: University of Pittsburgh Press, 1971], 105).

2. Ibid., 151, 147-53.

3. Not until the 2nd of December, 1961 did Castro declare himself to be "a Marxist-Leninist," and the Cuban revolution "a Socialist and anti-imperialist revolution" (*New York Times*, December 3, 1961).

4. This was the tactic that Theodore Roosevelt employed at Panama in 1903. Hitler and Mussolini had also employed it in the Spanish Civil War, and more recently, the Russians in Hungary.

5. Bowles' memorandum suggested an alternative which pre-visioned the 1962 quarantine of Cuba: "If . . . the Soviet Union should attempt to provide an aggressive Castro with substantially larger amounts of arms, including naval vessels, we would have the power to throw a blockade around Cuba and to extend it, if necessary, to petroleum supplies. Technically, this, too, would be an act of war. However, I believe we would find it vastly easier to live with direct action of this kind in the face of what we would fairly describe as an open Soviet move to establish Cuba as a military base than with the covert action now under consideration" (Chester Bowles, *Promises to Keep: My Years in Public Life* [New York: Harper & Row, 1971], 327-8).

6. Roger Hilsman, *To Move a Nation* (New York: Doubleday, 1967), 31.

7. Schlesinger, *A Thousand Days*, 247-8.

8. Ibid., 260-1.

9. Bowles, *Promises to Keep*, 444.

10. Ibid., 343.

11. Schlesinger, *A Thousand Days*, 262.

12. *RN: Memoirs of Richard Nixon* (New York: Grosset and Dunlop, 1978), 234. For Nixon, a principal use of international law was to provide "cover stories" to disguise real intentions. In *Six Crises* he relates how he reacted to a speech of Kennedy's during the 1960 presidential campaign, in which Kennedy came out for assistance to the Cuban forces fighting for freedom. Knowing of the invasion plan, which he had vigorously supported as Vice President, Nixon concluded that the right response for him was to misrepresent his own position to the voters: "There was only one thing I could do. The covert operation had to be protected at all costs. I must not even suggest by implication that the United States was rendering aid to rebel forces . . . I must attack the Kennedy proposal . . . as wrong and irresponsible because it would violate our treaty commitments." This he proceeded to do, though he was convinced it would hurt his campaign chances. "The average voter is not interested in the technicalities of treaty obligations. . . . He favors the candidate who wants to do something . . . dramatic and forceful—and not the one who takes the 'statesmanlike' and the 'legalistic' view" (Nixon, *Six Crises* [Garden City, N.Y.: Doubleday, 1962], 354-6).

13. Schlesinger, *Robert Kennedy*, 476-7; Powers, *The Man Who Kept the Secrets*, 132-5.

14. Powers, 133-43; Schlesinger, *Robert Kennedy*, 475-80; U.S. Senate, Select Committee to Study Governmental Operations with respect to Intelligence Activities, *Alleged Assassination Plots Involving Foreign Leaders*, 94th Cong., 1st sess., 1975, S. Rept. 94-465, pp. 141-8 (hereafter cited as "Alleged Assassination Plots").

15. Schlesinger argues that the Kennedys probably did not authorize assassination, but Powers argues strongly that they must have done so, though it was a fundamental stratagem to keep such authorization out of discussion at meetings, and never to put it in writing. Schlesinger, *Robert Kennedy*, 488-98; Powers, 153-8. The Senate's committee studying intelligence activities cited an inspector-general's report that the subject of assassination of Castro was raised at one meeting, and it told of the deletion of a reference to assassination from a memorandum of the meeting, at the instance of a CIA official who expostulated against "the inadmissibility and stupidity of putting this type of comment in writing" (*Alleged Assassination Plots*, 161-2).

16. *Dept. State Bull.* 45 (1961): 461.

17. *Dept. State Bull.* 46 (1962): 281.

18. *See* chapter 3. The Missile Crisis has been so intensively researched and reviewed that a brief resume of the relationship of legal and political considerations should here suffice. Among the best accounts are Robert F. Kennedy, *Thirteen Days* (W.W. Norton & Co., 1969); Elie Abel, *The Missile Crisis* (J.B. Lippincott Co., 1966); Graham T. Allison, *Essence of Decision* (Little Brown & Co., 1971); Abram Chayes, *The Cuban Missile Crisis* (Oxford

University Press, 1974). The book by Chayes focuses specifically on the role of law.

19. Chayes, *Missile Crisis*, 15-6.

20. Ibid., 16, 65. Chayes notes that several of the participants in the discussion took legal positions which accorded with the bureaucratic perspective of the government offices they represented. He wrote: "It is almost impossible that legal considerations should *not* enter the process of decision. They will always tend to favor one or more of the players in the game, who will see that they are brought to bear" (ibid., 35).

21. John Bartlow Martin, *Adlai Stevenson and the World* (Garden City, N.Y.: Doubleday and Co., 1977), 725-35.

22. Exchange of letters, October 27-28, 1962, *Dept. State Bull.* 47 (1962): 743-6.

23. *Dept. State Bull.* 52 (1965): 738.

24. It is reported that General Palmer, who was sent to take command of the American force the day after the first Marines had gone ashore, was told: "Your unstated mission is to prevent the Dominican Republic from going Communist" (Abraham Lowenthal, *The Dominican Intervention* [Cambridge, Mass.: Harvard University Press, 1972], 116). The degree of actual danger that communists would gain control of the regime which would have resulted from a rebel victory had there been no American intervention remains a matter of debate. The rebels were committed to the return of Juan Bosch, as the constitutional president of the country, and no one thought Bosch to be a communist. The armed struggle brought retirement from the battle of some older civilian leaders on the rebel side and replaced them with young military officers who were more militant and possibly more radical. The decision-makers in Washington, driven by their fear of "a second Cuba," repeatedly asked the American embassy and the intelligence services to send them information about communists and communist activity, and they naturally got in return reports which stressed any possible communist connection to the exclusion of other kinds of relevant information. Lowenthal, 82, 110, 153-5. On May 5 Stevenson reported in detail to the Security Council what was known by the United States about communist activity in the Dominican Republic. He spoke of several attempts by Castro before 1965 to infiltrate paramilitary insurrectionists into the country, and he listed nine Dominican communists who were active in the current rebellion. He conceded, however, that most of the participants in the rebellion were not communists. *Dept. State Bull.* 52 (1965): 881-2. In actuality, there was no more than a suspicion that the revolt's leaders *might* turn it in a "Cuban" direction. Senator William Fulbright wrote: "Intervention on the basis of Communist participation as distinguished from control ... was a mistake in my opinion which also reflects a grievous misreading of the temper of contemporary Latin American politics. Communists are present in all Latin American countries, and they are going to inject themselves into almost any Latin American revolution and try to seize control of it. If any group or any movement with which the communists associate themselves is going to be automatically condemned in the eyes of the

United States, then we have indeed given up all hope of guiding or influencing even to a marginal degree the revolutionary movements and the demands for social change which are sweeping Latin America" (*Congressional Record*, 89th Cong., 1st sess., 111: 23858 [Sept. 15, 1965]).

25. Lowenthal, 86, 106.
26. *Dept. State Bull.* 52 (1965): 746.
27. Ibid., 739-41.
28. Ibid., 741. The next day the OAS foreign ministers, with only Chile abstaining, voted to send a five-member committee to the Dominican Republic to offer good offices and aid in the re-establishment of peace.
29. UN Security Council, *Official Records*, 1198th Meeting (May 3, 1965).
30. *Dept. State Bull.* 52 (1965): 862-3.
31. Peacekeeping efforts of the OAS and the UN are summarized in *Yearbook of the United Nations* (1965), 152-5, and *Yearbook* (1966), 125-31.
32. Leonard C. Meeker, "The Dominican situation in the Perspective of International Law" (an address before the Foreign Law Association on June 9), *Dept. State Bull.* 53 (1965): 60-5. There is no indication whether Meeker was asked for advice before the decision to intervene, or what advice he would have given in such a case. He was here performing the role of defense counsel after the fact.
33. J. Ann Zammit, ed., *The Chilean Road to Socialism* (Brighton, England: Kensington Press, 1973), 255 ff.
34. Henry Kissinger, *White House Years* (Boston: Little, Brown and Co., 1979), 653.
35. Ibid., 671.
36. *Alleged Assassination Plots*, 227-8.
37. Seymour M. Hersh, *The Price of Power* (New York: Summit Books, 1983), 259, 274-6.
38. *Alleged Assassination Plots*, 228.
39. Ibid., 256.
40. The domestic causes of Allende's downfall are emphasized in Paul E. Sigmund, *The Overthrow of Allende and the Politics of Chile, 1964-1976* (Pittsburgh: University of Pittsburgh Press, 1977).
41. *Covert Action in Chile, 1963-1973*, Staff Report of the Select Committee to Study Governmental Operations with Respect to Intelligence Activities, U.S. Senate, Dec. 18, 1975, 94th Cong., 1st sess., 1975, Committee Print, 39.
42. U.S. Senate, Select Committee to Study Governmental Operations with Respect to Intelligence Activities, *Final Report*, 94th Cong., 2d sess., 1976, S. Rept. 94-755, Book 4:122.
43. Kissinger, *White House Years*, 674.
44. *Alleged Assassination Plots*, 242-3, 254.
45. Kissinger, *White House Years*, 655, 659.
46. In his effort to show that Allende intended to establish a dictatorship (*White House Years*, 656) Kissinger quotes out of context from Regis Debray, *The Chilean Revolution: Conversations with Allende* (New York: Pantheon Books, 1971). But the Debray interviews, read in their entirety, support the

opposite conclusion. Allende explained that when he spoke of Chile's need for revolution he meant revolution "from the sociological point of view." To a later question he responded, "We have arrived through the polling booths. Apparently it can be said of us that we are mere reformers, but we have taken measures which imply that we want to bring about the revolution, *that is transform society*" (Debray, 116, 127, italics added). He spoke repeatedly of his intent to act within the laws: "The situation in Chile is such that the Constitution can be changed within the Constitution" (97). While speaking of the tendency of Chile's independent judiciary to act as a guardian of economic privilege, he added, "I shall respect the limitations imposed by a system which is not of our making while the three powers exist independently" (103-4). He had indicated his intention to propose laws to reform the judiciary (99). "In some countries," he said, "there is no alternative to the armed struggle: where there are no parties, no trade unions, where there is dictatorship. . . . There, elections offer no hope" (127). This was not the situation of Chile. When Debray referred to the power of money to control the mass media, Allende replied, "We are not going to suppress the communications media which are in bourgeois hands, but we are going to coordinate our own, we are going to increase them . . ." (113). With respect to the "Statute of Democratic Guarantees," he explained that while its introduction was a tactical necessity in order for him to secure election by the Congress, its provisions were entirely consistent with his party's program (119-20). He said that he expected the fact that his government was acting within the Constitution to prevent any United States intervention (126). Allende emphasized his commitment to national independence, saying that the reason he founded the Socialist Party rather than becoming a Communist was that he felt the need for a party that was "free of ties of an international nature" (62). For Chile, national liberation meant the achievement of economic independence, by the nationalization of those fundamental sources of national wealth that were in foreign hands (70-1, 85).

47. *Covert Action in Chile*, 44-5.
48. *Dept. State Bull.* (August 1979): 57, 60.
49. Ibid., 58.
50. *Dept. State Bull.* (November 1979): 56.
51. *Washington Post,* May 8, 1983. In addition to the legal obligations stemming from the relevant treaties, Jefferson's neutrality law of 1794 provides penalties for anyone within the United States who "knowingly begins or sets on foot or provides or prepares a means for or furnishes the money for, or takes part in, any military or naval expedition or enterprise to be carried on from thence against the territory or dominion of any foreign prince or state . . . with whom the United States is at peace." 18 U.S.C. Sec. 960. It is still in force, but the executive branch chooses not to enforce it.
52. TIAS 1598.
53. *Dept. State Bull.* (December, 1983): 6.
54. *Dept. State Bull.* (June, 1983): 5.
55. Statement of Deputy Secretary of State Dam to the House Committee on Foreign Affairs, *American Journal of International Law* 78 (1984): 203.

56. Detlev Vagts, "International Law Under Time Pressure: Grading the Grenada Take-Home Examination," *Am. Jour. of Int'l Law* 78 (1984): 171.

57. *New York Times*, Nov. 4, 1983.

58. *New York Times*, Sept. 19 and Sept. 23, 1983.

59. This episode is documented in H. Gordon Skilling, *Czechoslovakia's Interrupted Revolution* (Princeton, N.J.: Princeton University Press, 1976).

60. *Current Digest of the Soviet Press* 20, no. 46 (Dec. 4, 1968): 3.

61. Skilling, 729. "Socialist community," used in some translations, is a more accurate rendition from the Russian.

CHAPTER 8: DECISIONS CONCERNING AFRICA

1. Georges Abi-Saab, *The United Nations Operation in the Congo 1960-1964* (New York and London: Oxford University Press, 1978), 41. Abi-Saab examines the role of law in UN decisions, but does not consider U.S. decisions, except incidentally.

2. *Public Papers of the Secretaries-General of the United Nations*, vol. 5, *Dag Hammarskjold 1960-1961*, ed. Andrew Cordier and Wilder Foote (New York: Columbia University Press, 1975), 3-4.

3. Abi-Saab, 38, 44-5.

4. Urquhart, *Hammarskjold*, 430, 435. Conor Cruise O'Brien, who served the UN in the Congo, notes that, where Lumumba saw the central problem as Belgian intervention, which had caused the secession of Katanga, Hammarskjold saw it as "the incapacity of the central government—the provincial government's decision to call in Belgian troops being, in his view, a consequence of this. . . . Hammarskjold did, I think, share the very widespread and sometimes unconscious European assumption that order in Africa is primarily a matter of safeguarding European lives and property. On this assumption Tshombe was and is preferable to Lumumba" (O'Brien, "The Congo, the United Nations and Chatham House," *New Left Review* 31 [May-June 1965]: 8). Eisenhower and his advisers, even more clearly than Hammarskjold, sympathized with the Belgian viewpoint. This was partly a "NATO reflex," but more importantly, they saw Katanga as an "isle of stability" and preferred Tshombe's "reasonable attitude toward Belgians and whites" to Lumumba's fiery nationalism. Stephen Weissman, *American Foreign Policy in the Congo 1960-1964* (Ithaca, N.Y.: Cornell University Press, 1974), 74-5.

5. *Alleged Assassination Plots*, 53.

6. Lumumba was an admirer of Ghana's President Kwame Nkrumah, whose goal of Pan-Africanism inspired Lumumba when he travelled to the first Pan-African Conference in Accra in December 1958. Rajeshwar Dayal comments: "Neither [Lumumba nor Kasavubu] was inspired by ideology in the accepted sense of the term. Ideas such as Communism or anti-Communism were entirely alien to their consciousness. Both wanted an independent Congo, free of the rival power blocs, a Congo that was master in its own house"

(Dayal, *Mission for Hammarskjold* [Princeton, N.J.: Princeton University Press, 1976], 296.

7. *Alleged Assassination Plots*, 14.

8. This is the conclusion of Thomas Powers, who conducted a careful review of the evidence concerning the covert efforts apparently authorized by President Eisenhower to assassinate Lumumba and Trujillo (the dictator of the Dominican Republic), and by President Kennedy to assassinate Fidel Castro. Powers, *The Man Who Kept the Secrets*, 119-58.

9. Dayal, who arrived in the Congo to replace Bunche on September 5, wrote: "The serious differences between Lumumba and the UN were common knowledge, and there were rumours that a change of government would be welcomed by the harried UN officials. . . . The Western embassies had been openly urging Lumumba's overthrow" (Dayal, *Mission for Hammarskjold*, 31).

10. *Public Papers, Dag Hammarskjold*, 160.

11. Weissman, *American Policy*, 91. *See also* Cordier's account in *Public Papers, Hammarskjold*, 161.

12. Wainhouse, *International Peacekeeping at the Crossroads* (Baltimore: Johns Hopkins University Press, 1973), 282.

13. *Public Papers, Dag Hammarskjold*, 161.

14. Kasavubu later joined in the appointment of the "College of Commissioners" whom Mobutu named to run the government.

15. Weissman, *American Policy*, 95-9; Andrew Tully, *CIA: The Inside Story* (New York: Wm. Morrow, 1962), 220-2; Catherine Hoskyns, *The Congo Since Independence* (New York: Oxford University Press, 1965), 215; Madeleine Kalb, "The CIA and Lumumba," *New York Times Magazine* Aug. 2, 1981, 48.

16. Dayal, *Mission for Hammarskjold*, 66. A close relationship with Mobutu was established by Lawrence Devlin, U.S. military attache and CIA station chief in the Congo at this time. Devlin returned to the Congo in 1965 "just before Mobutu's second *coup*" (Dayal, 65; cf. Powers, *Man Who Kept the Secrets*, 146). Sources interviewed by Weissman confirmed CIA support of the Mobutu coup (Weissman, 95).

17. Mobutu ordered all Soviet diplomats and technicians expelled from the Congo.

18. Dayal, 46. He reports that Hammarskjold also "was unhappy about the closure of the radio station and airports and considered both their legality and necessity doubtful."

19. Dayal, 116.

20. Urquhart, *Hammarskjold*, 477.

21. Ceylon, Ghana, Guinea, India, Indonesia, Mali, Morocco, the United Arab Republic (Egypt), and Yugoslavia were opposed; Canada, Ethiopia, Ireland, Liberia, Pakistan, Sweden, and Tunisia abstained.

22. Richard Mahoney, *JFK: Ordeal in Africa* (New York: Oxford University Press, 1983), 55-6, 69-71; Urquhart, 504-5.

23. Security Council Res. S/4741 (1961).

24. *Dept. State Bull.* 44 (1961): 359-65.

25. Mahoney, 82-7.
26. Mahoney, *Ordeal in Africa*, 105.
27. Hilsman, *To Move a Nation*, 253.
28. *Dept. State Bull.* 46 (1962): 12.
29. This is Hilsman's characterization of the options (Hilsman, 265).
30. Total gross cost of ONUC (excluding the civilian operation) was $408,323,396, of which the United States contribution (32.4%) was $132,298,802, a very small amount in comparison to U.S. peacekeeping costs for operations in which U.S. forces are used.
31. *Second Report of the Secretary-General on the Plan for an Emergency International United Nations Force*, Nov. 6, 1956, UN Doc. A/3302, General Assembly, *Official Records*, ES-1 (1956), Annex 5. The "other" costs included costs of rotation of troop contingents, operation of aircraft, rations, and special equipment, supplies and services.
32. *Public Papers, Dag Hammarskjold*, 236, 438.
33. General Assembly Res. 1731 (XVI), 1732 (XVI), and 1739 (XVI), December 20, 1961. Although the United States was not listed among the sponsors of these resolutions, it was reported that the projects of the bond issue and the appeal to the International Court had originated in Washington. *New York Times*, Jan. 16, 1962; Martin, *Adlai Stevenson and the World*, 700.
34. House Committee on Foreign Affairs, *Hearings on S.2768*, 87th Cong., 2d sess., 1962, 21, 26-7, 43, 60, 75, 99-100, 153.
35. *Dept. State Bull.* 50 (1964): 901-5.
36. H. Conc. Res. 343, *Congressional Record*, 88th Cong., 2d sess. (1964) 110: 19886, 20574.
37. *Dept. State Bull.* 51 (1964): 688-9, 826-7.
38. *UN Yearbook* (1964), 44. The challenge was rejected in a vote in which the Soviet Union was allowed to participate.
39. UN Doc. A/5916/Add. 1 (Sept. 30, 1965), General Assembly, *Official Records*, Annexes (XIX) 21: 86.
40. Nicholas, "The United Nations in Crisis," *International Affairs* 41 (1965): 446.
41. *Report of the Secretary-General*, Feb. 4, 1963, Security Council, *Official Records*, 18th year, Supplement for January-March 1963, 92.
42. Weissman, *American Policy*, 227-34.
43. Ibid., 245-6. State Department Africanists grumbled, says Weissman, "This would never have occurred under JFK." According to him, President Johnson "gave many the impression that he wanted a quick anti-Communist solution and had little empathy for African opinion" (ibid, 225).
44. George W. Ball, *The Past Has Another Pattern* (New York: W.W. Norton, 1982), 322-5.
45. Weissman, 246-54.
46. On Mobutu's connection with the CIA, *see* note 16, above.
47. *UN Yearbook* (1975), 863-4.
48. South Africa's interest lay in the fact that the party fighting against it for the independence of Namibia drew support from Angola.

49. For further details, see Nathaniel Davis, "The Angola Decision of 1975: A Personal Memoir," *Foreign Affairs* 57 (Fall 1978): 109-24.

50. Colin Legum, "A letter on Angola," *The New Republic*, Jan. 31, 1976.

51. Statement by Secretary Kissinger to the Subcommittee on African Affairs of the Senate Committee on Foreign Relations, Jan. 29, 1976, *Dept. State Bull.* 74 (1976): 174, 182.

52. In 1978 President Neto was helpful to the Carter administration in ending attacks on Zaire by Katangan exiles based in Angola. Calling themselves the National Front for the Liberation of the Congo, this group has been described as "lineal descendants" of Tshombe's Katanga gendarmerie. When they invaded Zaire's Shaba province (the former Katanga) in 1977, and again in 1978, Mobutu's army proved unable to deal with them without outside help. France and Morocco responded to Mobutu's appeal for help in 1977, and in 1978 French and Belgian forces, this time transported by the United States, again drove out the invaders. While President Carter initially charged that Cuba had trained the invaders and did nothing to stop them from crossing the border, it was later revealed that Castro had informed the United States on May 17, 1978, after that invasion began, that he had learned the raid was contemplated and had urged President Neto to prevent it. Neto undertook to disarm the returning rebels to prevent further attacks (*New York Times*, June 10, 1978). In this case the sending of foreign troops to help the government of Zaire repel an invasion of its territory seemed not inconsistent with the accepted consensus respecting legitimate uses of force. Cuba and Angola evidently concurred in the opinion that for them to participate in the invasion would be illegitimate.

53. Cervenka, *Organization of African Unity*, 93-4.

54. *Dept. State Bull.* 77 (1977): 845.

55. News Conference, Feb. 10, 1978, *Dept. State Bull.* 78 (1978): 14; Cyrus Vance, *Hard Choices* (New York: Simon & Schuster, 1983), 73-4, 85-91.

56. *New York Times*, Feb. 22, 1978; Vance, 85-88.

57. General Assembly Res. 390A (V), Dec. 2, 1950; *UN Yearbook* (1950), 368-70.

58. International Court of Justice, *Reports* (hereafter cited as "I.C.J. Reports"), 1950, p. 128.

59. General Assembly Res. 1142 (XII), Oct. 25, 1957.

60. General Assembly Res. 1361 (XIV), Nov. 17, 1959.

61. *Dept. State Bull.* 55 (1966): 567.

62. I.C.J. *Reports* (1966), 6.

63. *Dept. State Bull.* 55 (1966): 523, 567-8.

64. General Assembly Res. 2145 (XXI), Oct. 27, 1966.

65. Security Council Res. 276 (1970).

66. I.C.J. *Reports* (1971), 16.

67. Security Council Res. 418 (1977).

CHAPTER 9: IRAN AND AFGHANISTAN

1. After the coup American oil companies acquired a 40% interest in a new consortium to market Iranian oil, under the terms of a settlement made by Iran with the Anglo-Iranian Oil Company.
2. Harold Temperley, *A History of the Peace Conference of Paris* (London, 1920-1924), 6: 5-9.
3. *British and Foreign State Papers* 114 (1921): 900.
4. Temperley, 6: 211-6.
5. British and French occupation of Syria and Iraq roused anti-allied feelings in Iran, and the British feared that if Russia were defeated Iran would bow to German pressure to end British control of Iranian oil. Churchill, *The Grand Alliance*, vol. 3 of *The Second World War* (Boston: Houghton Mifflin Co., 1950), 478.
6. *For. Rel. U.S.* (1941) 3: 393.
7. Churchill, *The Grand Alliance*, 482.
8. *Documents on American Foreign Relations* (1941-42), 678.
9. *British and Foreign State Papers* 144: 1017.
10. *For. Rel. U.S.* (1946) 7: 299-301.
11. The Soviet Union retaliated by complaining to the Security Council against the presence of British troops in Greece. This was another indication of Russian (and British) willingness to compromise on spheres of influence, which the United States opposed.
12. *For. Rel. U.S.* (1946) 7: 340.
13. Ibid., 348.
14. Quoted in Joseph Jones, *The Fifteen Weeks* (Harbinger Books ed. 1964), 54.
15. *For. Rel. U.S.* (1946) 7: 535.
16. Ibid., 563.
17. Acheson, *Present at the Creation*, 506.
18. Ibid., 507.
19. Ibid., 506.
20. Ibid., 508.
21. I.C.J. *Reports* (1952), 93.
22. Acheson, *Present at the Creation*, 662.
23. The operation is described in detail by Kermit Roosevelt in *Countercoup: The Struggle for Control of Iran* (New York: McGraw-Hill, 1980).
24. Roosevelt, 210.
25. Roosevelt, 9.
26. Mottahedeh, "Iran's Foreign Devils," *Foreign Policy* 38 (Spring 1980): 19-34.
27. Brzezinski, *Power and Principle*, 354-98; Vance, *Hard Choices*, 326-48.
28. Brzezinski, 396-7.
29. William H. Sullivan, "The Road Not Taken," *Foreign Policy* 40 (Fall 1980): 175-86.

30. Vance, 369.

31. Later, on May 24, 1980, the court gave judgment for the United States, deciding that Iran had violated its obligation to the United States under conventions in force between the two countries, "as well as under long-established rules of international law." It reaffirmed the previous order, and decided that Iran was under obligation to make reparation to the United States. The form and amount of such reparation was reserved pending further proceedings. I.C.J. *Reports* (1980), 3.

32. Security Council Res. 461, Dec. 31, 1979.

33. Vance, *Hard Choices*, 400-1. The statement spoke also of willingness to take steps to lift the freeze of Iranian assets and to resume the supply of military spare parts to Iran.

34. Testimony of John E. Hoffman, Jr., a lawyer for Citibank, before the Senate Banking Committee. Abridgement published in the *New York Times*, March 1, 1981, sec. 3.

35. Texts of the various declarations and undertakings constituting the agreement are in *Dept. State Bull.*, February 1981.

36. State of the Union Address, *Dept. State Bull.*, February 1980.

37. Brzezinski, *Power and Principle*, 426-32, 443-7.

38. As reported by UPI, *Albuquerque Journal*, March 7, 1980; cf. Brzezinski, 445.

39. Vance, 391.

40. Carter's emphasis on human rights was effective in improving conditions for dissidents in those countries which were, to an important extent, dependent on American economic support. It produced amelioration of abuses of human rights in several Latin American countries. It had little effect in the Soviet Union and Eastern Europe, except to damage the atmosphere in which inter-governmental arms control talks were conducted. The administration's statements on human rights also deceived American domestic opinion by giving an erroneous impression that by their treatment of their own citizens the Soviet rulers were violating international law in an eggregious way. Ambassador McHenry, for example, denouncing the Soviet intervention in Afghanistan in a speech to the UN Security Council on January 6, 1980, characterized it as "a gross and blatant violation of the most important principles of international law and of the UN Charter." This was true enough with respect to respect to the principle "that one state must not use force against the territorial integrity and political independence of another state." But he was wrong to refer to respect for human rights as a legal obligation of similar sort. The Charter does not include it in its list of principles of obligatory international conduct. Respect for fundamental human rights is referred to in the Charter only as an aspiration and a long-range goal. In a similar way, administration spokesmen had repeatedly spoken of Soviet "violations" of the human rights provisions of the 1975 "Helsinki Agreement," characterizing those provisions, as President Carter did in his address to the UN General Assembly March 17, 1977, as "solemn commitments . . . [which] must be taken just as seriously as commercial or security

agreements" (*Dept. State Bull.* 76 [1977]: 333). Yet the human rights principles, repeating the language of the non-binding UN Declaration on Human Rights, were put at Helsinki, not in treaty form but in a "Declaration" which was part of the Final Act of the Conference on Security and Cooperation in Europe. The Soviet Union, along with other participating states, signed with the clear understanding that it was *not* a legal commitment. Thus, President Ford said of it on July 25, 1975, "I would emphasize that the document I will sign [at Helsinki] is neither a treaty nor is it legally binding on any participating state" (*Dept. State Bull.* 73 [1975]: 205). See Oscar Schachter, "The Twilight Existence of Nonbinding International Agreements," *American Journal of International Law* 71 (1977): 296-304; Schachter, "International Law Implications of U.S. Human Rights Policies," *New York Law School Law Review* 24 (1978): 63-87. For a view that "a crucial . . . condition for improvements in respect to human rights in the East is the continuation of detente itself," see Karl Birnbaum, "Human Rights and East-West Relations," *Foreign Affairs* 55 (July 1977): 783-99. Birnbaum warned against taking measures in the name of human rights which could be construed as interference in internal affairs, and believed it essential "to convey to the governments of the Warsaw Pact countries that Western support for human rights movements in the East does not reflect an aspiration to upset the political and social systems in those states." In his memoir, Secretary of State Vance noted that "some groups saw the [human rights] issue primarily as a powerful instrument in the political offensive against the Soviet Union." For their part, the Soviet leaders "felt our human rights efforts were aimed at overthrowing their system." The issue contributed to a "growing polarization of U.S.-Soviet relations" (Vance, *Hard Choices*, 46, 99-103).

CHAPTER 10: QUESTIONS OF NEUTRALITY

1. TIAS 2976.
2. Council on Foreign Relations, *The United States in World Affairs* (1954), 324-5; Bowles, *Promises to Keep*, 478-80.
3. TIAS 4190.
4. Bowles, 481-503.
5. Kissinger, *White House Years*, 187.
6. Ibid., 687.
7. Ibid., 701-2.
8. Ibid., 184-6, 191, 193.
9. Minutes of meetings, printed in *The New York Times*, Jan. 6 and Jan. 15, 1972.
10. Kissinger, *White House Years*, 905-6.
11. Ibid., 910-11.
12. Ibid., 899.
13. *Dept. State Bull.* (August 1981): 83.
14. The islands were first settled, in 1764, by the French, who called them Les Malouines after the town of St. Malo (hence the Spanish name, Islas

Malvinas). France transferred the islands to Spain in 1767. A British settlement made in a different part of the islands in 1766 was the subject of controversy between Britain and Spain and was abandoned by the British in 1774. The government of the United Provinces (Argentina), as successor to Spain, established control of the islands in the 1820s and granted a concession to found a settlement to a Frenchman, Louis Vernet, who was appointed governor. A dispute with U.S. sealers led to an attack on Vernet's colony by an American warship in 1831 and to British reassertion of its old claim to the islands. Julius Goebel, *The Struggle for the Falkland Islands* (New Haven: Yale University Press, 1927).

15. General Assembly Res. 1514 (XV), Dec. 14, 1960.
16. Alexander Haig, *Caveat: Realism, Reagan, and Foreign Policy* (New York: Macmillan, 1984), 272.
17. *New York Times*, April 3, 1982.
18. Secretary of State Haig reports that Galtieri suggested to the U.S. ambassador "that Washington should acquiesce in the invasion as a quid pro quo for Argentine support for the United States in the Southern Hemisphere." Haig, *Caveat*, 275.
19. Ibid., 266.
20. *New York Times*, May 30 and June 6, 1982.

CHAPTER 11: SUMMING UP

1. David McClellen and David G. Acheson eds., *Among Friends: Personal Letters of Dean Acheson* (New York: Dodd, Mead & Co., 1980), 103.
2. A recent book on United States recognition practice finds a growing tendency to deemphasize recognition and to continue diplomatic relations with new regimes. L. Thomas Galloway, *Recognizing Foreign Governments: The Practice of the United States* (Washington: American Enterprise Institute, 1978). In a preface to Galloway's book, Professor, later Judge, Richard Baxter quoted a statement on normalization of diplomatic relations by Deputy Secretary of State Warren Christopher. This said, "The premise of our present policy is that diplomatic relations do not constitute a seal of approval.... The reality is that, in this day and age coups and other unscheduled changes of government are not exceptional developments. Withholding diplomatic relations from these regimes, after they have obtained effective control, penalizes us. It means that we forsake much of the chance to influence the attitudes and conduct of a new regime.... Isolation may well bring out the worst in the new government. For the same reasons, we eschew withdrawal of diplomatic relations except in rare instances—for example, the outbreak of war or events which make it physically impossible to maintain a diplomatic presence in another capital."

Baxter thought this policy had been influenced by "the fact that various forms of diplomatic relations . . . have been carried on with political entities or governments that the United States did not recognize," and he reached the conclusion that "whether recognition should be granted or withdrawn has become a nonproblem." Without denying the hopeful nature of the recent policy trend, this conclusion seems overdrawn. Denial of recognition, where it is accompanied by refusal to be governed by legal norms in the conduct of relations with the unrecognized entity, raises very real problems for the administration of international order.

That American policy in this area has also led to considerable confusion is indicated by President Carter's answer to a question about Cuba at a citizen meeting in October 1979. He was asked why his administration would not accept "the fact that the Cuban government was here to stay." He replied: "Until Cuba can bring their own troops back from unwarranted involvement in the internal affairs of other countries, until they release the hundreds and hundreds, even thousands of the political prisoners they have in jail, we will not recognize Cuba" (*New York Times*, Oct. 17, 1979). The President was apparently unaware that the United States had never withdrawn its recognition of Cuba, as an independent state, or of the Castro government, which the U.S. recognized in 1959 when Batista fell from power.

INDEX

Acheson, Dean G., view of the UN, quoted, 13; and Berlin crisis, 36-38; advice not to ask declaration of war in Korea, 46; and 38th parallel, 50, 52; opposes intervention in China, 60-61; on recognition of the Chinese Communist government, 62-66, 80; recommendation to protect Formosa, 61, 69, 71, 218-219; policy concerning Indochina, 84-87; opposition to intervention in Iran, 102-103; and Soviet missiles in Cuba, 125; and Iranian oil nationalization, 183-185
Adams, John Quincy, 8, 73
Adee, Alvey A., 74
Afghanistan, British influence, 179; Soviet intervention (1979), 197-199, 237
Allende, Salvador, 132-137, 253-254
Allison, John, 49
Anglo-Iranian Oil Company, 179-180, 183-185
Angola, 169-172, 258
Arab League, Pact of, 18
Arbenz, Jacobo, 103-106
Argentina, action concerning Central America, 140, 212; conflict over the Falkland Islands, 210-215, 261-262

Ball, George, 160-161, 165, 169
Bangladesh, struggle for independence, 204-205, 207-208
Baxter, Richard, 262
Belgium, intervention in the Congo, 149; Stanleyville rescue operation, 169
Berlin, Soviet attempts to end Western occupation rights, 31-38; Berlin wall, 38; treaty settlement (1971), 39

Bishop, Maurice, 143
Bonsal, Stephen, 120, 250
Bosch, Juan, 127, 128, 130, 132
Bowles, Chester, 122-123, 157, 160, 250
Brandt, Willy, 39
Brezhnev Doctrine, 147
Brown, Harold, 198
Brzezinski, Zbigniew, 189, 198
Bundy, McGeorge, quoted, 29-30
Bush, George, 207

Cabral, Reid, 127, 130
Canning, George, 73, 222
CARICOM (Caribbean Community), 143
Carter, President, recognition of Chinese Communist government, 102; and Nicaraguan revolution, 137-138; and El Salvador, 138; and conflict between Somalia and Ethiopia, 173; and South Africa, 177; and Iranian revolution, 189-191; hostage crisis, 191-197; Soviet intervention in Afghanistan, 197-199, 201; military aid to Pakistan, 209; human rights policy, 260-261
Castillo-Armas, Colonel Carlos, 104
Castro, Fidel, 107, 119-120, 123, 229
Central Intelligence Agency (CIA), covert interventions, 19, 92, 102-107, 120-124, 133-136, 140-142, 153-155, 168-169, 170-171, 185-187, 222, 246-247, 249-250, 251; aid to Iranian secret police, 188
Chayes, Abram, 140, 252
"Chicken" games, 30-41, 224-225
Chile, 132-137
China, Communist, alliance with the Soviet Union (1950), 18; agreement with India (1954), 18; intervention in Korean War, 56-57;

warning against entry of UN forces into North Korea, 54, 55-56; recognition question, 61-67, 78-80, 98; warning concerning foreign intervention in the French-Vietnamese war, 246; and Nationalists' off-shore islands, 99-101; visit of President Nixon, 101-102, 200; military aid to North Vietnam, 117; supports Pakistan against India, 204-209; conflict with India (1962), 204; conflict with Vietnam, 19, 238
Chou En-lai, 55-56, 63-66, 70, 79, 95, 99, 206, 244
Christopher, Warren, 138, 262
Churchill, Sir Winston, "percentages agreement" with Stalin, 12; opposes military intervention in Indochina, 92; and Iran, 181, 182, 185, 187
Citibank, negotiations with Iran, 195
Clay, General Lucius, 31, 34, 239
Clubb, Edmund, 65-67
Colby, Breckenridge, 75
Coolidge, President, 76
Corbett, Percy, 235
Cordier, Andrew, 150, 153-155
Cuba, under Castro, 119-124; relations with Grenada, 143; sends troops to Angola, 170-172, 258; and Ethiopia, 172-174
Cuban missile crisis, 40-41, 124-127

Dam, Kenneth, 142, 144
Dayal, Rajeshwar, 154-155, 158
Debray, Régis, 253-254
De Gaulle, Charles, advice to President Kennedy on Vietnam, 112-113, 249
Department of State, opinions of legal adviser, 105, 125, 130-131, 165-166, 208, 237
Dien Bien Phu (battle), 88-89, 93
Dominican Republic, U.S. intervention, 127-132, 252-253
Dulles, Allen, 102, 121, 122, 185
Dulles, John F., advice concerning action north of 38th parallel, 49-50; advice concerning Formosa, 68; policy concerning Indochina, 87-97; and covert operations, 87, 92, 102-107, 187; policy of nonrecognition, 98-99; mutual defense treaty with Nationalist China, 99-101; and U.S. intervention in Iran, 187; and Guatemala, 103-104; and Suez negotiations, 107-109; alliances with Turkey, Iran and Pakistan, 200, 203

Eden, Sir Anthony, 91-92, 94-95, 106-111, 187, 246, 247
Egypt. See Suez Canal; Suez crisis
Eisenhower, President, and Berlin crisis (1959-60), 34-37; and Indochina, 87-97; determination not to recognize Chinese Communist government, 98; mutual defense treaty with Nationalist China, 99-100; opinion concerning nuclear weapons, 100; covert intervention in Iran, 102-103, 185-187; covert intervention in Guatemala, 103-106; and Suez crisis, 107-110, 247, 248; plan to overthrow Fidel Castro, 106, 120; and Congo crisis, 151-157; relations with India and Pakistan, 203-204
El Salvador, 138-139
Eritrea, 173-174
Ethiopia, 172-174

Falkland Islands conflict, 210-215, 227-228, 261-262
Fitzgerald, Frances, 114
Ford, President, 117, 170
Formosa. See Taiwan
France, in Indochina, 83-97; and U.S. intervention in Guatemala, 104-106; aid to Sandinist government of Nicaragua, 138-140; and U.S. intervention in Grenada, 144; policy concerning the Congo, 153, 160; and UN peacekeeping costs, 163; and India-Pakistan conflict, 207-208; gives up colonial possessions in India, 213
Fugh, Philip, 63-64, 243
Fulbright, Senator William, 13, 121, 252-253

INDEX 267

Gandhi, Indira, 205
Geneva Conference on Indochina, 88
Gizenga, Antoine, 156, 158
Goa, forcibly incorporated in India, 212-213
Goldberg, Arthur, 167, 176
Good Neighbor Policy, 238
Great Britain, position on military action in North Korea, 51, 53, 56; view of U.S. action concerning Formosa, 70-71; recognition policy, 73-75, 244; restoration of French rule in Indochina, 83; and U.S. intervention in Guatemala, 105-106; opposes intervention in Grenada, 143-144; policy concerning the Congo, 153, 158, 160; and UN peacekeeping costs, 162; and Somalia, 172; and Eritrea, 174; relations with Iran, 178-188; sphere of influence in Afghanistan, 179, 199; and India-Pakistan conflict, 207-208; and Falkland Islands, 210-215, 227-228
Greece, U.S. aid in civil war, 14-16, 236-237
Grenada, 142-145
Gross, Ernest, 176
Guatemala, U.S. intervention in, 103-106, 247

Haig, Alexander, 139, 213-214, 262
Hammarskjold, Dag, and situation in Guatemala (1954), 105; and UN operation in the Congo, 149-159, 162, 255
Hays, Congressman Wayne, 165
Helms, Richard, 133-135
Helsinki Agreement, 260-261
Hemingway, Ernest, 120
Henkin, Louis, 239, 248
Hilsman, Roger, 122
Ho Chi Minh, 83-87, 90, 97, 112, 114, 115, 220
Hodge, General John R., 43
Holland, Henry, 104
Hoover, President, 77, 245
Huang Hua, 63-64, 208
Huerta, Victoriano, 8, 75

Human rights, U.S. policy concerning, 260-261
Huyser, General Robert, 190

India, agreement with China (1954), 18; opposition to UN military action in North Korea, 53-55; interest in Indochina, 92; and UN operation in the Congo, 158, 160-161; and UN peacekeeping expenses, 163, 175; wars with Pakistan, 202-209; view of U.S. military aid to Pakistan, 203, 210; policy of non-alignment, 203; border conflict with China, 161; purchase of arms from the Soviet Union, 204; Indian-Soviet friendship treaty, 207; seizure of Portuguese Goa, 212-213
Indonesia, war for independence, 82-83; use of force to acquire West Irian and East Timor, 212-213
International Court of Justice, compulsory jurisdiction, 25, 140-141, 175-176, 185, 192; UN peacekeeping expenses, 164-166; Namibia, 174-177; Anglo-Iranian dispute, 184-185; case concerning U.S. staff in Iran, 192-193, 260; Nicaraguan complaint against the United States, 140-141
International law, of war, 7; on the use of force, 17-26, 217-218, 237; national interpretation of, 26, 216-217; intervention, 19-26; recognition, 25, 71-81, 221-222, 244, 250, 262; bearing on national decisions, 216-217, 252
Iran, 178-197, 199-200; extra-territorial jurisdiction in, 178, 180, 188; foreign concessions, 178-180; spheres of influence and Allied occupations, 179-183; treaty with Soviet Russia, 179-181; U.S. call for Soviet withdrawal (1945), 182; dispute with Britain over oil concession, 183-185; U.S. intervention in 1953, 102-103, 185-188; revolution and seizure of U.S. embassy, 189-197; war with Iraq, 19

Israel, conflicts with the Arab states, 2, 23, 41, 109-110, 202, 229, 238

Jefferson, Thomas, 8, 72
Jessup, Philip C., 68, 242
Johnson, President, 112, 114, 116, 148, 249

Kasavubu, Joseph, 153-156, 168
Katanga, 149-161, 258. *See also* United Nations, operation in the Congo
Katzenbach, Nicholas, 125
Kellogg-Briand Pact, 10
Kennan, George, 14, 246
Kennedy, President, and Berlin, 37-39; and Cuban missile crisis, 40-41, 124-127, 241; and Vietnam, 112, 114, 116; and CIA operations against Castro, 120-124, 127; policy concerning the Congo, 157-161
Kennedy, Robert, 41, 123, 125, 126
Khomeini, Ayatollah, 188-190, 194
Khrushchev, Nikita, and Berlin, 32-38; and Soviet missiles in Cuba, 41, 126
Kipling, Rudyard, 8
Kirkpatrick, Jeane, 212-213
Kissinger, Henry, 133, 135-137, 170-171, 205-209, 253
Knowland, Senator William, 67
Korea, before June 1950, 42-45; North Korean aggression, 45-48, 238; issue of military operations north of 38th parallel, 48-57

League of Nations, 10, 46, 78, 174-175
Lehman, Senator Herbert, 67
Lichenstein, Charles, 145
Lie, Trygve, 79, 242
Limited war, concept of, 46-47, 57, 115-116, 219-220, 223
Lodge, Henry Cabot, 104-106
Lumumba, Patrice, 152-158, 255

MacArthur, General Douglas, 51-53, 56-57, 68, 244
Malvinas. *See* Falkland Islands conflict
Mao Tse-tung, 63, 64

Meeker, Leonard, 125, 130-131, 147, 253
Mexico, policy towards Nicaragua, 138, 139; and UN peacekeeping expenses, 163
Mobutu, Joseph, 154, 156-159, 169, 170
Monroe Doctrine, 7, 9, 225-226
Montevideo Convention on Rights and Duties of States (1933), 140, 235, 237
Moore, John Bassett, 75-77, 236
Mossadegh, Mohammed, 102, 178, 183-188

Namibia, 174-177
Nasser, Gamal Abdel, 107-109, 187
National interest, 1-2, 230-233
Nehru, Jawaharlal, 53, 56, 158, 203, 238
Neto, Agostinho, 169-170, 172, 258
Neutrality, in international law, 21-25; policy of, 7, 202, 204, 207, 228; U.S. neutrality act, 254
Nicaragua, 137-142
Nixon, President, quoted, 123, 251; and Vietnam, 116, 118, 249; advice to invade Cuba, 123; and Chile, 132-137; sides with Pakistan against India, 205-209; policy towards China, 200, 205-209
North Atlantic Treaty, relationship to UN, 14, 18
Nuclear weapons, implications for decisions respecting use of force, 29-30
Nuremberg Military Tribunal, 237

Organization of African Unity (OAU), 18, 21, 170-171, 173
Organization of American States (OAS), Charter, 18; and situation in Guatemala (1954), 103-105; and Cuban missile crisis, 40; excludes Castro government from meetings, 124; and situation in the Dominican Republic (1965), 128-131; and Nicaragua, 137-138, 226; and Grenada, 144; and Falkland Islands conflict, 215
Organization of Eastern Caribbean States, 143

Pakistan, wars with India, 202-209; alliance with the United States, 203-204, 208; alliance with China, 204, 207-209
Panch Shila, 238
Poland, Yalta Declaration concerning, 12

Radford, Admiral Arthur, 89-90, 92-93
Reagan, President, and Central America, 139-142; and Grenada, 142-145; military assistance to Pakistan, 209; and Argentina's invasion of the Falklands, 212-215
Recognition, policy, 62, 65-67, 71-81, 98-99, 101-102, 221-222, 250, 262-263
Ridgeway, General Matthew, 89, 245
Rogers, William, 177, 207
Roosevelt, President Franklin D., 76, 82, 83, 182, 238
Roosevelt, Kermit, 185-187
Roosevelt, President Theodore, 8, 235, 250
Rusk, Dean, 49, 68, 121-122, 165, 243
Russia (Tsarist), sphere of influence in northern Iran, 179

Schachter, Oscar, 261
Schlesinger, Arthur M., Jr., 121, 251
Schneider, General René, 134
Scoon, Sir Paul, 144-145
Shanghai Communiqué, 18, 101
Somalia, 172-173
South Africa, intervention in Angola, 170-171. *See also* Namibia
South West Africa. *See* Namibia
Soviet Union (USSR), policy concerning Eastern Europe, 12, 145-148; alliance with China (1950), 18; in North Korea, 1945-49, 42-45; boycott of UN Security Council, 47; and Korean War, 47, 238, 242; recognition of Ho Chi Minh government, 87; policy changes after the death of Stalin, 88; proposes conference on Indochina, 88; and U.S. intervention in Chinese civil war, 101; in Cuban missile crisis, 40-41; and Middle East, 41; trade agreement with Cuba, 119; aid to Nicaragua, 139, 140; interventions in Eastern Europe, 145-148; policy concerning the Congo, 152-158; and UN peacekeeping costs, 162-163, 166; aid to Angola and Ethiopia, 170-173; encroachments on Iran, 178-183; Soviet-Iranian treaty (1921), 181; intervention in Afghanistan, 197-201, 237
Spanish civil war, 24, 244
Spheres of influence, 12, 19, 41, 137, 145-148, 179, 182, 224-226, 259
Stalin, Josef, 12, 182
Stevenson, Adlai, 125-126, 127, 128, 157, 158, 166-167
Stimson, Henry, 76-78
Stuart, John Leighton, 59, 62-64
Suez Canal, London Conference (1956), 108-109
Suez crisis, 107-111
Sullivan, William, 190

Taft, Senator Robert, 46, 67
Taiwan (Formosa), 57-61, 67-71, 99-102, 206, 218-219; mutual defense treaty with U.S., 99-102
Taylor, General Maxwell, 123
Thompson, Llewellyn, 124
Trujillo, Rafael, 127
Truman, President, and Yalta Agreements, 12; aid to Greek government in civil war, 14-16; and Berlin blockade, 31-32; and Korean conflict, 45-57, 242; decision not to ask Congressional declaration of war, 46; decision on crossing the 38th parallel, 48-57, 219-220; decision to neutralize Formosa, 57-71, 218; policy concerning Indochina, 83-87; and Iran, 182, 183-185
Tshombe, Moise, 149, 151-152, 159-161, 168

U-2 spy plane, 240-241
United Fruit Company, 103, 247
United Kingdom. *See* Great Britain
United Nations, American expectations concerning, 11, 12-13; and

Greek civil war, 14-15; declaration on principles of international law concerning friendly relations and co-operation among states, 17, 20; definition of aggression, 17, 20; declaration on the inadmissibility of intervention, 20, 22; declaration on the granting of independence to colonial countries and peoples, 20, 210-211; in Korea, 44-57; Security Council resolutions authorizing military action, 47-55, 219; and conflicts between India and Pakistan, 202, 204, 207; and Guatemala (1954), 104-105; and situation in the Dominican Republic (1965), 127-130; and Nicaragua, 139-140; operation in the Congo, 149-161; peacekeeping costs, 161-167; and Eritrea, 173-174; and Namibia, 174-177; and Iran's detention of U.S. hostages, 192-193; and Soviet intervention in Afghanistan, 197; and situation concerning the Falkland Islands, 210-215; and Argentina's resort to force, 211-215; and seizure of territory by Indonesia, 212-213. *See also* UN Charter

UN Charter, U.S. ratification, 10; provisions of, 13, 17, 20, 21, 105, 163-167, 237, 238, 239, 242; and civil wars, 19-20; and neutrality, 21; and peacekeeping expenses, 162-167
UNEF (United Nations Emergency Force), 150, 162, 163
USSR. *See* Soviet Union
U Thant, 146, 160, 167

Vance, Cyrus, 137, 173, 189-191, 261
Vandenberg, Senator Arthur, 15
Vietnam, declaration of independence, 85; France's war in, 83-97; U.S. intervention, 112-118, 223, 248, 249

Waldheim, Kurt, 192-193
Ward, Angus, 65-67
Wilson, President, 8-10, 74-75
World communism, 24-25, 69, 103, 114, 220-221, 228-230

Yalta agreements, 12
Yugoslavia, and Greek civil war, 15-16, 236

Zaire. *See* Congo

ABOUT THE AUTHOR

Edwin C. Hoyt is a lawyer and political science professor at the University of New Mexico. He is a graduate of Harvard College and Harvard Law School, and holds the Ph.D. from Columbia University. Harvard awarded him a scholarship for study at Cambridge University, England (1938-39). After law school he served in the U.S. army, ending with assignment to the legal division of the quadripartite Allied Commission for Austria (1945-46). He practiced law in New York City and continued graduate studies at Columbia's Russian Institute and in international law and relations, obtaining the Ph.D. in 1958. He taught international law at Columbia and international relations at Hamilton College, and held a research fellowship at University of Michigan Law School, before moving to New Mexico in 1960. His published work includes *The Unanimity Rule in the Revision of Treaties: A Re-examination* (The Hague: Martinus Nijhoff, 1959) and *National Policy and International Law: Case Studies from American Canal Policy* (University of Denver Monograph Series in World Affairs, 1966).